Kellogg's Corn Flakes versus TELMA + CREST TOOTHPSTE.
.1 Paris-style show of brutal strength
:2 Mohammed directed his followers to face
3 On Medineh and Mecca and folorn J
Cars blacken air – no catalytic converte
1:2 BOOK – The Smokescreen.
1:1 (20 yrs to have a road approved?)
2 Sensations about Driving tests and off
1:1 THE BETTER ECONOMY OF SYRIA?!
2 parking offences
:4 Tomatoes rotting in fields / spoiled .
WORD Insolvency
4:3 Arabs reject Palestinians – they are stateless!?

THE FALL OF ISRAEL

THE FALL
OF ISRAEL

BARRY CHAMISH

CANONGATE PUBLISHERS

*To my wife Sasha, our son Ariel and
the little girl who will be born with this book*

First published in Great Britain in 1992 by Canongate Publishers
Ltd., 14 Frederick Street, Edinburgh EH2 2HB

ISBN 0 86241 355 9

British Library Cataloguing-in-Publication Data.
A catalogue record for this book is available from the British
Library.

Typesetting by Falcon Typographic Art, Fife, Scotland
Printed in Great Britain by
Butler & Tanner Ltd, Frome and London

Contents

Acknowledgements

I wish to thank my politico/economic adviser, Joel Bainerman; Benny Saidel, my invaluable researcher; Dr Alvin Rabushka for his lessons on economics and for reviewing the banking chapter; Jacob Sullum, editor of *Reason* for his advice on charity and philanthropy; Dr Rachelle Fishman for correcting the sections on health and sanitation; Dr Ezra Sohar who taught all us reformists about the dangers of the Israeli bureaucracy; Charles Hoffman, whom I have never met but who nonetheless opened up the secrets of the Jewish Agency for me and Dr Steven Plaut for the compressed lesson on private industry.

Nor can I properly express gratitude to Richard Ayles for discovering my rough stone, or to Judy and Neville Moir for polishing it and Stephanie Wolfe Murray for displaying the finished jewel. And finally, thank you to Evelyn Cowan, the matchmaker and Philip Levy who suggested I present my ideas to Evelyn. It is my hope that this book somehow rewards all these fine people with a reformed and more secure Israel.

Introduction

It's as if Israel's Arab enemies had hatched a sophisticated plot to destroy the country by planting agents throughout the ruling classes. Israel is on the way to a total collapse because Israelis with power are making life an unbearable misery for everyone else. *The Fall of Israel* will document the widespread crime and corruption of the Jewish state in the probably futile hope of generating reform from without. The author is an Israeli patriot and war veteran. This is not another instance in a long and ignorant series of Israel-bashing by enemies of the country but a sincere plea for change before the title of the book becomes prophetic.

Readers will recognise names like Shamir, Peres and Sharon but will not be so familiar with the less well known personalities, political parties and organisations. The best advice the author can offer is to soak in the atmosphere without dwelling on the details. It is the intention of the book to paint a picture of severe moral degradation and if the reader finds himself 'entertained' by the indignation, so much the better.

Life for the Israeli caught in the midst of the moral breakdown is far from entertaining, however, and this must be kept in mind even if the reader has been deliberately amused. Most Israelis are living wretched existences thanks to the politicians who rule them. They have almost no control over who rules them. The 'only democracy in the Middle East' is a farce. Candidates for public office are not selected by the people, but rather the central committees of the various parties hold their own internal elections. The candidate who receives the most votes from his own party members will become first on the party list and thus his party's candidate for prime minister. The second-highest vote collector will have gained enough internal support to choose whatever ministry he wants if his party wins a general election, and so on down the line. In this way, 70-year-old Yitzhak Rabin wrested the Labour Party leadership from 68-year-old Shimon Peres in 1992. No one less geriatric could mount a serious challenge to their doddering presence.

Political appointees and a totally centralised economy have left Israel's health system in tatters, its water diseased, its schools barely functioning, its army demoralised, its diplomacy a mockery. Israelis are unemployed, underemployed or recently impoverished.

Back in 1985, inflation had reached 450% and the government formed a conspiracy with the national trade union and industrialists to save the economy from impending ruin. All savings and salaries were tied to the Cost of Living (COL). The COL was computed by registering changes in the Consumer Price Index. This basket of indicators included the prices of food, books and clothes but had nothing to do with salaries or the price of capital. So if a locust plague raised the price of coffee in Brazil, it would affect the value of money in Israel. At the same time that savings were linked to the COL and thus were devalued by some 20% a year, wages were not adjusted to the full COL. In 1991 the wages of most Israelis lagged behind the COL by 2% by government decree. Joel Bainerman, one of Israel's most astute economic writers, estimates that in the six years since the economy was tied to the COL, purchasing power has fallen by 35%. One result is that Israelis have found themselves in debt. The average personal debt is now $15,000, by far the highest in the world.

Without money to cover the bare expenses of living, Israelis became deeply indebted to their banks. The book will illustrate in vivid detail that Israeli banks are crooked beyond belief. This is a reflection of their owners, the government, which took over 90% of Israeli banking after the banks hoodwinked the public out of a third of its savings in 1983. The gap between real lending and borrowing rates in Israel is an incredible 30%. With the public forced to borrow because of its dwindling buying power, it cannot come even close to keeping up with the usurious repayment rates. There are currently 1.8 million police debtor files and, according to the head of Israeli Police, Yaacov Terner, there are 560,000 warrants out for bad debts. This in a population of just under five million. Because the government controls the courts and police, debtors are pursued incessantly. In one out of every three Israeli households, there is an unbearable fear of repossession and jail.

To understand this formula for corruption let us try analogies with two other democracies. Americans are requested to imagine the end of elections for the president, congressmen and senators. Instead, at the next Democratic or Republican convention, the delegates themselves will choose the candidates. The politician with the most delegate votes will be the candidate for president and all other appointments will be decided by diminishing delegate support. In order to win delegate support the politician will make promises – be they of government jobs, unjustified tax exemptions or straight cash. And no matter how obvious the patronage, the politician cannot be removed from office because he represents no state and no district.

British readers are asked to imagine the end of political constituencies. Citizens no longer have a Member of Parliament representing them personally. MPs can only be removed by their own parties, most of whose members are immersed in the gentle arts of bribery, graft, deceit, embezzlement and blackmail.

The Israeli electoral system ensures that no matter how deep the scandal, politicians almost always stay in power for good. With 18 parties sharing 120 seats in the Knesset, no one party can form a government by itself. So the biggest party invites small, narrow-interest parties into a coalition. If one or two of these insignificant parties leaves the coalition, the government will fall. So no matter how much money politicians steal from the public, they will not be ousted for fear of toppling the coalition.

The book begins with the example of Arye Deri, Israel's Minister of the Interior. As of this writing, he has been investigated for the misappropriation of at least $50 million in public money for over a year and a half. Yet, despite a police investigation and the horrible stench of graft, he sits in the highest law-making body of the nation, the government cabinet.

And he is not the only suspected thief in that august body. This book will offer solid evidence of crimes committed by a wide spectrum of high-ranking politicians including Sharon, Olmert, Peres, Beilin and Shaki among others. Those politicians not justifiably suspected of misusing public funds are shown to be deeply incompetent and they include Shamir, Levy, Rabin and Peretz. The combination of corruption and stupidity is destroying the country.

According to Bainerman, 'The government foisted this plan on the public supposedly to halt inflation but really to cut wages and earn money through debt collection. They're willing to impoverish the whole country to enrich themselves. Israel isn't a democracy, rather a kleptocracy. The government is cleaning up while the people turn into paupers.'

The signs of a desperate people are everywhere. There are now

40,000 hard-drug addicts in Israel. In the first half of 1991, 23 wives were murdered by their spouses. Just a decade ago 50 murders a year was considered shocking. And Israelis have become cheats; there is almost no choice if they wish to survive. They cheat by trading currency illegally, withholding taxes and most sadly, by short-changing their own people far too often. Trustworthiness is not a virtue, it is a sign of weakness in an Israeli society rotting from a tragic lack of moral guidance from its leaders.

The book documents the degradation of Israel but does not blame Israelis. In this book, the politicians are the villains and the Israeli people are rightfully portrayed as decent, caring and criminally exploited. Lest any reader think this book is an attack on Israel, let that perception end right now. The book is a defence of an embattled and moral Israeli public savagely victimised by the travesty of their government and bureaucracy. And let there be no mistaking one revolting fact. Israel is a police state, for it is the police who carry out the decrees of the state and spread terror throughout the country.

So why don't Israelis rebel against this intolerable life? They do; they leave. In 1985, Dr Ezra Sohar, a brilliant economic reformist wrote, 'From 1949 to date, over 400,000 Israelis have left Israel for good or over 10% of the Jewish population.' Sohar correctly blames their flight on Israel's, 'socio-economic system; a system of total government control of the economy that breeds inefficiency, waste, nepotism and corruption'.

But Sohar's figures are far too conservative. Many other sources, including those released by the passport office, indicate that 400,000 Israelis live in America alone. It is estimated that 150,000 babies that would have been Israeli are instead American.

All over the world in places as far flung as Toronto, Johannesburg, London and Melbourne there are expatriate Israeli communities. The total number of Israelis who have permanently left the country is around 700,000, some 18% of the Israeli Jewish population. No country in the world, not Turkey, not Haiti, is witnessing such a torrent of people abandoning their land. And the figure would be much higher if there weren't ties to family, friends and the Hebrew language. Israelis love their country but despise what is happening to it so much, that close to a fifth of them have waved goodbye for good. And they are not alone. After Israel totally botched up the mass immigration of Soviet Jews between 1989 and '91, the immigrants began looking for a way out of the country. By the summer of '91, 5,000 Soviets were applying for passports and more and more, Israel became a way-station for Soviets, not a final home.

Life in Israel means harassment by endless authorities, tension and injustice. Every year, over 20,000 Israelis seek new countries to live in. According to one watchdog group, one out of every three graduates of an institute of higher learning will emigrate. Change and reform seem so unlikely that despair is leading to mass abandonment. If the crumbling infrastructure and decayed government doesn't lead to the fall of Israel, then depopulation might.

The reader will ask, why haven't I heard all this before? If he could read Hebrew, none of this would be a surprise since the Israeli press is filled with stories of corruption and social sickness. But the reader who has never perused a Hebrew paper is dependent on foreign journalists to tell the story of Israel, and they do it very, very badly. Major publications do not hire Israeli bureau chiefs, but instead send their own nationals on two- or three-year stints. These journalists speak not a word of Hebrew, rely on their predecessors' contacts for quotes and remain lost and confused while professing expertise on Israel. Their main focus is on the Palestinian issue, and they miss the true disaster which surrounds them.

The Fall of Israel will correct the gross inadequacy of foreign reporting from Israel. It will reveal how overseas aid and charity are propping up a deeply corrupt political system and turning proud Israelis into beggars. It is the author's hope that all such monies will be cut off until there is some assurance that Israel is on the road to complete reform.

The author's style is sometimes irreverent but let the reader not confuse this with flippancy. The amorality of Israel's power structure is leading to the demise of a country that is home to the author's wife and son, much of his family and most of his friends. The state of Israel's decline is absolutely heartbreaking to the author of this book.

PART ONE

The Diseased Democracy

CHAPTER ONE

Deri Products

Arye Deri is hardly a well known politician outside Israel, yet he is the Minister of the Interior and wields a great deal of power. He is also known in Israel as possibly the most corrupt cabinet member (or the least astute for being so blatant about it). He has been under police investigation since the spring of 1990 on charges of fraud and embezzlement.[1]

Deri's problems began in November of 1989 when the Jerusalem city treasurer, Yaacov Efrati, was accused of improperly transferring $170,000 to religious institutions in the city. Two city councillors, Yehuda Meir and Deputy Mayor Ornan Yekutieli, initiated a private investigation into the affair and reached the conclusion that the Interior Minister had threatened to withhold funds to the city unless a good part of the money was directed to institutions run by his political party, Shas.

Most of Israel's local governments are deeply in debt and despite high municipal taxes throughout the country, without government allocations, towns and cities would be unmanageable. Deri's ministry controlled the 750 million shekels ($335 million) that would be allocated at his discretion to local governments. The two Jerusalem councillors discovered that their city was not an isolated case. Throughout the country councils received their bail-out allocations only after agreeing to shift a percentage of the funds back to Deri. Yekutieli and Meir produced 80 documents demonstrating the extent of the kickbacks. Of the six projects to receive Interior Ministry funding in Dimona, five were Shas-run. In Bnei Brak, where no more than 15% of the population support Shas at the polls, fully half the $3.4 million allocated went directly to Shas institutions.

The two councillors made public their findings, presented their evidence to the State Comptroller and demanded an investigation. Thereafter they were harrangued with violent threats that upset their lives dramatically. There was no shortage of political

9

threats as well. Jerusalem's mayor, Teddy Kollek, demanded their resignations.

The Deri scandal took a long breather because of a government crisis in March of 1990. But before attempting a logical explanation of the events, one other accusation by the two Jerusalem councillors is vital. In their demand for a government probe of Deri's shenanigans at the Interior Ministry they added that Deputy Finance Minister, Yossi Beilin, had been aware of the Deri kickbacks since the end of October, 1989.

Beilin was chief aide and deputy to the Finance Minister, Shimon Peres. Peres, at the time, had been the head of the Labour Party since 1977. He had run for Prime Minister four times and had yet to win a victory. He served as Prime Minister for half a term as a result of a tie in 1984 but had failed again in his bid for power in the 1988 elections. Because the ruling Likud Party was reluctant to form a coalition with the religious parties, its leader, Yitzhak Shamir, opted to share power with Peres, offering Peres's party the Finance and Defence Ministries. For reasons later explained, Peres accepted the post of Finance Minister but he wanted only to be Prime Minister. If he could persuade Shas, with its five seats, to leave the government and form a coalition with Labour, he would get his wish.

But such an option appeared impossible. Shas was the party of Sephardic (Middle-Eastern origin) Jews who were both religious and right-wing (Shas itself did not have a right-wing foreign policy, but its constituency certainly did) while Peres and his party was mostly Ashkenazic (European origin) and secular.

Yet in March 1990 the impossible happened: Deri became a left-wing peace dove and led his five-member party out of the government coalition, causing a parliamentary vote of no confidence and the fall of the Likud coalition. The issue was whether to accept demands on Israel for a regional peace initiative from the American Secretary of State, James Baker. Labour was willing, but Likud and all the religious parties were opposed to the American pressure. All, that is, except Shas, and that didn't last for long.

While the parliamentary crisis continued for well over two months, Deri's behaviour as Interior Minister stayed out of the news. But once the crisis abated the full extent of the corruption charges became public knowledge. First the state Attorney-General, Miriam Ben Porat released the results of her investigation of Deri and his Shas Party. She uncovered details of how the party shifted vast sums of public monies into its private coffers.[2]

With the heat on high, one of Deri's public servants, Moshe Glenzer, resigned from the ministry, taking with him some very damning documents. They found their way into the hands of two reporters from Israel's largest and most influential daily, *Yediot Achronot*. Two reporters, Mali Kempner and Mordechai Gilat, wrote a series of articles documenting alleged but genuinely shocking misbehaviour.

Deri was publicly accused of:

—Bribing the Jerusalem Municipal Council with $900,000 of government money to appoint his brother Yehuda, the chief Sephardic rabbi of a large Jerusalem district called Ramot. Further, Jerusalem Municipality contributed $180,000 to be used towards buying a school for the minister's brother.[3]

—Ordering the mayor of Or Akiva, Shabtai Shalom, to exempt a religious leader from paying back taxes of about $450,000. Deri promised to make up the loss out of government funds.

—Transferring $3 million to the allegedly unsavoury town council of Hadera but only recording a $2.5 million transfer on the public ledger. No one knows what became of the missing half million.

It appears Deri's methods were to involve people in crime and then threaten to expose them if they opened their mouths. But he involved too many people to ensure secrecy and, though he could corrupt almost everyone he wanted to, almost wasn't enough. Once the accusations went public, two private citizens took out police complaints against Deri. The police acted against the complaints and raided his office. The results shocked Israeli Inspector General of Police, Yaacov Terner, who claimed he had 25 separate charges against Deri and intended to pursue them in the courts.

With his back to the wall Deri went on the offensive. First the newspapers were filled with large advertisements proclaiming support for Deri. The sponsor of the ads called itself 'Sephardic Jews For Fair Media' and might have been more effective if it wasn't headed by the principal of a school which received its funding directly from Deri. In effect, Deri was funnelling public funds towards a campaign to defend himself to the public. The public, however, was having none of it, so in June 1990, Deri appeared on a public affairs television programme displaying the results of lie-detector tests he had 'volunteered' to submit himself to. He was innocent on all counts, which was fine except many of the questions focused on a side issue: how he managed to purchase a very expensive home on his public servant's salary. The minister protested far too much and his credibility sank even further. As a result, he or his supporters adopted far more sinister tactics.

First, the reporter who unveiled the Deri affair, Mordechai Gilat, became the victim of a combined campaign of threats and attempted discrediting. By phone and letter the threats poured in. But when these tactics failed, his home was bugged twice. The wiretappers, in the tradition of Shas incompetence, were caught. One of the seven was a gentleman called Tsuberi, a parliamentary aide to another Shas Member of the Knesset, Arye Shlomo Gamliel. The network of criminals surrounding Deri widened with the police investigation. One of Deri's closest aides, Zvi Jacobson, was arrested on suspicion of illegally transferring $315,000 of Interior Ministry funds to a religious seminary run by his father. When arrested he was carrying a list of instructions on how to wear the police down during interrogation. More confusing was a cheque for over $4,500 found beside the stalling instructions which Jacobson could not explain at all.

But Jacobson was not alone in his delaying tactics. Deri became so exasperating that the Minister of Police, Ronnie Milo, accused him of refusing to co-operate in the investigation. This was a major slap in the face by a government coalition partner and a hint that perhaps it would be best if Deri stepped down from his ministerial post unless he co-operated with the police.

It is hard to imagine any democracy in the world where a high-ranking minister would not be asked to step down in the face of embezzlement, fraud, blackmail and illegal surveillance charges. But Israel has no written constitution and members of the government are immune from prosecution. So long as Deri stayed in the government, he could not be charged with any crime.

He went on the rampage in order to hold on to his ministry. He claimed not to be ashamed of the illegal wiretapping of a journalist but was angered when one tape revealed a conspiratorial conversation between the Police Inspector General and the reporter about the minister. Further, Inspector General Terner was heard on tape slurring Sephardic Jews.[4]

Deri took every opportunity to obfuscate the issue. If Terner really was in cahoots with the journalist then he would have to resign his post. But no court in the land could listen to the tape since it would be inadmissable as evidence and would prejudice the whole investigation. After planting doubts about the legality of the police investigation against him, Deri went straight for the jugular of Israeli society, the supposed prejudice against dark Sephardim by light Ashkenazim.

From 1948 to about 1957, some 800,000 Jews were forced to leave their homes in Arab lands. Around 600,000 of them arrived in Israel where they were rudely treated by the mostly European Jews of the land. The Sephardim were traditionally religious and many were from the merchant class. They were badly treated by the secular rulers of the time and forced to adopt manners foreign to them in order to survive. Workers could not get ahead unless they joined the ruling Labour Party or its union. Most couldn't bear the régime and, lacking assets, became a true underclass.

In 1977, Menachem Begin was elected Prime Minister, in no small part because of the support of the Sephardim. It was during his term of leadership that various Sephardic appointments were made – the President of State, vice-Prime Minister and, most significant of all, Army Chief of Staff. Begin's greatest accomplishment other than the still contentious Camp David Accords, was bringing Sephardim *en masse* into Israeli society. And for that reason, the 50% of Israel that is Sephardic will mostly vote for a Likud government for the foreseeable future.

Deri is a Sephardi of Moroccan origin and was, previous to the exposure of his alleged misdeeds, comfortable in the Ashkenazic world. But once the allegations started flowing, he revived the wounds of Sephardic mistreatment. First he accused Police Inspector General Terner of slurring all Sephardim, then he accused all his tormentors – the police, media and political establishment – of harassing him because he wasn't 'white' enough. In one public rally he compared himself to a sacrificial lamb carrying out 'holy work', but being stopped 'by the devil', or all Ashkenazim. The next night he accused European Jews of turning Sephardim into drug pushers, prostitutes and murderers. He rhetorically asked his followers, 'What have they done to us?'

But stirring up ethnic hatred still did not do the trick so Deri deftly pulled out the joker from his pack. He threatened to pull his party out of the ruling coalition and bring down the government. At the time of the threat, in September 1990, the Likud-led coalition had a majority of two in parliament. Had Shas, with its five members, left, they would have succeeded in bringing down the government.

At the time of writing, over a year since this affair erupted, Mr Deri is still the Minister of the Interior and is still responsible for the distribution of almost $335 million worth of government funds. The Likud, more interested in power than honesty, have not forced this alleged thief and blackmailer out of his position and have learned to live with him in their midst. And taxpayers' money still flows through his sullied fingers. If ignorance is criminal, then the ruling Likud is a partner in the Deri affair.

But the then opposition Labour leader, Shimon Peres, may well have played a more direct role in the whole nasty business. From the beginning of Israeli statehood, Labour has bought electoral support by using public money to fund their own hospitals, banks, sporting clubs and places of work mainly through the workers' union, Histadrut. Shas was just following practices entrenched in government behaviour by Labour. However unseemly these practices under Labour were, they were done openly. Deri has been accused of misusing public funds to line his own pocket as well as those of friends and associates. According to city councillors Yekutieli and Meir, he did so with the full knowledge of the Deputy Finance Minister, Yossi Beilin.

In a private interview, Yekutieli claimed: 'In informal talks, Beilin admitted to knowing about Deri's misappropriations back in October of 1989. He not only knew about them, he boasted that soon Labour would have Shas in its pocket . . . Beilin knew something terribly crooked was taking place but told me that's what makes the system tick.'

Meir went further: 'Beilin . . . told me it was cheaper to buy a religious party than to start a war. I told him it was a waste of money. The religious parties can't be bought for long. He told me this time one would stay bought.'

According to Israeli parliamentary law, the Finance Minister is responsible for the legal use of all ministry allocations. If the Finance Minister's deputy was aware of the illegal use of public funds, would he be duty-bound to report his knowledge to his superior, in this case, Shimon Peres? According to Moshe Negbi, a well known Israeli legal commentator, 'There is no constitution in Israel, so parliamentary law is always hazy. However, if any private citizen refuses to report a crime, he can be charged as an accessory. And ethically this applies more to a law-maker.'

So Beilin, if the charges against him by two respected municipal politicians are to be believed, was at least an accessory to a crime and, of course, the ultimate victims were the country's taxpayers. But is there any proof that Peres used the knowledge to blackmail Shas out of the government and into his own coalition? Meir believes there is: 'I saw a letter to a top official from Peres delivered on the very eve of the no-confidence vote. In it Peres promises to give a certain religious organisation a large sum of money. I think Peres is more guilty of a moral crime than Deri. Deri used most of his illegal money to advance a cause. Peres used Deri's to advance himself.'

CHAPTER TWO

Government in Permanent Crisis

To the interested outsider, swallowing the story of Israel's government paralysis in one bite is far too daunting a task, so an attempt will be made to give explanations in digestible pieces between the chronicles of contemporary corruption.

By January 1990, Shimon Peres had made his first move to bring down the government. The Science Minister, Ezer Weizman, who retired from politics in February 1992, had recently met with high-ranking PLO officials in London, and Prime Minister Shamir wanted him removed from the cabinet. Peres manipulated his party to close ranks behind Weizman and threatened to leave the government if Weizman was forced out. This was good strategy by Peres. It was bound to split ranks in the Likud. It is illegal for Israelis to meet PLO members and in one celebrated incident, Abie Nathan, Israel's best known peace activist, was jailed for six months on the charge. Nathan first gained notoriety by flying his Piper Cub to Egypt in 1966, to present the government with his personal peace proposals. The Egyptians mercifully did not shoot him out of the sky but he returned to Israel without meeting an official of any rank.

For two decades he has operated a floating radio station in the eastern Mediterranean which broadcasts messages of peace. Clearly this venture is a notable failure but it does give him an opportunity for self-aggrandisement. Nathan attempted to make his subsequent imprisonment a *cause célèbre* but succeeded only in making a little splash. Very few Israelis want any association with the PLO. After his release from prison, Nathan was hardly rehabilitated. He returned to Tunis for more meetings with the PLO and was arrested and charged upon his return to Israel. This time he tried a hunger strike to publicise his case but still stood trial.

Weizman is now a member of the Nathan School of Idealism, though it was not always that way. A founder of the Israeli Air Force, he spent most of his political career as a hawk. With these credentials in hand he was appointed Defence Minister in the first

Likud cabinet and was a chief negotiator for the Camp David Accords. The Egyptians flattered him and eventually softened him up enough to persuade Prime Minister Begin to accede to practically all Egyptian demands. In the end (March '82) Israel gave up two airfields a few miles into the Sinai at a loss of $5 billion, every cent of investment in the Sinai oil fields as well as a town of 2,200 people, a few metres into former Egyptian territory.

In time Weizman isolated himself from Likud thinking and formed his own peace party which won a paltry three seats in the 1984 elections. Despite his clear lack of drawing-power Labour offered him high status and a cabinet post in any government of theirs if he abandoned his own party by melding it with theirs. Weizman, seeing Labour was desperate for allies, took the offer.

When Weizman met the PLO officials, he knew he was breaking the law but he was also aware that as a member of the cabinet he was immune from prosecution, and would not become another Abie Nathan, left to wallow lavishly in some low-security luxury prison.

But Weizman was not just another altruistic disc jockey. He was a former Minister of Defence and Air Force Chief of Command. If kidnapped by the enemy, he could reveal the defence infrastructure of Israel.

And Peres chose the flimsy cause of his errant party comrade to fell the ruling body of the nation. But Shamir knew Peres's intentions and sought a compromise to prevent the end of the government. This was no easy task since one faction in his government, led by Industry Minister Ariel Sharon, would threaten to leave the government if Weizman stayed on. However, a compromise was reached and Weizman was demoted from the inner to the outer cabinet.

Peres was in the government and was plotting to destroy it. A few months later he did and we shall dissect the plot shortly, but first a few words from Israeli writer Yosef Goell:

> It is only rarely one can attribute blame for a marked deterioration in a political situation to just one person. But in the present case there is not the slightest doubt that the man most responsible is not the Likud's Yitzhak Shamir but Labour's Shimon Peres . . . When Shimon Peres brought down the unity government . . . his behaviour was the reverse of that required by the dictates of national responsibility.[1]

To those unacquainted with the workings of Israeli government, an obvious question would be, how does a plotter against the government manage to become a Minister of Finance within it?

In brief, Israel's political system combines the best of Britain and Italy to produce a nightmare. When a voter chooses a party, he does not choose who should be on that party's list of candidates. That is taken care of by the central committees of each party. This is where the trouble begins. A few hundred men, mostly old, jockey for positions on the list. Being in a low place on the list guarantees exile in the political wilderness, so each committee candidate must garner votes amongst the low-ranking cadre. That means promising people everything from jobs to government funds in return for immediate support. If the party is elected, it must first return favours to the rank and file and this is stage one of political appointments, and a very good reason for any ambitious Israeli to join a political party.

But since up-and-coming politicians are not likely to be given an influential post, the rank and file, many already paid off, back the high-ranking politicians. This effectively blocks newcomers from the high places on the list and keeps faces from changing in the cabinet. Shamir is 76, one of the oldest leaders in the world. His predecessor retired at 70 and while that makes the Likud seem old, they are spring chickens compared to Labour, whose leader is a spry 70; the average age of their Knesset members hovers around 60.

Peres managed to lose four elections in a row but had such resources of political patronage[2] that his party found it difficult to overthrow him. In fact, he almost single-handedly has destroyed a party considered invincible when he took it over.

Israel today is divided electorally as follows: 40% right, 35% left and 15% religious. That leaves about 10% undecided and expensive elections are held every four years or so to sway a paltry 200,000 people to change positions. In 1984 Labour lost an election because of the rigidness of the electorate. The Likud had enmeshed the country in a war in Lebanon that had lost its justification two years previously. Inflation stood at 450% and the charismatic Menachem Begin had resigned as leader leaving the listless Shamir to run the party. Yet distrust of Peres was so high that the election ended in a tie between the two big parties.

In any given election the voter has a choice of some 60 parties. To sit in the Knesset a party must capture 1% of the vote. The small parties represent narrow interests and about 20 of them find their way into the seats of power each election. Up to 1984 whichever party collected the most seats in the 120-seat Knesset could garner a few allies in ideologically similar parties and form a government, taking with it other small parties wanting to taste power. In 1984 neither Labour nor Likud was close enough to forming a majority with its allies, so both were forced to seek new partners from parties whose sole *raison d'être* was to promote fundamental religious precepts.

Making alliances with religious parties is hardly a new concept in Israel. David Ben Gurion, Israel's revered but overrated first Prime Minister, started the ball rolling in this direction by trading army service for students of yeshivas (seminaries). When he made the deal only a few hundred young men entered yeshivas every year. Today, some 20,000 orthodox religious adolescents of both sexes, or two full army divisions, shirk their military duty, driving a huge wedge between the majority who serve their country and sadly, die for it, and those who pray in safety for it.

One religious party called Agudat Yisrael is composed of black-coated Hasidim, whose roots lie in the Polish and Russian ghettos of 300 years ago. They were deeply opposed to Zionism from their inception in 1912, claiming that Israel cannot be revived until the messiah presages it. Since the messiah had not lately been seen in Poland, the founding of Israel had to be a scriptural impossibility.

When the very real state of Israel was founded, Agudat Yisrael, amongst other Hasidic groups, took the position that, in fact, Israel had really not been revived because it doesn't actually exist. Agudat Yisrael, which seats five members in the parliament of the country does not recognise the state of Israel and its supporters do not serve in its army.

In 1984, Agudat Yisrael declared that one of its conditions for joining a government was an amendment to the Law of Return and they dragged other religious parties with varying enthusiasm into a debate that became known as 'Who's a Jew'. Even though the issue of Who's a Jew in the 1984 elections was minor compared to 1988, the law had just missed being passed by the Knesset in 1985, by 62 votes to 54.

Because Jews were dispersed around the world at the time of Israel's founding in 1948, it conferred automatic citizenship on any Jew landing in Israel who requested it. Knowing who was a Jew was not a great problem since strict records were kept by the rabbinical courts of the diaspora. By definition a Jew was any person born of a Jewish mother, a wise contingency for a people subject to rape in strange lands. But events in America were changing accepted notions. There, the threat of assimilation prompted the establishment of new religious movements, the most powerful becoming the Conservative and Reform, who together outnumber the Orthodox today by five-to-one. Each movement makes its own laws. The Conservative movement attempts to walk a fine line between staunch Orthodoxy and the cultural reality of its adherents. Reform, which is responsible for most synagogues west of the Mississippi, has diluted Judaism almost beyond recognition by adjusting its tenets to the superficial spirituality of a materialistic constituency.

Among the changes instituted by the American Jews were the sanctioning of female and homosexual rabbis, driving cars on the sabbath (a necessity in suburbia) and the removal of prayer caps in synagogues. As shocking as these changes were to the Orthodox, they were merely changes in liturgy. One Reform law, however, threatened the nature of the Jews as a unique people. The Reform movement changed the rules of the religion to include children of Jewish fathers and gentile mothers as Jews. The old way was not only a method of accepting the products of rape into the fold but also a foolproof test for nationhood. With a million Jews in California itself, and without a deep examination of the sexual mores of this progressive state, it is guaranteed that under the new patrilineal law, not a few non-Jews will slip through the fence.

To protect the children of Israel, Agudat Yisrael desperately wants a change in the Law of Return. If they had their way, and they may yet, any Jew who underwent conversion by a Conservative or Reform rabbi would have to be converted again by an Orthodox rabbi before becoming eligible for automatic Israeli citizenship. At present the power of the Orthodox is so great that they have flouted religious freedom and blocked Reform and Conservative rabbis from gaining recognition by the state. Such rabbis may perform religious functions such as marriages, but the marriage will not be registered unless an Orthodox rabbi is present.

And all Israelis must abide by the Orthodox if they want to get married, divorced, register a baby or die. There is no civil marriage in Israel and anyone who doesn't wish to be betrothed in the Orthodox manner flies abroad, often to Cyprus, to return to Israel as sinful citizens. The children of such unmarried couples can be labelled bastards if the marriage is one which could not have been permitted religiously.

More absurdly, a tattoo can prevent a religiously legal burial since it is forbidden for Jews to wear one. In one perhaps fanciful case, an Israeli with a tattoo on his arm asked his rabbi to bury the arm in a gentile cemetery and the rest in his family plot.

American Jews tolerated their exclusion from the Israeli religious mainstream but the threatened change in the law governing Who's a Jew challenged their legitimacy too much by far. If enacted, tens of thousands of Jews converted by Reform or Conservative rabbis would cease being Jews in Israel and the very legitimacy of their movements would be mortally threatened in the Jewish state.[3]

Labour could not possibly acquiesce on the issue because, not only did it cause deep revulsion amongst its mostly secular followers, but one close ally, the Citizen's Rights Movement (whose Hebrew acronym is 'Rats'), owed most of its six seats to its opposition to Orthodox hegemony. Forming a cabinet with Rats and Agudat Yisrael would be akin to a government run by a council of Stalin, Reagan, Churchill and Mussolini. But Likud was capable of retaining power by giving in on the Who's a Jew issue. The Orthodox parties share with Likud a total reluctance to give up Biblical Jewish land for what would be a most tenuous peace. The Likud will not compromise on territory for military and nationalistic reasons, while the Orthodox consider it a sin to surrender any part of the land promised to the Jewish people by God. They may have taken different routes, but the Likud and the religious parties share the same perspective on this one very vital issue.

To gain power without a change of the Who's a Jew law, Peres courted the religious party leaders and their spiritual mentors, and offered political support for a wide variety of basic changes in society if they would join his coalition. But Agudat Yisrael, smelling victory, refused the first offers. So Peres increased the stakes, lavishing promises of high cabinet positions. But still Agudat Yisrael rejected the proposal so Peres offered money, a great deal of money, in well placed government posts, in outright allocations of cash and in up-front payments of public funds. But still it was no government without an amendment to the Who's a Jew law.

Now it was Shamir's turn. The religious parties upped their stakes and so did Shamir. All the better for them when they took the Shamir deal back to Peres to ask him to top it. But they didn't realise the extent of American Jewish pressure to back off Who's a Jew. Shamir couldn't budge on that one other than promising to introduce the bill into the Knesset at some vague moment in the future when the American squeeze was off. But he did offer some new and imaginative proposals on 'diverting' public money legally at various ministries and posts.

The religious parties were intrigued but still held out for Who's a Jew.

Exasperated beyond recognition, Shamir and Peres had no choice but to form a government together. After a good deal of haggling a crazy quilt government was formed. Peres would be Prime Minister for the first two years, Shamir the last. Shamir would be the first Foreign Minister, Peres the next.

The reader must try and imagine the results. For the first two years the Prime Minister was declaring his government's willingness to trade land for peace while his Foreign Minister was declaring that not an inch of holy land will be given up. Then the next Prime Minister devoted energy to expanding settlements in the disputed territories while his Foreign Minister was in distant lands trying to give away the settled land to the nicest bidder. This was not merely a government at cross purposes. This was a government paralysed by schizophrenia.[4]

CHAPTER THREE

A Government Falls

Although Peres spent the last two years of the unity government plotting its downfall, the government lasted its full tenure and new elections were called in 1988. In the four years since the previous election, a new factor had arisen that could severely affect the upcoming results and, for once, the unity government took unified action. If they had so desired, Labour and Likud governing as one could have outlawed all religious parties and given the nation separation of 'church' and state. But the will was never found. However, an exception was made for Rabbi Meir Kahane and his Kach Party.

Kahane was elected four years previously on one major issue, the expulsion of all Arabs from Israel. Such a platform was shocking and, at the time, his election was considered an embarrassing fluke. After four years of unrelenting and brutal terrorism, the electorate had changed their mind about Kahane and his ideas.

In July 1988 the respected Jaffee Institute for Strategic Affairs polled a wide cross-section of Israelis on the subject of legitimate ways of resolving the Arab uprising which had begun eight months previously. Most respondents (51%) thought 'transfer' (the euphemism for expulsion of Arabs) the most appealing choice. Land for peace came a poor second at 39%. That same figure of 51% has since recurred in other polls.

Far more frightening to the big parties were pre-election polls that showed Kahane's Kach Party receiving anywhere from five to eleven seats if elections were held the next day. If the forthcoming election was as split as the last, and all the polls suggested it would be, then an arrangement with Kahane would have to be made in order to avoid another 'unity' government. Labour would never be able to make a deal with this pariah, but Likud had another worry – he was cutting deeply into their own constituency. So, hand-in-hand, they passed a bill in the Knesset banning all racist parties from seeking election, followed by a vote declaring Kahane racist.

There were a number of problems with Kahane's expulsion. First he invited people of all colours, white, brown and black to join his movement. He was quite colour blind. If anything he was a Jewish chauvinist not a racist. Secondly, another party called Moledet (Motherland) – whose platform differs from Kach only in that it would exclude Israeli Arabs from any expulsion, preferring only the forced removal of territorial Arabs – was allowed to run for the Knesset where it won two seats and today boasts a cabinet post. Finally, Kahane was a rare honest politician, unencumbered by financial scandals in his political career. A significant part of the populace saw Kahane as victimised and this affected the final results dramatically.

Kahane expected such action from Labour but felt betrayed by Likud whom he viewed as a natural ally. (The joke in Israel was that in any Likud government, Kahane would be made Minister of Transport.) He campaigned furiously amongst his many supporters to abandon the Likud and vote for any other party.

He achieved his intended results. The campaign was bitter, with Labour running entirely on a peace campaign, claiming they were the only party capable of reaching an agreement for peace. This is a rather spurious contention since Labour fought four wars in 30 years of power compared to Likud's one war since 1977 and it was Likud who made the first deal with an Arab country at Camp David, Maryland. Likud focused more on the economy, making empty promises to free the tired citizens of bureaucratic strangulation.

In the end, the central issue turned out to be the concerted attack on Kahane. Labour kept its usual dwindling constituency but failed to win converts to Peresism. But poor Likud lost significantly to parties farther to its right and especially to the religious parties. When all the votes were tallied, the religious parties had 18 seats and effectively controlled the make-up of the next government. Or so they and everyone else thought.

Peres had other ideas. It was mathematically possible for him to form a government if he somehow persuaded almost every new Orthodox member of the Knesset to join his proposed coalition. So he donned a *kippa* (skull cap) and approached the rabbis who advised the political parties. He offered even more cabinet posts, more money, more positions with free cars and secretaries and more ways to have access to public funds. But the same old issue stumped him again: Who's a Jew?[1]

If Peres was stalled permanently on the issue, Shamir announced a willingness to give in and support a change in the Who's a Jew law.[2] Never has the American Jewish community reacted so quickly to any announcement from Israel. One by one came the big fund-raisers, congressional lobbyists and local leaders, large and small, to change Shamir's mind. In the end he decided that Who's a Jew was worse than forming another untenable government of 'unity' with Labour.

This time round he had more cards to play since Labour had no chance whatsoever of coming to an agreement with the religious parties. In the end Peres was happy to receive the Finance Ministry as it gave him the power to bail out both the kibbutzim and the bankrupt industries of the Labour Party. Yitzhak Rabin, a Prime Minister who had resigned for reasons of former banking illegalities became Defence Minister, possibly the saddest aspect of the new deal. Shortly after the government was formed, an uprising called the *intifada* began and Rabin was charged with putting it down. His methods resulted in a textbook case of turning a small rebellion into a prolonged tragedy.

After using enough government money – to keep his interests solvent for a few more years,[3] Peres decided it was time to play his Deri card and try to remove the government from power: having failed to cause enough of a crisis over the Weizman issue, he saw another opportunity given to him by James Baker. Baker is another in a long line of American Secretaries of State who have decided to get their fingers burned solving the Arab–Israeli dispute. After consultations in Cairo, he came up with a five-point plan agreed to by the Egyptian government, awaiting confirmation by the Israeli government.

However, there was one major sticking point. Israel will not negotiate with the PLO, and any government that agrees to do so could literally foment a civil war. Baker proposed that Israel meet with Palestinian representatives who were expelled from Israel for PLO activism. He also insisted on Israel negotiating with Arabs from East Jerusalem. This point could not easily be broached. East Jerusalem had been annexed to Israel and if there is one issue that both left and right agree on, it's that Jerusalem will not be divided in any future agreement. By negotiating with East Jerusalemites, Israel would be sending a clear message that Jerusalem could become a divided city again for a price. Shamir was forced to reject both clauses of the plan and Peres decided this would be the issue to bring down the government. His message was 'Say yes to Baker', and failure to do so would result in his calling a

vote of no-confidence in the Knesset. This normally wouldn't pass
but Shamir had angered the religious parties by rejecting them in
favour of another unity government. And what Shamir didn't know
was that Peres had found a way to get the five members of Deri's
Shas Party to vote against the government.

In short, Shamir said no to Baker and Peres manipulated the fall
of the government. By Israeli law, Peres had three weeks to form
a new coalition. If he failed it would be Shamir's turn to try. For
88 days, both leaders outdid each other bribing the small parties
to join them in a coalition. Peres had convinced Shas to support
his vote of no-confidence but he made the mistake of thinking that
meant the party would join his government. Shamir appeared to be
finished. His party is deeply factionalised and in the past months
a large faction led by Ariel Sharon had left the Likud. Another
faction called the Liberals, led by Yitzhak Modai, abandoned the
party taking with it five seats. Before he could attract new partners
to any coalition, he would be forced to get his old ones back in line.
And it wouldn't be cheap.

While Shamir was busy mending fences with public money, the
rank and file of Shas finally understood that Deri had betrayed
them by taking a right-wing party to the left. Deri became a victim
of public death threats on posters, by mail and by phone. He was
viewed increasingly as a traitor by his party's supporters.

Shas and two other religious parties obey the commands of a 93-
year-old, half-deaf rabbi from Lithuania named Eliezer Shach. To
stop the schism in Shas, he took the extraordinary step of appearing
before 20,000 of his supporters in a sports stadium. One evening
Israeli television shifted its prime-time schedule to broadcast the
legendary event live. Viewers were mostly disappointed since Rabbi
Shach is almost toothless and hasn't the power to raise his voice
above a whisper. Very few understood what he was saying but
the interpretations the next day were clear. He condemned the
Israeli left for 'Eating rabbits' on their kibbutzim and for generally
demeaning the values of Judaism. The message was clear: no Shas
deal with Peres.

The religious defections continued. Two of the five members of
Agudat Yisrael defected to Likud and one member of Shas resigned
from his party to throw his lot in with the Likud. He is Yitzhak
Peretz, the current minister for Absorption. The two Agudat Yisrael
defectors were well rewarded by Shamir later on. Both received
deputy ministerships with their $3,500-a-month salaries, million
dollar budgets, free cars and hired help. Avraham Verdiger is now

Deputy Minister of Jerusalem, a meaningless post, while Eliezer Mizrahi is the current Deputy Minister of Health, a position which carries significant power.

Shamir was making gains but Peres still had the advantage. He had three members of Agudat Yisrael still with him and the makings of a deal with the Liberal faction: But Peres's period of government-making had ended and legally, he should have turned over to Shamir the right to form a government.

However, the President of Israel, Chaim Herzog, a member of the Labour Party, came to the rescue. The Presidency is a cosmetic position somewhat like the English crown. He is the moral guide and conscience of the country and can open or close parliament. Herzog, apparently not spotting a moral conflict of interest, extended Peres's right to form a government by fifteen days. It may not be unusual for the President to grant extensions, but in this case it was a blatant act of partisan politics which served to act as a stay of execution for Peres.

Peres sustained another blow when an 86-year-old Brooklyn rabbi, who has never been to Israel and is viewed as the messiah by many members of Agudat Yisrael, stepped into the fray. Rabbi Menachem Schneerson, known as the 'Lubovitcher Rabbi' decreed that his followers in Agudat Yisrael were not to support a Peres government. That left Peres begging the Likud defectors from the Liberals. He offered Avraham Sharir[4] ministries in the next two of his cabinets and upped the stakes with Yitzhak Modai, offering him the ministry of his choice. Both men decided not to give their answers until Shamir had his chance to form a government.

Then the horse-trading got serious. Modai announced that he would not enter into negotiations with Shamir unless he was given a $10-million bond, cashable if Shamir did not form the next government. Modai is the current Finance Minister. There was no need to cash his bond. Sharir is still another Deputy Minister. Meanwhile, the same tactic was applied by Shamir to Labour. He found one disaffected Labourite named Ephraim Gur and made a deal with him if he would defect. Gur announced that he would join the Likud if Peres was unable to form a government. He is today the Deputy Minister of Transport.

All this wheeler-dealing took time and President Herzog was forced to give Shamir a three-week extension on his formation period. But at the end of 88 days, Shamir put together the most tainted cabinet in the country's history. The price to the public was enormous. In a country whose population is less than five million, there is a total of 33 ministerial and deputy ministerial positions, each with budgets of between one and two million dollars. But the real sign of money politics was the allocation, rather gift, rather bribe, of $100 million of public money handed out to the religious parties just for joining a government.[5]

CHAPTER FOUR

Rogues' Gallery

For 88 days Israel had no government whatsoever. Most government activities ground to a halt while the leaders of the two big parties scrambled madly to patch up some kind of make-do coalition of remarkably differing interests and philosophies. What finally emerged in 1990 was the most incompetent, dogmatic and greedy collection of people ever assembled to rule Israel. What follows are some portraits of the current Israeli cabinet, the highest and supposedly most trusted leaders of the land.

ARIEL (ARIK) SHARON

Sharon will be remembered as the boldest and perhaps best general in Israeli military history. He salvaged a victory from the debacle of the Yom Kippur War by personally leading his troops across the Suez Canal, thereby accommodating the encirclement of two Egyptian armies. In 1977 Sharon ran under his own party, called 'Shlomtzion'. After the election he joined the Likud. Sharon exemplifies the impossibility of displacing a highly placed Israeli politician no matter how great a scandal. In 1982 Sharon was Defence Minister at the time of the infamous Sabra and Shatilla massacres. The Kahan Commission, which officially investigated the massacre, found Sharon guilty of gross negligence and recommended his removal from the cabinet. But the rest of the cabinet, led by Shamir, were most reluctant to let Sharon go since with him would go the votes of his followers and a good number of seats from the Likud. So expediency ruled the day and he was fired from his position as Defence Minister but allowed to stay in the cabinet, eventually as Minister of Industry, where he caused more damage to the Israeli economy than he managed to do to Lebanon's.

Menachem Begin was once asked why he didn't appoint Sharon Defence Minister and in a now famed retort he replied that he'd be frightened to see tanks surrounding the Knesset. But even Begin, a man of great principles, was bulldozed into accepting Sharon as Defence Minister after a barrage of PLO artillery and rocket attacks against northern Israel led to a public demand for a more aggressive response.

Sharon gave most of the public what it wanted after the British Ambassador was shot and the Israeli Defence Forces (IDF) attacked Lebanon *en masse*. While giving the military their orders, Sharon was informing the cabinet of entirely different commands. At the outset of the war he told them that the goal was to secure a line 40 kilometres north of the border, the range of a Katyusha rocket.

Begin, not knowing that Israeli troops were already 100 kilometres inside Lebanon, announced the war aim of 40 kilometres. Reporters seized on what appeared to be a blatant lie by Israel but in fact, it was only Sharon who fomented the falsehood.[1] Day after day he lied to the cabinet about the war aim and stategy. As one cabinet minister noted, the only way to get the truth out of Sharon today is to read tomorrow's papers.

The Lebanon War was a public relations disaster for Israel but up until Sabra and Shatilla, it was a beneficial war for the country.[2] With a relatively mild Israeli loss of 200 war dead, the PLO were forced to evacuate to lands far from easy reach of Israel's borders.

If at that point Sharon had declared victory, Israeli troops could have returned home with everlasting honour. However, Sharon's plans were more grandiose than simple military triumph. He was going to leave Israel the legacy of a friendly neighbour to the north. And he probably would have managed this to a certain extent, had his ally of sorts, President Bashir Gemayal, not been blown up by the Syrians.

Using the pretext of restoring order after the assassination, Sharon ordered his troops into Moslem West Beirut and they ended up positioned outside the Sabra and Shatilla refugee camps, which are better described as villages. Within these villages were a number of armed PLO fighters in contravention of the expulsion agreement arranged by Philip Habib and the Lebanese government. Israel wanted these men out but was wary of being responsible for any more casualties. With this in mind, Sharon, a mere two days after the assassination of President Gemayal, asked Lebanese Maronite troops to enter the camps. They did so with relish, murdering some 800 people over a weekend. Sharon was forced to resign as a result of sanctioning the whole débâcle. He was not the only one to be rebuked by the Kahan Commission, however. When leaked news of the massacre reached Ze'ev Schiff, a journalist with *Ha'aretz*, he immediately tried to contact members of the cabinet to find out what action would be taken against the murderers. The first man he spoke to was the then Foreign Minister, Yitzhak Shamir, whose reaction was to reprimand Schiff for interrupting his holiday meal. (The massacre took place on *Rosh Hashana*, the Jewish New Year.) Shamir's apparent decision that his dinner was of more importance than mass murder may well have prolonged the bloodshed by a day and cost hundreds of lives. In any normal democracy, that would have been the end of his career – as it was, he escaped unscathed and went on to become Prime Minister.

Sharon was now merely the Minister of Industry, a result, no doubt, of the expertise in commercial technology he had amassed as a soldier and rancher: he owns the largest sheep ranch in the country. For an Industry Minister, he took a decidedly monopolistic step. He raised tariffs on imported sheep, thus saving the nation from Scottish lamb. He then set about making local goods unprofitable by initiating a Free Trade Agreement (FTA) with the United States which is supposed to reduce and finally eliminate all tariffs and duties on trade between the two countries. Upon first glance, the idea seems advantageous to Israel which is a small market that has privileged access to the biggest market in the world. Up until the FTA, Israeli products survived in the home market as a result of high duty on foreign goods which more than doubled their prices. Once the agreement took effect, the whole plan backfired. Israel's consumer goods are shoddy compared to America's and the few manufacturers of quality items didn't have the budget to crack the highly competitive American market; nor did they possess sufficient selling skills as a result of living in a protected market for so long.

Once the prices on Marlboros dropped, the Israeli cigarette monopoly, Dubek, started going broke. Crest toothpaste cut deeply into the sales of the Israeli products, which are often akin to chalk immersed in sheep dip. Kellogg's Corn Flakes seem to out-taste Israel's Telma product and so on down the line of consumer purchases.

Sharon's foray into world trade caused other reverberations back in the Knesset. The government earns more from import duty charges than from income tax. Every time someone in Israel buys even the cheapest, smallest and flimsiest car, the government adds another $7,000 to its coffers. If American cars could come in without duty then the government would lose more revenue than it could recoup by taxing outgoing Israeli products like chocolate-covered orange peels and appliance adaptors. Sharon's plan was robbing the government of its vein of gold and there seemed no simple way of producing equal quantities of unearned cash from the weary populace. All in all, Sharon had to get Israel out of this signed, witnessed and most legal agreement between the two countries.

Sharon took an all too typically Israeli tack. He sought instances of arguable American abuses of the treaty and claimed America was taking advantage of Israel. He made such a public issue out of the minor discrepancies that the Americans set up a special commission to oversee the administration of the agreement. After a delegation of Israelis flew to Washington to air their complaints, the Americans came to the correct conclusion that the Israelis were taking great efforts to renege on the whole thing. The treaty is still on the books but the Fords and Buicks without duty are nowhere to be found in a land of Fiats and Metros.

Having shattered the treaty he fathered, Sharon decided to take a break from industrial matters for four months. He had sued *Time* Magazine for libel as a result of their claim that he planned the Sabra and Shatilla massacre with Phalangist leaders. If *Time* was right, Sharon would not have been merely negligent but an accessory to mass murder. But *Time* was horribly wrong and Sharon's name was cleared.

But he spent four months in America, the first two fund-raising for his trial, the next two staying at a very expensive suite at the Plaza Hotel. Choosing not to take a temporary leave of absence, he left no one in charge of the Ministry's affairs for a third of a year. And for that time no one was in charge of creating industrial jobs, new technology or useful products. And since some 800 of Israel's 1,300 significant factories are owned directly or indirectly by the government, the period when Sharon was away from the office was one of slowdown to outright stagnation.

On the other hand, while he was away, there was a marked reduction in bare-faced patronage. To assure permanent hegemony, *Ha'aretz*, the respected newspaper, reported on 19 September 1985 that, 'of the 27 new directors appointed by Ariel Sharon during his tenure of Minister of Industry and Trade, 23 are active Likud members.' Being a director means a large salary and perks. Most of these juicy and unprofitable jobs went to his own followers, not of course, to experts on trade and industry.

Miriam Ben Porat, the respected and totally honest State Comptroller, noted in her 1990 report that 'Haphazard methods, poor planning and flagrant violations of the law characterise the workings of the Ministry of Industry and Trade.'

She found a number of fine examples of his work ethic, a typical instance of which was hiring one of his supporters to be his advisor on agricultural affairs. Unfortunately, no such position in the ministry existed or was approved by the Civil Service Authority – a 'technicality' Sharon circumvented by hiring the man as 'an outside contractor'. No one knew what this man was contracted to do, though he was apparently so proficient at whatever it was he was doing that Sharon gave him yet another position, 'Advisor to the Minister on Development Areas'. This post never existed before but must have involved simple tasks since the new advisor was not asked to give up his outside contractor job. In short, the fortunate follower drew two salaries for doing nothing. As Ben Porat notes: 'It is clear that he was and continues to be employed in violation of the law. In the opinion of the state comptroller, the behaviour by the ministry . . . should be viewed in a grave manner.'[3]

He abused his power in other ways too, in one instance awarding substantial research and development grants to projects already completed, and in another case (after his request for their transfer had been turned down by the Civil Service Authority), luring two women from other ministries to work for him by offering them greatly enhanced salaries paid for out of public funds.

It appears that Sharon ran a crooked Industry Ministry but after the formation of the new government in May 1990, he was given an even more important task to mishandle: creating new accommodation as Minister of Housing. The timing of this appointment, the most ideological position in the cabinet short of Prime Minister, was important. By May 1988, perestroika and glasnost had engendered the emigration of Soviet Jews, resulting in a tidal wave of new Israelis. Israel's population might be increased by 25% as a result of the human flood.

Israel has been waiting a long time for an increase in its Jewish population to offset the frightening birthrate of the Arabs within its borders. Jewish emigration was still a ticklish question in the Kremlin with all its vital ties to the Arab world and nothing was allowed to upset the testy feelings of the Soviet leadership.

But the cabinet decided to put massive emigration at risk for the sake of ideology. Sharon had many times publicly given his vision of several million Jews settling in the Jordan Valley (better known as the West Bank). The Soviets implicitly stated that populating the West Bank with their Jews would endanger the whole enterprise. What better man to placate their fears than Sharon at Housing?

And he didn't let anyone down. Sharon owns a thousand-acre ranch but still felt a little constricted, understandable in his case, so he bought a home in the Moslem Quarter of the Old City of Jerusalem. There is an unwritten law dividing the Old City and keeping its residents in separate quarters. Sharon's home was a deliberate provocation and a message that a Jew could live anywhere he chose in his own land – perhaps a noble sentiment, but costly to Israelis who don't share it. Besides the cost of the house, an eight-man guard is stationed permanently outside it, their salaries paid by an already beleaguered and overtaxed public.

The Easter before there had been another surprise, this time for residents of the Christan Quarter of the walled city. A hundred and fifty Jews moved into a building in their quarter. The churchmen protested and the world watched Israel suffer another blow to its image as black-garbed priests carrying large crosses clashed with soldiers in Easter processions. This was not a constituency Israel could afford to alienate. Religious Christians, especially in America, are amongst Israel's most devoted supporters, largely because they see the Jewish state as prophetic and presaging the Second Coming.

The purchase of the building was legal. The owner received $4.6 million for the property, far above its actual value and he set up shop well away from Israel with the money. The land was not holy, in fact it was quite run down, and in any other city, the transaction would have been ethical. But in Jerusalem it was viewed as an intrusion guaranteed to spark violence. Still, it was a private transaction, wasn't it?[4]

No, it wasn't. The Housing Ministry, at the time run by David Levy, had contributed significant funds towards the purchase of the property. Public money had once again been used to stir up trouble in the promotion of Likudan ideology. The Americans were so incensed by the revelation that the government had had a part in the purchase of the building that they subtracted the government's contribution from their next economic aid package.

And the provocations continued. Shamir announced that with the big new population coming from Russia, a big new Israel would be required.[5] The Arab states are terrified by the Soviet emigration and used this statement as proof that the government was using Soviet Jews to fill the disputed territories. They succeeded in forcing Gorbachev to threaten to stop the emigration if Shamir was stating policy. In fact, he may have been, but less than 1% of Soviet Jews have chosen to live in the territories and James Baker took great offence at the Soviet leader's threat to emigration and forced him to back down. Soviet Jews continued to flock to Israel despite Sharon's mis-management of the housing operation.

Sharon continues to be deliberate in his timing. When James Baker visited Israel after the Gulf War to push his new 'window of opportunity' peace initiative, Sharon authorised the dedication of two new settlements. As a result, when Sharon arrived in Washington a month later, Baker called him an obstacle to peace and refused him the right to attend a White House meeting with American Housing Secretary, Jack Kemp.

Sharon's tenure at Housing has been a disaster not only for young couples who have been priced out of the housing market by government policies, but especially for new immigrants who were initially being housed either in army camps or three families to an apartment in civilian areas. The fiasco of housing will be examined at length but many of the causes for the disaster lie in the enmity between Sharon and Finance Minister Yitzhak Modai.[6]

YITZHAK MODAI

Mr Modai, as the reader will recall, agreed to join the new coalition only if Shamir gave him a cheque of $10 million, payable if Shamir failed to form a government. He was rewarded for his monetary craftiness with the Finance Ministry.[7] To his credit, he hasn't been as blatant in handing out government money to his allies as was his predecessor, Peres. His style of maintaining order and the status quo is, however, much more sinister: he withholds funds. A fine example was his refusal to fund retraining programmes for Soviet doctors, about 7,000 of them so far. Israeli doctors can only earn serious money after finishing their government health-plan hours, when they can offer real treatment in their expensive private clinics. Too many modest-living Soviet competitors would have cut deeply into their pockets.

Modai has displayed his concern for public welfare by warning all Israelis that their standard of living must fall to accommodate the new immigrants; then he proposed legislation to lower the minimum wage to less than $2 an hour as well as to tax pensions, government or otherwise, and savings funds. And he will not give Sharon what he needs to build housing. Every plan Sharon proposes, Modai rejects. It reached the point in May 1991 that the two of them had it out in a ministerial meeting. According to bystanders, Sharon made the foundations tremble. Witnesses to the meeting left in disgust, one noting that 'two governments are sabotaging each other'. Another Likud witness admitted sadly, 'It just isn't working.' So Sharon makes plans for housing which Modai rejects. The result is a threatening housing shortage that may well send hundreds of thousands of Israelis into the streets, either to live or to riot. Of the 45,000 housing units Sharon planned for the year 1990, only 4,500 were completed. That number of immigrant families is arriving every four months. Simple mathematics shows that trouble is brewing over accommodation.[8]

Modai's most blatant act of patronage was in using his position to get his 32-year-old adviser, Silvan Shalom, appointed head of the Israel Electric Corporation with a salary of $60,000. Six years before, Shalom had been head of a Likud student organisation. *Jerusalem Post* writer Joel Bainerman expresses his contempt for Sharon and Modai, and the corrupt system that supports them: 'That as Finance Minister, Modai could put a 2.4 billion shekel budget [$1.8 billion] and 10,000 employees into the hands of someone with absolutely no corporate experience says something about his professional acumen . . . Clearly Modai was serving his own interest.'[9]

Modai's unsavoury tactics have not gone unnoticed by the rest of the government either, as Asher Wallfish explains: '. . . Modai is branded by the Likud as a blackmailer who got his way . . . The worst kind of a blackmailer is a successful one . . . All this creates a fine scenario for parliamentary skulduggery, mainly at the expense of the national economy.'[10]

To get even, the rest of the cabinet fight Modai on every one of his proposals. This is the state of financial affairs in the nation of Israel: everyone in government despises the Minister of Finance and tries to prevent him from doing his job. Oh the glories of anarchy!

DAVID LEVY

The Likud is divided into three major factions. The most powerful of these is led by Shamir and represents the original Herut (freedom) Party whose roots extend back to Poland of the 1930s. From the foundation of the state until Begin's election to power in 1977, Herut was the loyal opposition of the Knesset.

The second major faction is headed by Sharon, who left the military a hero and used his popularity to unite some directionless but influential politicians behind his banner. This faction is the most nationalistic of the Likud and, when bargaining for a cabinet post during the government formation of 1990, Sharon gladly opted for Housing which was a perfect springboard for controlling the settlement of the disputed territories.

There are smaller factions within the Likud, such as Modai's liberals. To appease Modai's thirst for power, Shamir let him get his hands on the nation's purse-strings, giving him the post of Finance Minister.

The third major faction is led by David Levy and is best described as the blue-collar constituency. This faction is vitally important to the Likud since most blue-collar Jewish voters in Israel choose the Right in all elections. If Levy were to lead his followers out of the Likud, the party would never again hold power. While Sharon wanted his cabinet post to advance his ideology, and Modai, his to gain undisputed financial power, what Levy wanted more than anything else was respect. In May 1990 he found the perfect vehicle to achieve this, the post of Foreign Minister. Unfortunately, few people in the whole government were less qualified to be in this essential position than Levy and most of the country prayed he wouldn't buy himself the job. But the nation's hopes were not to be realised.[11]

Because Menachem Begin owed his election in no small part to the Sephardic blue-collar vote, it made sense for him to appoint a working-class Sephardi to a powerful cabinet post. The highest-ranking candidate was Levy, a contractor of Moroccan descent from a development town in the north of the country.

Levy's *curriculum vitae* hardly inspired high cabinet rank. He is a self-made building contractor who never finished his secondary school education. More discouraging was the fact that though perfectly able, he never served in the armed forces. In Israeli politics, the army has produced a good number of leaders such as Generals Dayan, Rabin and Sharon.

To sum up the present pathetic situation, the Foreign Minister of Israel, who has a strong say in the highest-level military decisions, has never served a day in the army and the same minister, who must fly to Washington to confer with graduates of Georgetown and Harvard, never made it through high school. But the situation gets worse. Because of the vital ties to America, Israel has always chosen Foreign Ministers like Abba Eben or Moshe Arens who speak English. With so much at stake with every verbal nuance, knowledge of English is a prerequisite for the Foreign Minister – that is, until Levy came along. He is the first Foreign Minister in Israel's history to be totally ignorant of basic English.

Begin knew Levy's shortcomings and offered him a less important

cabinet post at that time, namely Housing. But as a sop to
the Sephardic community, he also appointed Levy as vice-Prime
Minister.

Levy used Housing as a springboard to power. At one Likud
convention his followers tried to brawl their way to the top by
hurling chairs, punching rivals and creating pandemonium. As
unseemly as the display was to a repulsed nation, this ploy, to
topple Shamir and gain control of the party, was repeated by
Sharon's faction just before the fall of the government in 1990.

Taking his post of vice-Prime Minister seriously, Levy was
insulted when Shamir left the country on business and kept
important decisions from him even though he was, in theory,
leading the nation while the real Prime Minister was abroad.
Finally, realising that his vice-premiership was a fraud, Levy, in
a televised speech before his congregants, pronounced his view of
his position with the infamous words, 'Nigger work, nigger go.'

The nation was appalled by his crudity, but not surprised since
Levy was the butt of half the jokes invented in the country.
Americans have Polish jokes, the British have Irish jokes: Israel has
David Levy jokes. It is said that a fire swept through his home and
destroyed his library. Both books were lost and he hadn't finished
colouring one in yet. And on and on by the dozen. And though
Levy hired image-makers who blow-dried his hair and furnished
him with a pair of spectacles in a bid to make him look intelligent,
he never stopped being a joke amongst all educated Israelis and a
good chunk of the remainder who had any common sense.

Once the nightmare of Levy as Foreign Minister sunk in, a round
of Levy humour circulated in Israel, such as this joke told just before
Levy flew to Washington for the first time as Foreign Minister.
The Hebrew word for aftershave lotion is 'aftershave'. Levy is in
a Washington chemist shop and asks his interpreter, 'How do you
say aftershave in English?'

The trip itself was a joke but Levy didn't get it. He was
totally elated by his meetings with Secretary of State James
Baker whom he now called, 'My friend Jim', undoubtedly much
to Jim's chagrin.[12]

He claimed to have swayed Jim on all of Israel's basic positions
vis à vis the approaching Gulf War and the anticipated attempt
to reach agreement of the Israeli/Arab dispute after it was over.
In fact, thanks to the unique chemistry between him and Jim,
American/Israeli relations had been strengthened, trust had been
restored and 'a good era' of understanding initiated. From now on

he and Jim would be in constant contact, ready to exchange ideas at a moment's notice.

As usual, the reality of the situation escaped him. Levy, addressing a gathering of American Jewish leaders announced: 'We are at the opening of a new era in relations between Israel and America. I am very happy about that and I am very happy that I was the instrument to bring this about.'

But one American at the meeting believed Levy had been taken in by the cordial atmosphere of a first meeting. Levy had not even left America when Baker announced he was flying to Syria to strengthen ties with Israel's most implacable enemy.

Levy did not make much of an impression in Washington and the word used by certain state department officials to describe him was 'lightweight'. But the state department has nothing against lightweights from Israel. With just the right amount of flattery and some fancy verbal footwork, they can be made malleable to American interests. And Levy was just as anxious to work with the Americans as they were to have him in their camp. A peace treaty would finally bring Levy the respect of all those who mocked him in Israel. It was Levy who negotiated a $400 million loan to house incoming Soviet Jews. He sent a letter to Baker that outlined conditions attached to the loan. Two were totally unacceptable to the vast majority of Israelis on both the left and the right. First Levy promised not to settle Soviet Jews in areas which were not under Israeli control before 1967. This includes a number of districts in Jerusalem. Secondly, he agreed to report to the Americans on every new building project in all areas – but implicitly in East Jerusalem.

This was an incredibly stupid mistake by Levy, which Baker seized and exploited to the full. He persuaded President Bush to declare East Jerusalem and all outlying neighbourhoods formerly in Jordanian hands, essentially, occupied territory. Occupied thanks to Levy. The Jerusalem neighbourhoods in question such as Ramot, French Hill and Gilo are home to over half of Jerusalem's Jewish population and they have yet to be informed they are living in areas open to negotiation by any American administration, let alone their own Foreign Minister. Only the pressure on Bush and Baker from prominent American Jews got Levy out of this snafu.

No French Jews rescued Levy from his snafu with Mitterrand. In a private conversation[13] the French President told Levy that his government knows the importance of Jerusalem both strategically and historically to Israel and understands Israel's refusal to put the city up for auction. This was diplomatic of Mitterrand and not intended as a policy statement – which Levy turned it into when he made public this conversation to the media while still in France. Mitterrand was deeply embarrassed by Levy's revelations and made some denials, but Levy stuck to his guns, thereby humiliating the French leader even more.

But his principal failing ground is America, where his good friend Jim abuses him with impunity. Since Camp David in 1977, Egypt and Israel have been receiving approximately equal amounts of American aid. Egypt has managed to turn easy loans into a $7-billion debt since then. Israel's, in comparison, is $4.5 billion. In the days leading up to the Gulf War, America agreed to waive all of Egypt's debt as a reward for joining the coalition against Iraq. The same offer was not made to Israel though the debt was acquired as a result of the same peace treaty, and America was obliged to show a modicum of evenhandedness to both parties.

Levy flew to Washington to ask Bush to waive Israel's debt as well. The President expressed his appreciation of Israel's 'low profile' during the Gulf Crisis and assured him that America's new ties in the Arab world had not changed the relations between Israel and his country. But no debt was waived. After Levy's meeting with Baker, he spoke to reporters, stretching credulity by saying 'We didn't come here to discuss money.'

But that was not quite how Israeli politicians viewed things. Shimon Peres, speaking before party members said, 'David Levy calls James Baker "Jim", but the fact is for the first time the US has waived the debts of one side only, while in the past it always helped both sides. Under the cosmetics and smiles lies a dire political reality.'[14]

Levy, after the Gulf War ended, became the peacenik of the Israeli cabinet, supporting the American position time after time in opposition to his own government. Levy had been turned into an apologist for the shifts and inconsistencies of Baker's latest peace proposals. Israel began the procedure with significant accommodation, agreeing to Baker's proposal for a regional conference to settle differences. But when Syria and Saudi Arabia refused to participate, Baker backtracked and accepted their proposal of an international conference with UN participation. Everyone but Levy, who continued to support Bush wholeheartedly, knew that such a proposal would be an ideal opportunity for all sides to gang up on Israel.

This angered the cabinet. Shouting matches between him and

such ministers as Yuval Ne'eman (Science), Sharon and Modai led to calls for his resignation, prevented only by a fear of the government falling and everyone losing out. Levy has split the government by switching ideologies in midstream. He hasn't the intellectual prowess or nerve to deal with Washington confidently and he is unwittingly creating discord between the two allies as no other minister has done. Yet the outside view lately is that Sharon and Shamir's 'intransigence' is more of a root cause of disharmony than Levy's incompetence.[15] Things have reached the point that Shamir reportedly gets sadistic pleasure out of rejecting Levy's proposals. Still, as little as he respects Levy, Shamir will not sacrifice his blue-collar support by sacking him. Meanwhile the Israeli public asks what Levy's toughest three years were. The answer is fifth grade. But the humour, derivative as it is, barely masks the outrage, exemplified in the writing of Yosef Goell:

> Levy is the wrong man in the wrong job at the wrong time. The Likud has better candidates . . . [certainly the handsome and well spoken, Benjamin Netanyahu]. The primacy Prime Minister Shamir accorded to internal Likud Party calculations in giving in to Levy's insistence on becoming Foreign Minister, for the sole purpose of serving as a stepping-stone to the premiership, has all the makings of a full-blown calamity.[16]

MOSHE ARENS

Arens is Shamir's closest cabinet ally. He had been a competent Foreign Minister in 1990, when Levy pushed him out of the post. Shamir's cabinet is filled with backstabbers, coup fomenters and religious fanatics, so he needs at least one reliable ally. Thus he appointed Arens Defence Minister, knowing full well his unsuitability for the position. He had been Defence Minister before, and his short tenure (1983–84) was so filled with anguish that his reappointment in 1990 was nothing short of indefensible.

Arens had taken over the post from Sharon who had resigned in disgrace over the Lebanon débâcle which led to the deaths of hundreds of Arab non-combatants. By 1983, it was clear to a majority of Israelis that there was no longer any reason to stay in the land of Cedars. The PLO had mostly been removed and that was the supposed war aim. With the assassination of Bashir Gemayal, the secondary aim of a peace treaty was beyond reach. Israel was now in Lebanon for nothing.

But Arens refused to budge. As Israeli soldiers by the dozens were killed in Shi'ite explosions, the country became deeply demoralised.

Reserve soldiers dreaded their call-up notices and once in Lebanon were terrified to go home on leave for fear of car-bombs. Yet Arens would not leave Lebanon. It took the next Defence Minister, Yitzhak Rabin, to make the decision. For one year, Arens oversaw the squandering of young Israeli lives.

His next act of demoralisation concerned the building of a fighter plane called the Lavi. The decision to build the Lavi was taken in the mid-1970s while Arens was the Israeli Ambassador to the USA. Arens, who had contributed to the design of the successful Kfir jet, used his position in Washington to release $150 million of American government money to seed the project. From then on he treated it like his own baby.

By the time he became Defence Minister, his baby was very expensive to feed. Just producing a prototype was chewing up 20% of the defence budget. Furthermore, thousands of the country's best weapons engineers, about a third of all available talent, were tied up in designing just one weapon. At least 10,000 workers were dependent on the Lavi for their income. And, just as had happened in Lebanon, it was all for nothing. The plane would cost over $75 million if it was ever built, far more than the cost of an American F-15. On top of that, the likelihood of recouping losses through overseas sales dwindled to nothing when the US, which had already blocked Kfir sales to Ecuador and Taiwan, requested that Israel stop building the Lavi.

But Arens displayed that famous stubbornness and dragged the country into an ugly public debate over the worthiness of his flying white elephant. When the smoke cleared the Lavi was dead and thousands of people were unemployed. Reportedly, dozens of Israel's top engineers were lured to South Africa where employment prospects in the arms industry were very bright. As for Israel, billions of dollars, once again, had bought nothing.

The worst fiasco, however, was the Bus 300 affair, which demoralised Israelis even more than the Lavi adventure into high-tech aeronautics. Four teenagers armed with automatic rifles and grenades took over an inter-city bus near the coastal city of Ashdod. Arens viewed the 'busjacking' as an event to change his image from the intellectual to the fighter, in the greater tradition of Rabin, Dayan and Sharon. He showed up at the scene of the drama dressed absurdly in a crooked battle helmet and declared in front of the cameras that no terrorist would leave an attack in Israel alive.

When the troops stormed the bus, one teenage girl was killed but the rest of the hostages were saved. The army announced that all four terrorists were killed in the shoot-out. Unfortunately, a press photographer filmed one terrorist being led away very much alive after his capture. In fact two terrorists were taken alive and were interrogated then killed by Shin Bet, the Israeli secret service. Shin Bet is answerable to the Prime Minister's office, not the Defence Ministry – this was a joint operation with paratroops.

Most Israelis know when the army announces that all terrorists were killed in a raid that some really weren't. Enough men have participated in anti-terrorist operations to ensure that this is common knowledge. This is not an issue in Israel, or it wasn't until Arens publicly let the cat out of the bag.

By announcing beforehand that no terrorist would survive the attack, the photograph of the living prisoner being taken away had added significance. The order to kill him seemed to be coming from the Defence Minister himself.

The issue was basic: Israel is ruled by democratic law and anyone charged with a crime, no matter how heinous, has a right to defend himself in court. Israel's civil libertarians were outraged that the captured terrorist was denied due process of law, and accused the army of murder. The issue was taken to the Supreme Court which supported these accusations. The army was about to go on trial for misconduct, but who in the army sets policy? The answer is the Chief of General Security Services (GSS), whose identity is kept secret for fear of a kidnapping by the enemy. The Chief was nonetheless subpoenaed over the Bus 300 affair and if he actually appeared in court, his cover would be blown forever.

Once again the country was dragged through a wrenching debate. The court ruled against a strong majority of public opinion which was glad the terrorists were killed and wished the civil libertarians a not dissimilar fate. Nonetheless, the Security Chief was handed a court order and would have to expose his identity, thus exposing the country's highest-ranking secret commander.

The affair, hand-made by Arens, seemed to have no solution short of endangering the security of the state to make a legal point. But where there's a will there's a lawyer in Israel. The country's President, Chaim Herzog, came to the rescue.

As the moral conscience of the nation, the President, whose role is mostly ceremonial, can grant pardons from criminal prosecution. It is usually considered more dignified for the President to remain above the fray and not get involved. Herzog cares little for decorum though, showing a remarkable similarity to less important politicians in his desire for as much public cash as he can get his hands on during his term in office.

In an obvious attempt to provide himself with a comfortable retirement he appealed to the Knesset to provide presidents and past presidents with an advisor, assistant, spokesman, secretary and chauffeur for life.[17]

The Chief of General Security met with Herzog, and the President had a sudden brainwave during the meeting. The Chief of Security would admit that the army had overstepped the law in the Bus 300 incident and the President would grant him a pardon. Thus Chaim Herzog became Israel's Gerald Ford.

The Bus 300 affair ended but not without severely diminishing the integrity of the President and the almost sacred shrine of the presidency. Speculation about what the Security Chief had on the President circulated throughout the country with a common theory involving financial irregularities in some African business deals. Whatever the truth actually was, the presidency was besmirched, though eventually the President himself was appointed to a second term of office. And Moshe Arens was appointed to another term as Defence Minister in 1990.

EHUD OLMERT

This somewhat critical look at the Likud members of the cabinet will end with Health Minister Ehud Olmert. He is the only other minister widely known abroad. Because of his good looks and passable English he has become an important spokesman, especially in Britain. He made national headlines in 1990 after being set up by the BBC to debate with a PLO member. Olmert won this unwanted encounter hands down and gained a great deal of respect.

But back at home one currently feels the first simmerings of scandal which may or may not boil over. Let it be restated that conflicts of interest have nothing to do with being a Knesset member. Such parliamentarians may keep whatever jobs they choose on the outside while promoting laws to benefit said jobs on the inside.

Olmert, one of the priciest lawyers in Israel, was accidentally discovered to be one of the most unscrupulous also. In 1987 police investigating the files of the North American Bank, which was involved in an embezzlement of at least $37 million, turned up some rather revealing information about Ehud.

It seems Olmert had directed one client to the bank who deposited $1.6 million. The client, according to Olmert's own explanation, was a criminal fighting extradition charges and Ehud felt his money would be safe in this obscure bank. And the bank appeared to be grateful for at least this patronage. Olmert was rewarded with a $50,000 loan, of which not a penny was ever returned. Naturally such a classic case of corruption would be the end of Olmert's career anywhere else. But in Israel he is considered a candidate for the leadership of Likud sometime after the present generation burns out.

MOLEDET

The Likud is supported by three secular parties to the right of its platform, Moledet, Techiya (revival) and Tzomet (crossroads). Techiya and Tzomet share ultra-nationalistic philosophies and the difference between them is mostly style. All three parties bolted the government in January 1992, Techiya and Moledet in protest of the Baker peace process, Tzomet, admirably, demanding electoral reform. But fear not readers. They will reappear in the next cabinet, that will be formed probably in July. It was their abandonment of the coalition that precipitated the 1992 elections. Techiya – led by the occasionally hysterical Geula Cohen, who interrupted Sadat's address to the Knesset and was thrown out of the chamber, and by Science Minister, Yuval Ne'eman, an internationally respected nuclear physicist – is bombastic; while Tzomet, led by Raful Eitan, Minister of Agriculture, is far more thoughtful. Neither party has yet been caught in the web of corruption engulfing most other parties.

In fact, Eitan has displayed a great deal of integrity and is becoming a strong moral voice in the Knesset. This surprises those who remember him less than fondly as Military Chief of Staff during the Lebanon War and who blame him for the embarrassment of Sabra and Shatilla and the 600 Israeli war dead. When he entered politics many thought his obsession would be the disputed territories and, in fact, early in his political career he caused a stir with his statement that settlements would surround and trap Arabs 'like drugged cockroaches in a jar'. Although the allegory may be militarily accurate, not all Arabs enjoyed being compared to cockroaches and a good many Jews sympathised with their anger.

Despite beginning in character, Eitan has displayed consistent honesty since. He is a farmer and so remains one of the few ministers suited for his post. As Agriculture Minister he has done more to alert the public of the quickly deteriorating and disappearing

water supply than any predecessor, declaring states of emergency and
strictly restricting supply when politically feasible.

The Likud went 30 million shekels ($13.5 million) into the red
financing its last election, in no small part, according to a Likud
newsletter, because of excessive spending by Ehud Olmert. To cover
its losses it introduced legislation, twice since 1988, to force the public
to pay all party deficits. Naturally Labour also liked the idea of their
bill being footed by the public and has supported the legislation, as
have the numerous smaller parties. Only Tzomet and the middle of
the road Shinui (change) Party, have refused to take a penny from the
budget to cover their own party expenses. And for this decent position,
Eitan's personal standing rose, even amongst his declared enemies to
the left.

But his star has risen over the issue of electoral reform. The single
most important thing that could save Israel from its self-created
morass of filthy politics is a drastic change in the way Knesset
members are elected. Eitan has introduced legislation calling for
the direct election of Members of Parliament which would make
each Member personally accountable to his constituency. This change
would mean the end of the majority of high political careers, since
almost everyone currently running the government would be likely
to lose a public popularity contest. But most beneficial of all, it would
toll the death knell for the small parties who would need a majority
of a constituency to gain a seat, not merely 1% of all votes cast.

The Likud, which desired electoral reform when it was in opposition, has now taken a strong stand against it, pushed by the
religious parties who would lose their disproportionate power in
any fair election. This unholy cabal flexed its muscles in November
1990. Eitan had given the government an ultimatum: introduce my
electoral reform bill or I leave the government. Had Eitan taken his
two seats out, he would have deprived Shamir of his majority. But
Shamir is craftier than the decent general. He managed to buy Agudat
Yisrael and its five seats at a tremendous cost and thereby, fearless
of his government weakened beyond taking action, outflanked Eitan
practically on the eve of his ultimatum day.

Once again reform was shelved, but Eitan and his Tzomet Party
gained elevated status. Zelda Harris, secretary of the Committee of
Concerned Citizens, a leading activist organisation fighting for reform,
is a grudging fan of Eitan's, noting that, 'He's a man of the earth, a
farmer who has a clear and simple vision of right and wrong. He is also
uncorruptible and that puts him at a disadvantage. Decency doesn't
often triumph these days.'[18]

And indeed in the case of Moledet strong evidence for gross indecency exists on a famous tape-recording.

Moledet is the party whose central platform is 'transfer', or the expulsion of territorial Arabs from Israel. For this same stand, the Knesset, including the Likud, expelled Rabbi Meir Kahane from parliament on trumped up charges of racism.

A further source of trouble was Shamir's promotion of the Moledet leader, Rehavam Zeevi, to a cabinet post. In 1979 an FBI document accused Zeevi of consorting with drug smugglers. This led to a police tap on his phone. In one recorded conversation a gentleman named Oshri, who was later convicted of murder, appealed for Zeevi's help with his police problems. Zeevi agreed to do what he could.

Ehud Olmert somehow got his hands on the tape and presented it to Shamir to dissuade him from approving Zeevi's appointment. Shamir was unmoved and Olmert threatened with bodily harm.[19]

Another MK, Mordechai Virshubsky, raised the matter of Zeevi's friendship with killers and drug smugglers in the Knesset debate on his cabinet approval, understating: 'For a cabinet minister to consort with murderers is not done.'

But done it was and for very good political reasons. Polls suggest that Moledet, like Kach would have done before it, will pick up about five seats in the next general election. With Zeevi in the cabinet, the Likud will pick up the seats, thus lessening its dependence on the religious parties and forever putting off another unity government with the fickle and conniving Labour. With such advantages, what difference is it to Shamir, that a man linked to organised crime now sits with him in cabinet meetings? Who knows, some day the Prime Minister might need a hitman.

CHAPTER FIVE

Holy Corrupt Parties

Perhaps no political change in recent days has been so divisive as the rise in the fortunes and misfortunes of the religious parties. With sanctimonious greed, they have plundered the Treasury while forcing the enaction of repressive and unjust laws on the secular majority.

The story of the religious parties is not new, it's just been deeply intensified since 1984, when the secular voters became polarised almost equally between the two major parties and their natural allies. With both parties unable to form viable coalitions amongst themselves, they turned to wooing the parties of God whose agendas are very different from their own.

The alliance between religious and secular is said to have officially begun in 1947 when the UN sent an inquiry commission to report back on the viability of a Jewish state. All voices were to be heard including that of Agudat Yisrael, which represented Orthodox interests in pre-state Israel. Founded in 1912 solely as a political movement aimed at fighting Zionism, it seemed likely to oppose the founding of a Jewish state.

Their fears of a Jewish state undercutting their position were not totally unfounded. The Jewish Agency, then the official Jewish governing body, was run by David Ben Gurion and his followers, practically every one of them atheistic or agnostic socialists who felt untold revulsion at the thought of founding a state based on traditional ghetto religious superstitions.

Only the fear of losing UN backing for statehood pushed Ben Gurion into the reluctant arms of Agudat Yisrael, which suspected their rights might be better protected under further Christian or even Moslem rule. Ben Gurion promised Aguda that the new Jewish state's civil laws (governing marriage, divorce, birth and death) would be under Orthodox supervision and control, that all state-owned eateries would be kosher and that schools would be divided between the parochial and mainstream with separate administration but equal validity.

48

After achieving statehood, religious influence increased with the addition of the pro-Zionist National Religious Party (NRP) to the Knesset. Although they were serious rivals, the combination of two religious parties working towards common goals pressured the first governments of the new state to make accommodations. Ben Gurion would promise legislation on behalf of the religious, then demur until the religious parties would demand action; he would demur again and the government would fall, only to be reconstituted along the same lines the next time around.

Along the way legislation was enacted that restricted travel and commerce on the sabbath or the sale of pork, but enforcement was made nearly impossible by a secular majority unwilling to bend to the religious minority no matter how much it had the law on its side. Sometimes side-stepping the law was costly and silly. Kibbutz Lahav, which raised pigs, had to go to court to prove the animals provided a humanitarian justification for raising them (their skin is used in grafts mainly for burn victims), and once so proven had to erect large wooden platforms below the pigs so their feet wouldn't soil the holy ground of Israel.

As the observant Yosef Goell notes: 'The game produced a messy system, irrational compromises, a deep disrespect for the law, which was often seen as a mere piece of paper to be ignored, and a deepening sense of disdain and even hatred for anything to do with official religion or the religious establishment among a younger generation of secular Israelis.'[1]

Although the religious parties didn't gain anywhere near the full extent of their agendas, they did get their hands on some lucrative ventures. As part of the various coalition agreements, they were usually assigned such ministries as Religion or the Interior with all the funds those posts entailed. And as the protectors of civil functions, they could collect the fees for licences and paperwork. It was enough to keep them alive, body and soul. In fact, it was enough to keep the Orthodox flourishing while their numbers were small.

However, success was planting the seeds of collapse from within. Until the founding of the Jewish state, the Orthodox Ashkenazic yeshiva or seminary was restricted to only the most brilliant and promising religious scholars, mostly for financial reasons. Living in abject poverty, a European Jew could not afford to give up a son to pure study and only if his brilliance was noted would the community or yeshiva subsidise his education.

With the sudden and unexpected influx of funds from the Zionists, the religious community expanded their yeshiva system to include

every young boy of learning age, whether worthy or not, or capable
of withstanding the regimen of twelve-hour classes, without breaks
for leisure or sport. Such an education excluded the students
from 'useful' work after graduation since technical, scientific or
administrative skills were not part of the curriculum.

Because of the literal acceptance of God's ordnance 'be fruitful
and multiply', Orthodox families are huge. That same ordnance
denies birth control or abortion to the community, assuring further
steady growth and the highest rate of mongolism in Israel – even
the detection of Down's syndrome in the womb will not lead to an
abortion.

Learning nothing but *Torah*, these scholars, the vast majority of
whom are poor or average students, are not trained in any kind
of work. Thus the Orthodox leaders have managed to produce
a generation of men incapable of earning a living, exempt from
military service and raising huge families – since that is God's will.
They survive on whatever money their politicians can squeeze from
the state. Any funds they have been able to obtain, however, have
been at the expense of secular education. The amount of money
given by the government to institutes of higher education fell by
$45 million to $300 million in the ten years since 1980, lowering
academic standards and precipitating strikes by both students and
staff. In comparison, the end of the same period saw the yeshivas
receive $98 million, a rise of nearly $72 million. They were also
given $90 million in 'special allocations'.

To give this generation of scholars work, new yeshivas were
constructed and to populate them, duller adolescents became
permanent adult students, punching a clock and receiving stipends
from their yeshiva which in turn received the money from tax-paying
secular or traditionally religious Israelis who hardly want to
subsidise holier-than-thou layabouts.

By the late 1980s Israel was in its deepest recession ever with
unemployment passing 10% and a national debt surpassing $21.5
billion. The country could no longer support all the financial
demands of the Orthodox and their network had grown so large
that without massive aid, it was completely untenable. Hence one
of the principal reasons why the Orthodox parties steal.

The social consequences of the bed the Orthodox must lie in are
just emerging. Thousands of Sephardic students (far more than
Ashkenazic) enrolled by their parents in the yeshivas, have been
dropping out for lack of interest or ability to withstand the rigours
of a strict religious education. With no training, and alienated from

the part of Israeli society which earns an unsubsidised living, they are lost the minute they leave their yeshivas and far too often turn to crime.

There is one underfunded school, Bnei Reem, which attempts to rehabilitate Sephardi drop-outs from yeshivas. The task is daunting, as explained by the principal Shlomo Friedman.

> With nothing to do, how long do you think it takes these kids to discover drugs and petty crime? . . . We get these drop-outs but what can we do after instilling some basic humanity and self-confidence? We send most back to their yeshivas because there's no room for them in the marketplace . . . Most of these boys have manual or mechanical talents which should have been developed before. They never belonged in a yeshiva in the first place.

In the Ashkenazic Orthodox community, the situation is even more dire. Half a generation ago graduates of yeshivas could find jobs as teachers or functionaries such as scribes or circumsisers and thus earn a living. Today the well has dried up and these same graduates can only find subsistence receiving their government stipend for continued learning. Or by *shnorring*, which is Hebrew for begging.

Nahum Friedman, who runs the Mishkenot Yerushalayim, an organisation that aids Orthodox people seeking housing, was quoted in the Israeli press predicting a total breakdown of Hasidic society in Israel. There is not the money within Israel to support the infrastructure and, he claimed, over 50% of ultra-orthodox (haredi) men go abroad at some time to beg for money to support their families.

And yet, those with vested interests within the Orthodox community will not change the system. In fact, they resist change violently. Rabbi H, who teaches at a respected yeshiva and has published a successful book in the Orthodox community worldwide this past year notes: 'There is a lunatic fringe in the haredi community with interests in keeping the status quo. Let us say they engage in extra-legal activities when it suits them.'

Rabbi D runs the only junior high school yeshiva which trains its students in secular subjects and encourages a later choice between college or yeshiva in Jerusalem. He is discouraged by the over-crowding in other yeshivas and the insistence on a one-dimensional education for the students. He is also living in fear that those elements in his community who deeply fear secular intrusion will shut him down violently. At a similar institute, Rabbi Baruch Chait was run out of town after he was reportedly assaulted. He was forced to relocate 40 miles away in the isolated town of Matityahu.

Zvi Weinberger is the principal of the Jerusalem College of Technology, a technical college whose students are primarily religious and Sephardic. He is saddened by the situation: 'There's only one school left in all Jerusalem trying to train young haredim for a multi-choice future. Unless there is a change in their educational approach, the haredim won't be able to support themselves at all. A whole generation has passed without producing doctors, pharmacists, chemists or engineers. If the community doesn't adjust, the day of insolvency will approach quickly.'

Hence the situation the Orthodox parties find themselves in. The typical family is a ten-member unit living in a steamy two or three-bedroom apartment in an all-orthodox neighbourhood. The children are well cared for but sometimes badly fed. One case reported in the press concerned a woman watering down one egg to make omelettes for three children. Furnishings are bare, pictures do not grace the walls, television is forbidden and children intrude day and night. The husband's existence is his yeshiva, the overburdened wife takes care of the secular chores like paying bills and maintaining a budget, but cannot make do on what the yeshiva pays her husband to learn. It is a world of heated religious arguments flaring up in the stark and overpopulated ghettos of Orthodox Israel.

And it is up to the Orthodox politicians to hold the fort and maintain the money lifeline or if possible, increase it. With most of Israel opposed to subsidising the Orthodox world, squeezing money from their government requires new strategies which are not always pleasant.

What follows is a party by party look at Israeli religious politics, beginning with the party most trapped by its own deceit.

SHAS

The 1981 elections set a precedent that was to change and sully Israeli politics to this day. One Aharon Abuhatzeira, scion of a great Moroccan religious family, ran for the Knesset under a new party banner, Tami, which represented Sephardic religious interests. He did well for a first-timer, capturing two seats. This gave him enough power to request the Religious Affairs Ministry from Prime Minister Begin and get it.

By the time his tenure was over, he was arrested, tried and convicted for shifting large amounts of ministry funds to his own interests and receiving kickbacks for his trouble. He was sentenced to six months in jail but didn't spend a moment inside. Instead, he was ordered to report to the Jerusalem police station twice a week, which he did, while ensconced in a luxury hotel paid for by the public he had cheated.

Once again, it appeared that crime pays in Israeli politics. Abuhatzeira is today a loyal Likudnik and a sitting member of the Knesset. But his success in appealing to Sephardic voters did not go unnoticed by the Council of Torah Sages, the cabal of elders led by the 93-year-old Lithuanian-born Rabbi Shach, which had a strong influence on the direction of Ashkenazic religious affairs. He felt that a Sephardic party led by graduates of European-style yeshivas would further extend the power of the ultra-orthodox led by Agudat Yisrael. Thus Shas was born, ready-made for the 1984 elections. The impact of the new party was profound. On its first try, Shas garnered enough votes to become the fourth largest party in the Knesset.

The 1988 elections sanctified the power of Shas, as the party collected five seats and, more than any other religious party, determined coalition politics. Shamir tried desperately to form a Likud-religious coalition but appeared to give up when the price became unpayable. But even within a unity government with Labour, Shas's power was acknowledged by both big parties and a non-Knesset member, Arye Deri, was appointed Minister of the Interior.

Deri's own crimes have been summarised in previous pages but one example of his methods will serve to refresh the memory, no doubt by now clouding over with official crime. Shas set up an institute called 'The Centre for Torah Education of the Tradition of Jews of the East'. For all the mumbo-jumbo and pretension of the name, the institute was a front for channelling over a quarter of a million dollars in state funds into four Shas institutions. Or as the State Comptroller noted, 'a pipeline through which it was possible to bypass official policies'.

And that is part of the system Shas used to run an Interior Ministry based on kleptomania. Deri would withhold funds to local councils until they agreed to kickback money to his ministry. With this money the ministry would then fund institutions that were nothing more than fronts for the Shas Party.

The question remains, why would a party based on religious (and thus moral) principles turn so rotten, and why would its followers stand by it instead of protesting all the ethical outrages?

The answer lies in the constituency. While the leadership of Shas is haredi, the followers are not so strict and are willing to bend the rules when it suits them. They are the multitudes of poor Sephardim, more from Morocco than any other Middle-Eastern nation, who feel cheated by the Ashkenazim who have ruled them all their lives. They feel that the Europeans robbed them of their culture and denied them opportunities for wealth. Thus robbing the system that has been robbing them is justified.

More immediately, the Sephardic haredim also have their own system of yeshivas and charitable institutions and, like the Ashkenazim, their whole network of interlocking schools and charities is financially untenable and about to cave in, leaving the leaders high and dry. The difference is that the Ashkenazim have some alternatives to stay the execution.

The European haredim can turn to relatives and sympathisers throughout the diaspora, especially in America where the Orthodox population numbers about a million, most of whom work for a living. The Sephardi population, by contrast, was dispersed forcibly from the Arab lands and, never large to begin with, mostly settled in Israel. There is no significant hinterland supporting the centre.

The Ashkenazim are much more familiar with western ways of raising money. When they 'fund-raise', they aren't ashamed to apply high pressure until the victim acquiesces to rid himself of a pesty caller. The victim's name then enters a list for donations which is organised and filed for future use. Ashkenazi institutes run data banks while the Sephardi organisations, and especially Shas, are run by the seat of their pants by amateurs.

The Ashkenazim also are capable of making money make money and operate businesses – many legitimate, some scams – that help support the community. Many of the money-changers in Jerusalem's black market are European haredim, for example. They are astute observers of western finance and know when risks bring rewards.

The Sephardi haredim are restricted by the type of converts they can attract to the fold. Mostly their new members come from the poor of Israel. The Ashkenazi haredim actively seek new adherents from diaspora Jews, believing not only that their souls will be saved but their families abroad will contribute to their and everybody's well-being. There is one large Orthodox neighbourhood in Jerusalem populated mostly by newly observant American Jews, living in good part off monies sent from sources in the US.

Without the cushion enjoyed by the Ashkenazim, Shas was even more desperate to raise the funds necessary to support the endless needs of its community. And without the financial acumen to cover up its embezzlement, Shas was caught. Indeed, when the State Comptroller's staff investigated Shas Party finances, they were amazed how easy it was to discover stolen money from the unsophisticated characters Shas employed as accountants.

Shas also lacked the sophistication needed to maintain a political party in Israel. Labour, since the founding of the state, have enticed workers to join their union, the Histadrut, with the promise of advancement and have then taken their dues to support the party. They also own a bank and vast tracts of prime real estate, acquired naturally enough, with political influence on the local level. No matter how unpopular Labour is with the public, funds from one source or another will always keep the party afloat.

The Ashkenazi political parties have tried to copy Labour's model and one, the NRP, owns a major bank, Mizrahi, while Agudat Yisrael has shares in a smaller bank. Shas has no bank, no trade union, and little real estate. What it does have is a lot of people charged with crime.

Interior Ministry Deri's top financial aide, Yom-Tov Rubin, was held by police in 1991 on charges relating to graft and theft. Deri appointed him head of the town council of Lehavim near Beersheva. He then purchased worthless land in the area for a pittance. The land soon after was awarded a government building permit, very hard to acquire in Israel, and thus increased in value.

Another close aide of Deri's, Moshe Weinberg, was remanded on suspicion of bribery, embezzlement and fraud. Yet still another very close aide, Zvi Jacobson, was also arrested on suspicion of embezzlement. But if Deri and his closest aides are all under investigation for misappropriation of public funds, then it is only to the good of Shas attorney David Glass, who happens to employ Deri's own brother as a lawyer. The web of deceit spreads ever outwards, engulfing still another Shas ministry.

At the time of writing (but hopefully not of publication), Raphael Pinhasi is Israel's Minister of Communication and the other Shas minister in the cabinet. Police are currently investigating a charge made by former Shas MK, Yaacov Yosef, who happens to be the son of Shas's spiritual leader Ovadia Yosef, the former Chief Sephardic Rabbi of Israel. While a member of the Knesset, Yosef received a $225,000 cheque (for uses not yet disclosed). According to Yosef, Pinhasi took the cheque, forged Yosef's signature and cashed it. Added Yosef: 'Where is it written in the *Torah* that theft is allowed? Because he is a minister he

allows himself to steal? They all must be replaced. They are all
thieves.'[2]

The sudden burst of conscience by Yosef revealed his disgust at
Shas's policy of inflaming Sephardic feelings of injustice: 'Their
head is involved in the forging of signatures . . . and they scream
that they are being interrogated because they are Sephardim. They
will pay for their deeds.'[3]

Yosef was rewarded for his indignation with legal and physical
threats.

The police are investigating another Shas Knesset member, Yair
Levy, on suspicion of forging cheques worth $27,000 and depositing
public money into his private bank account. Levy met with police
inspectors and received permission to travel to America for a month.
Six weeks later he had still not returned, nor had he indicated that
he would. Some MKs were furious. Amnon Rubinstein of the Shinui
Party remarked: 'A public figure should have co-operated with the
police and come back quickly,' while a member of the Knesset for
Rats (Citizens' Rights Party) added, 'it would be a precedent of
historic and catastrophic proportions – an MK who goes AWOL from
the law.'*

And while the country wondered if Levy would ever return
to face charges,[4] another Shas MK, Rabbi Gamliel, had taken
unilateral action against the coalition. To protest the 'discriminatory
investigation' of Shas, he would not support any government
motion. The fact that his aide was being tried for bugging a
reporter's phone and house and that the trail could lead back to him,
undoubtedly spurred his decision, though he claimed his motives
were to fight anti-Sephardic treatment by the government.

With the whole party looking like a mafia family, the State
Comptroller took action to break Shas's back. The government
actually finances political party expenses in Israel. The State
Comptroller decided in the late winter of 1991 to cut some
$675,000 from Shas's government allocation as punishment for
all the illegalities she uncovered in four separate reports. With the
well of embezzled money drying up in the face of police scrutiny,
this smallish sum could mean the difference between life and death
for the party. Shas had signed long-term and expensive contracts
on behalf of its many institutions, and without the government
allocation, staff would go unpaid in violation of said contracts and
the party would be forced into bankruptcy.

---

* In January 1992, Levy was finally charged with stealing $250,000 by the police.

Perhaps the kleptocracy of Shas will lead to its downfall but again, predicting a Greek tragedy may yet be proved premature. Labour seemed to allow Shas to steal right under the Finance Ministry's nose in order to pressure the party into felling the unity government and joining a Labour coalition. When that failed, Likud kept two Shas ministers in the cabinet to prevent another government from collapsing, despite the relentless accusations and a police probe digging up reams of evidence against the party.

It is difficult to imagine any other democracy that would permit two ministers under a pall of suspicion about crimes of theft, fraud, forgery, graft and embezzlement, to continue in public office. But such is the appalling case in Israel.

YITZHAK PERETZ

A rabbi and former member of Shas, Peretz is now Likud's Minister of Immigration, a post of vital importance in view of the current massive exodus of Jews from the USSR. Needless to say, however, their arrival in Israel has been far from problem-free. Peretz did not act on the warnings he was given about the scale of the impending tidal wave of Soviets: though they would now process 250,000 immigration requests a year (as opposed to 20,000 previously), no new clerical staff were taken on at the Immigration Office. The clerks were not given a pay-rise to compensate for the extra work-load, nor were they provided with Russian translators to speed up the process. Most stupidly of all, the working day has remained 8 a.m. to 1 p.m. – the hours the Soviets ought to spend looking for work or accommodation or learning Hebrew – not waiting in interminable queues in the Immigration Office. It is difficult to see what more Peretz could have done to prevent their smooth entry to Israel.[5]

It was up to Peretz to run a friendly, efficient bureaucracy that would encourage the immigration process further, but he has failed miserably in his chosen task. Having no tolerance of non-religious Jews, he was never the man to absorb hundreds of thousands of mostly secular newcomers.[6] He accepted the post as a means of assuring the future religiosity of the heathen Jews arriving in their thousands every month. More than anything else, Peretz's ministry has been characterised by his insistence on maintaining the Jewish purity of the immigrants, persuading many of them to become 'more Jewish' with symbolic acts such as remarriage in the Orthodox manner, reconversion and circumcision. He has made immigration to Israel an excruciating process, many times exacerbated if one's Jewishness is remotely in doubt.[7]

DEGEL HATORAH

This is another party under the wings of Rabbi Shach's Council of Torah Sages. In the aftermath of the 1988 elections, the Techiya Party accused Degel HaTorah of cheating at two polling stations. They presented convincing evidence of ballot-rigging, including collecting the identity cards of the deceased still on the voter rolls and voting on their behalf. The evidence was convincing enough for the High Court to order the first re-election in Israel's history at the two contested polling stations.

In the winter of 1991, Degel HaTorah won again, though allegedly by further fraud. This time Techiya filed a formal complaint with the police, alleging bribery. Their report told of a 60-year-old woman who was offered a hundred shekels, a free taxi ride to the polling station and 'a nice gift' afterwards if she would vote Degel HaTorah. The report included another ten cases of similar bribes.[8]

When it comes to bribery Degel HaTorah is admirably non-discriminatory. When the results of the 1988 General Election rolled in, confused citizens were hard pressed to explain why over 2,000 Arabs, including Bedouins from the Negev Desert, who have little concern with haredi politics, voted Degel HaTorah. The mystery was later solved and a Degel supporter was sent to prison for bribing Arab voters with cash incentives.

Needless to say, Degel HaTorah is comfortably seated in the Knesset with two members and enjoys all the monetary benefits of being part of the ruling coalition, no matter how it got there.

NATIONAL RELIGIOUS PARTY (NRP)

This is the Zionist religious party currently split between the avid settlers and what it calls moderates. And, although the NRP's leader is up to his neck in alleged corruption,[9] this is not what characterises the party. Rather, they are distinguished by the fact that the most powerful faction within the party is Gush Emunim, the activist group who initiated settlement in the territories back in 1976.

Within the NRP-affiliated yeshivas there is taught a belief in populating the ancient territory of the Israelites as a holy act of redemption. In 1976 graduates and students of the NRP seminaries squatted on its first settlement illegally, eventually winning Labour Party approval and thus government sanction for its initiative. Since then, about 100,000 Jews, not by any means all NRP supporters, have joined them. Thus, one party's adherents have focused world attention on the issue of 'Israeli expansionism'.

That the settlers are peace obstructionists is hardly an Israeli consensus. The majority view the settlers as the last pioneers and idealists, willing to brave daily dangers for the ultimate security of the land. But even if the NRP-settlement movement is a divisive issue in Israel, at least it is not based on theft, graft, embezzlement, patronage, bribery or blackmail, but is founded rather on ideology.

While the ideology of the NRP may not be corrupt, their fund-raising is. For the past fifteen years, millions of dollars have been shifted to the party by Marcus Katz, a Mexico-based arms dealer who is deeply enmeshed in the morass of Central America (see *Dangerous Liaison* by Leslie and Alexander Cockburn).

Closer to home, NRP Knesset head, Avner Shaki, was investigated by the police in March '91 for shifting $400,000 in public funds to family members. He broke down during the interrogation in a Tel Aviv hotel room and asked God to save him. God's intervention was, as usual, unnecessary. He remains in the Knesset and not in jail.

AGUDAT YISRAEL (AGUDA)

Being non-Zionist enemies of the state Aguda resisted joining the current coalition until the price was right. On the very eve of Raful Eitan of the Tzomet Party's electoral reform ultimatum, Aguda joined Shamir's coalition. They received a few deputy ministerships worth millions of dollars but more importantly for them, Shamir agreed to introduce and support legislation restricting abortion, the production and sale of pork, public transportation on the sabbath and advertising which utilises pretty women, which is considered enticingly immoral.

Beginning with the last piece of legislation first: for the past decade billboard and bus-shelter advertising that has featured attractive ladies to sell a product have been defaced throughout the country. In Jerusalem defacement was not sufficient; dozens of bus shelters which had posters of women on them were burnt to the ground. The anger in the city amongst the secular population was so great a few years back that a synagogue was broken into and prayer-books were burned.

To the religious this was not retaliation of a kind. They are not aware of the deep feelings of many Israelis who consider freedom of expression more important in their lives than freedom of prayer. To such types, burning bus shelters because a woman revealed a bare arm was a gross infringement of their needs for artistic freedom and protection against exposure during a thunderstorm.

The arsonists were trapped, arrested and held, but always released without trial. Nonetheless they were somewhat humbled by the experience of handcuffs. The new Aguda legislation sanctioned the years of quasi-legal poster destruction.

The motivation behind the fires was not merely the protection of female dignity. In fact, the arsonists appeared to be deeply frustrated sexually and wanted no public reminder of what they were missing. As a rule, the ultra-orthodox marry in their teens, and not necessarily to the woman of their choice but rather to the whims of matchmakers, a necessity in the segregated world of the yeshiva. The wives may be as attractive as any in the general population but after a dozen children before the age of 40, haggardness sets in deeply. And in contrast to the modern Orthodox movement, make-up and fashion is unknown. A constant reminder of the availability of beautiful women to secular Israelis drives some ultra-orthodox men to pyromania.

Let it not be claimed that there is no hypocrisy in their attitude. Prostitutes in Tel Aviv and sex-shop owners (when their stores aren't burnt down) claim the majority of their clientèle are equally repressed Arabs and haredi men.

After agreeing to restrict beautiful women in advertising, Shamir accepted Aguda's anti-abortion demand. A fat lot of good that will do. In 1978, a similar law was passed because of Aguda pressure and the number of abortions in the country has risen steadily as Israelis discovered the sexual revolution with vigour. Mostly secular doctors ignore the religious prohibitions and the state has shown little enthusiasm for prosecuting its most educated and influential citizens.

Restricting sabbath travel hurts the masses of semi-traditional followers of religious and right-wing parties who don't always own cars that will withstand a trip to the beach on a hot day. It has no effect on the better-off supporters of the liberal/left who, mostly, wouldn't be caught dead dragging their families on an outing by bus.

Still, not just the poor were affected. In the Upper Galilee where it can be a three or four-hour trip to the population centres further south, the regional council petitioned the High Court to block the Agudat Yisrael-sponsored bill banning public transport on the sabbath. Its chairman accused the government of subordinating its 'administration and legal discretion to the dictates of the coalition agreement'. A rather obvious observation. Despite this and other legitimate objections, the laws governing sabbath transportation will be enforced vigorously or not depending on government determination to keep Agudat Yisrael in the coalition.

The ban on pork has been tried many times before but on this occasion the government seems determined to waste more taxpayers' money enforcing Aguda's will. After the planned law banning pork was announced, Jerusalem butchers hit the streets giving out free cooked pig flesh. While the public reacted in a mixed fashion – even violently against the display of non-kosher protest – two Jerusalem city councillors, Moshe Amirav and Ornan Yekutieli, backed the butchers, mostly out of disgust for the cynicism of the Aguda-Likud coalition agreement of November 1990. The two formed a new organisation called 'The Association Against Public Piggishness'. Yekutieli's slogan was, 'Get out of our plates'.

More seriously, once pork leaves the public domain, all health controls disappear. Israelis who choose to buy the meat will have to turn to Christian Arab raisers, whose standards are not always legal or palatable. Enforcing the law will be prohibitive and, as usual, will be financed by public money. Just closing down the pig farm at Kibbutz Lahav and the processing plant at Mizrah will cost the public millions of dollars and what will they gain as a result? Some people will stop sinning openly and buy non-kosher meat from Arabs. And once again, Israelis will ask what their tax money is going to. They have trouble meeting their food bill and some of the money that could be used for feeding their families will go towards stopping others from eating ham.

There is some hope, however. Most Likud members are secular and according to one Lahav resident, Ariel Sharon has been buying his pork there for years. But hypocrisy is rife in the government and even Sharon might be willing to skip a juicy meal to build more houses in the Judean Hills above Hebron. So Israelis might just have to buy a dime-bag of pork from a sleazy ham pusher for the foreseeable future.

Of course, the planned legislation did not thrill all law-abiding citizens of Israel. As radio announcer Idelle Ross resignedly said: 'It's going to be dull as hell here from now on. But at least there won't be any prostitutes, pork or posters.'

And, naturally, since the Likud-Aguda agreement of November 1990, religious oppression has increased substantially. Possibly the worst affected are those in the recreation and entertainment industry who do a substantial proportion of their business on the one night of leisure officially recognised in Israel, the sabbath. (Yes, Israel is the last country in the democratic world with a six-day work week.) They are forced to close on the sabbath, depending on the enthusiasm of local authorities.

In Tel Aviv, the municipality views sabbath offenders as a source of income. Yair Sinai, who owns a snack shop, has accumulated over $450,000 in fines for opening on the sabbath and trumped-up charges of littering, etc. Other businessmen throughout Tel Aviv, not believing the city would actually try to collect such fines, have run up similar amounts, enough to force them into debt for the rest of their lives. Yet they continue operating on the sabbath for commercial and ethical reasons, and each Saturday they get new fines of at least $90. Naturally, those with pull get the rare permit to operate on the sabbath while those unfortunate others without *shlep* or *protectzia* or a cousin in city hall, are harangued, not always into submission.

Yair Sinai knows of one businessman considering a conversion to Christianity to side-step the law and complains that Arabs are given preferential treatment by being allowed to desecrate a sabbath that isn't theirs. But others are also free to operate, as heavily-fined businessman Moshe Shaul observes: 'They leave the whores, thieves and addicts alone and instead bother someone who's trying to make an honest living.' Sinai has collected his share of fines and hopes: 'Some other government, someday, will overturn the sabbath law and cancel all our fines.' A noble sentiment, but impossible without a complete change in Israel's electoral system.

In contrast to Tel Aviv, the holy city of Jerusalem seems downright liberal. Judge Ayala Procaccio ruled in 1987 that the whole business of sabbath law was outside municipal authority and refused to prosecute those who violated the law. While religious city councillors want the sabbath rulings reimposed, enough secular councillors support Procaccio's judgment, with the result that Jerusalem is the country's most lively city on the sabbath – though compared to the stagnation of the provinces, the capital did not have to do much to win that recognition.

Despite non-Israeli conceptions to the contrary, the years that Jerusalem's celebrated mayor, Teddy Kollek, has spent in office have been a miserable failure. He has tried to run this city – which is incorrigibly religious – in a secular way. His vision, echoed in his party's name of One Jerusalem, has been mocked by the cruel reality of the city's segregation: Arab East Jerusalem is effectively closed to Jews; whole districts of Orthodox Jews are closed to secular citizens, while the secular neighbourhoods build social and economic barriers to stem the religious tide. A recent survey of divided cities placed Jerusalem first in the world ahead of Berlin, Boston or Belfast in terms of the sociological gaps between its main population groups.

The Jewish Quarter of the walled Old City of Jerusalem was planned as a half-secular area when it was first reopened to Jewish residents in the late 1960s. And initially, the first daring property speculators were non-religious. But once they proved that living so close to Arabs behind sixteenth-century Turkish walls was reasonably safe, Orthodox citizens began buying their share of the available property to be near the holy ground of the Temple Mount. (The so-called Wailing Wall is part of the territory.) Driven by a set of more immediate beliefs, they clashed constantly with the secular residents and drove most out by harassment. A television blaring on a Friday night might lead to a total electricity cut-off by means of stolen fuses in the building box a few seconds later. Unlawful appearances with loose teenage women could lead to shattered windows. Even the suspicion of unkosher habits might lead to neighbourhood reaction and defacement of property. Today, the planned mixed neighbourhood is almost all Orthodox, the secularists driven out a decade ago.

Deep as the intolerance of the Orthodox for the secular is, there are many secular-Orthodox friendships. But the secularist must give way every time a clash may occur. He will throw a party on a Saturday instead of Friday night for fear of offending his religious friends and will serve food on paper plates because his own may have inadvertently been polluted with a mixture of milk or meat. In social intercourse, the secularist must be more sensitive to the religionist. It is unavoidable. Over time, maintaining a friendship (or God forbid, a marriage) between the religious and the secular becomes such a daunting strain that the personalities drift apart.

Agudat Yisrael exploits and exacerbates the differences and widens the chasm. It is convinced that all Christians in Israel and those supporting the state from without are only interested in converting the Jews to Jesus Christ. Any Israelis associated with sympathetic Christian groups are branded proselytisers by Aguda's supporters and leaders. Even a man such as Nathan Sharansky, who spent a third of his life in Soviet prisons for his belief in Israel, was deigned an Aguda-Orthodox enemy for raising funds on behalf of a pro-Israel Dutch Christian group.

But Aguda prejudice goes beyond Christians; they also discriminate against fellow Jews. The Knesset had to introduce a new law in May 1990 to prevent schools refusing pupils on religious grounds, a move prompted by the discovery that Aguda schools in the city of Bnei Brak had turned pupils away because they were Sephardic.

One of the most active new government members has been Aguda leader, Menachem Porush, the Deputy Minister of Labour. One of his first actions was to prevent airport employees working on the sabbath, thus forcing foreign airlines to bring in their own mechanics, etc., if they wanted to fly out of the country on the holy day. The nation's third-largest industry – tourism – was necessarily badly hit as a result. Everything from hotels and tourist guides to taxis and cafés suffered, and El Al, Israel's airline, could have been threatened in kind by various foreign airports.

In addition, Porush has joined forces with Immigration Minister Peretz to make those arriving in Israel from the USSR on the sabbath wait until the following day before the interminable delays in processing their applications can even begin. Even culture is not safe from Porush's interfering hands. He has filed charges against people working or performing on the sabbath during the Israel Festival, a yearly extravaganza of poetry, opera and theatre.

When any government minister is foolish enough to challenge or criticise his blatant oppression, Porush responds calmly by calling the minister a Nazi – no lightweight insult in a Jewish state largely founded by Holocaust survivors.

Outsiders astonished at the level of religious intolerance in present-day Israel may be led to the erroneous conclusion that the country is swamped with God-fearing zealots. The truth, in fact, is that only 20% of the population is Orthodox in the haredi fashion. The power wielded by the religious factions proves on closer inspection to be more a case of the tail wagging the dog. The controlling minority is not only lowering the general public's standard of living, but is pushing people in directions they do not want to go. One often hears that there is nothing new in religious coercion, and that what is happening nowadays is no different from at any time in Israel's short history. But it seems today as if there is an Israeli Inquisition on.

During the May long weekend holiday in 1991, Deputy Minister Porush deployed a crack unit of Druze inspection teams to roam the country reporting on businesses remaining open during the religious holiday. The main points of attack were the boring but harmless Israel Festival, kibbutz industries and entertainment venues throughout the land. Porush's all-out war on sabbath and holiday violators, led by his gentile shock troops, would result in charges filed against honest businessmen by a government ministry willing to sacrifice huge amounts of public funds towards the legal costs of beating the recalcitrant sinners into submission.

The change of attitude is everywhere. Christians who have lived in Israel for decades are finding their visas suddenly difficult to renew, and are effectively being expelled from the country they've devoted themselves to.

But it is mainly Jews who are the common victims. In one absurd case, a 70-year-old woman had her passport application rejected because her picture was too sexy. She was wearing a sleeveless dress which is considered immoral by the Orthodox. The lady was forced to change her clothes and have another photograph taken before her passport would be approved lest some airport officer in a foreign land be titillated away from concentration on his *Torah* studies and loyalty to God.

The major difference between past and present scandals in Israeli politics is that the outrages of today surround supposedly religious men like Shas leader Arye Deri and Yair Levy. Six years ago, Deri was a mere yeshiva student while Yair Levy sold fish. The political deadlock has permitted novices to learn the system and its weaknesses and thus deprive the helpless public of money, of the right to earn a living, of protection against civil abuses and of secular peace of mind.

The damage caused by Shas has sent the good name of Sephardim spiralling backwards. Years of equality-building have been shattered by the new concept that Sephardi politicians are thieves. Even if Labour set all the precedents, the Orthodox parties took the lead in gross misbehaviour in the 1980s and 1990s. And when will it end? God only knows.

CHAPTER SIX

A Most Disloyal Opposition

The Labour Party and its leftist allies have not won an election in four attempts during the past fifteen years. This prevented large-scale corruption when Labour was out of power but did nothing to ameliorate it when the party shared power in two coalitions with the Likud.

Although there were certainly other personalities in the party who proved untrustworthy when in power, it has been decided to focus here on two Labour leaders only, namely Shimon Peres and Yitzhak Rabin. They are the only Labour politicians of any international standing left in the Knesset, the natural result of a party closed to fast-rising newcomers and kept out of ultimate power by the electorate for a period fast approaching two decades. An analogy can be drawn with American politics. The Presidency of the US is held with a tight grip by the Republicans because of the painful memories of Johnson and Carter, Vietnam and Iran. Israelis remember instead Meir and Rabin, Yom Kippur War and Maalot.

RABIN RISES, STUMBLES AND FALLS

Ask any Israeli who was the worst Prime Minister in his country's history and the name Golda Meir pops up far more than outsiders would expect. Few if any of her policies worked in the long-term. For instance, one of Meir's obsessions was the tightening of Afro-Israeli ties and she spent a fortune of public money sending experts in a variety of fields to Africa as a form of foreign aid. After the oil embargo of 1973-74 took effect, Arab pressure won out over Israeli benevolence and African countries, one after another, cut off ties to Israel, Golda or not.

Most serious of all was the fact that Israel almost ceased to exist in the early days of the Yom Kippur War. Meir's government was arrogant and not a little stupid. Misreading intelligence reports almost totally, the army was unprepared for the two-front attack

66

by Egypt and Syria beginning on 6 October 1973. Within 48 hours Syria had recaptured the Golan Heights and was within a short hike of taking the Eastern Galilee. Only some courageous fighting by the remaining Israelis on duty and a failure in the Syrian supply lines stopped a good chunk of Israel from becoming Syrian. The Egyptians did almost as well, retaking the Suez Canal and overrunning most Israeli positions in sight of the water within two days. It cost Israel the lives of 3,500 fighters to amend the mistakes of their government. Had the country been remotely prepared for an attack, the enemy would have been routed in hours.

Public outrage led to a government inquiry, the Agranat Commission, to determine the blame for the catastrophe. It was an unabashed whitewash, with the government coming out clean while much of the blame was directed at David Elazar, Chief of Staff at the IDF. Meir, however, quit as Prime Minister, leaving Yitzhak Rabin to lead her party in 1974.

Rabin's previous history as a general had hardly been impressive to say the least. A recent revision of Israeli history by Uri Millstein describes Rabin as one of the worst commanders of the 1948 War of Independence, bungling major battles such as Lod and Ramle and leaving more dead soldiers than almost any other high-ranking officer.

Worse, in many ways, was the *Altalena* episode. During a brief ceasefire in the war, Menachem Begin's Irgun – the underground fighting force which is a direct ancestor of the Likud – attempted to land a ship full of arms called the *Altalena*. Prime Minster Ben Gurion feared the huge arms cache would go directly to the Irgun and lead to an armed takeover of his government, but Begin quelled such doubts by allowing the shipment to be off-loaded at a Labour settlement. Ben Gurion still wanted to assert his authority and ordered the ship and its Jewish crew to be attacked by the army. Moshe Dayan refused to kill fellow Jews, but the obedient Rabin showed no such hesitation and gave the order to shoot, which resulted in the loss of the weapons and a few dozen Jewish patriots.

This same courageous Rabin was commander of the Israeli Defence Force (IDF) during the Six Day War. On the eve of battle he suffered a nervous breakdown and, according to Ezer Weizman,[1] had to be persuaded not to surrender before a shot was fired. Rabin later confirmed his breakdown but attributed it to an attack of poisoning.

During his brief tenure as Prime Minister, the country suffered miserably from terrorism. In attacks on the Galilee towns of Maalot and Kiryat Shmoneh, about 50 people, mostly high school students, were murdered.

And if Rabin had built untold enemies in the general public for his government's incompetence in the face of terrorism, he had two powerful enemies within the government determined to see his demise. The first of these was Shimon Peres (Simple Shimon), who was furious at being overlooked for the prime ministership in favour of Rabin. The second was the NRP whose members had been fired from the government by Rabin, in a rare act of secular conviction, after they refused to support him in the face of a political scandal that only makes sense in Israel. On Friday, 10 December 1976, a welcoming ceremony was planned for the arrival of the first F-15 planes from the US. They arrived 17 minutes into the sabbath causing the Orthodox parties to fell the government. There cannot be many Orthodox airmen serving at airbases and those that may exist are likely to be too loyal to the forces to report the incident to the press. So who did? Some suspected a religious party, while others believed the culprit to be Shimon Peres.

Even if Peres is guiltless in this incident, it hardly exonerates him from two decades of ceaseless rivalry in his bid to push Rabin out of the way, no matter how damaging the actions may be to his own party. The next press revelation was certainly beneficial to Peres's hopes of becoming Prime Minister.

In the midst of the 1977 election campaign, the media focused on a report that Rabin had a secret bank account in Washington in his wife's name. Israelis are not allowed to keep money in foreign banks (but can you imagine this law being enforceable?) and the Prime Minister was shown to be a criminal. He resigned in the face of illegal banking charges. Lucky Shimon took over the party leadership and led Labour to its first-ever failure in a general election.

In theory anyway, this should have been the end of Rabin. He was, after all, a politician who resigned in the face of criminal scandal. But Israeli politicians aren't through until they're legally brain dead. Take the example of Moshe Dayan. He was Defence Minister during the disastrous Yom Kippur War and despite 12,000 casualties and the great resentment of their families and friends, which means a good chunk of the whole population, Dayan was appointed Foreign Minister in the 1977 cabinet of Menachem Begin.

Rabin had a similar revival of fates, one that was a real disaster for the country. He was named Minister of Defence for the two terms of the '84 government and once again in 1988. By then,

Rabin's drinking problem had been a constant though subdued issue in the media and the Arabs of the Gaza Strip took to the streets violently. It was Rabin's duty to put a quick end to the uprising through Defence Ministry policy. Instead, the continuing rebellion became a festering wound on the country's political body, tainting the good name of Israel worldwide.

Rabin had two choices: negotiate or end the uprising quickly with force. Negotiations under the gun were never to be so it was up to Rabin to act Middle-Eastern and crush a rebellion hard.

The precedents are obvious. A month after Arabs under Israeli control rioted in the Gaza Strip, Palestinians next door in Rafiah under Egyptian control took similar steps. The Egyptian army fired mercilessly, killing many and thus ending their *intifada* in an afternoon. In Algeria 300 were killed by troops in a few hours, while 36 rioters were gunned down in Tunisia, both incidents occuring after the *intifada* had started. In Jordan students protesting against rises in tuition fees, as well as less educated citizens demanding political change, were treated to the same indiscriminate gunfire. Such is the way of the Middle East.

Israel, with its free press, cannot employ such tactics as policy but has, in the past, not been reluctant to apply brute strength when viewed necessary. Rabin took the middle ground, initially ordering troops to simply rough up rioters or as he put it, 'break their arms', hoping this would have some sort of deterrent effect.

When soldiers accepted the hint as official policy they were charged and sentenced with brutality. When commanders defended the rough stuff by pointing to Rabin's arm-breaking statement, Rabin denied ever making it. His indecisiveness left in its wake an army terrified of using force even if force was clearly called for.

Part of the failure was in initially giving the media a free run of the territories. The army never mastered the power of the media and the rioters had an instinctive appreciation of media exploitation. Much as Iranian students shouted anti-American slogans only when the cameras were rolling, the Arabs of the *intifada* knew a good news sequence and how to set it up. Provoking Israeli troops into action when the film crews arrived was child's play and for the first part of the uprising, Rabin had no media policy to balance the coverage. For all the world to see, Israeli was a bully, retaliating to rocks with bullets. Only too late in the game, after even Henry Kissinger advised Israel to restrict media activity, did Rabin take measures to stop the spread of misinformation.

Rabin's wishy-washy approaches have led so far to 800 Arab

and 35 Jewish deaths. But his handling of the *intifada* is not the only example of weakness leading to bloodshed. In the aftermath of the Lebanon War, about two dozen Israeli soldiers fell into enemy hands. Eleven, held in Lebanon, were exchanged for 5,400 Arabs held in Israeli prisons and Rabin approved the deal. Some of the exchangees were mass murderers including the killers of six students in Hebron and the Japanese who killed two dozen travellers, mostly Puerto Rican nuns, at Ben Gurion Airport.

Included in the deal was the right of about 600 terrorists to return to their homes in the disputed territories. Some 90% have since been rearrested and it is widely held that the experience of these hardened terrorists has made the *intifada* such a long-lasting rebellion.*

Yet despite such a record of failure, Rabin is currently viewed as the only one who can save Labour from the man who, more than anyone else, has relegated the party to the second division, Shimon Peres.

SIMPLE SHIMON

> Israeli Prime Minister Shimon Peres has been named fittest statesman in the world by an American body-building magazine. Dan Lurie, publisher of *Muscle Training Illustrated*, presented him with a gold-plated trophy in Jerusalem. 'From all my research, Peres seemed the fittest of all statesmen,' Lurie said.
>
> Peres, 62, is a heavy smoker who lists his chief recreations as reading and watching Arabic soap operas on television.[2]

This little item sums up Shimon Peres better than many an educated analysis which often miss the point. Constantly portrayed an an addicted deal-maker, selfish and egotistical or just plain untrustworthy, Shimon wants to be popular and will do anything to be liked, but comes off as transparently insincere. For example, just prior to the 1988 elections Peres put on a prayer hat for the cameras and emerged from his *Torah* lesson with a high Sephardic rabbi. Peres has little interest in *Torah* studies and none in the Sephardic style. He tried to be friendlier, more accessible to both the Orthodox and the Sephardim in one PR exercise, fooled no one and looked even more cynical than ever.

---

* A similar tale emerged in 1991. As part of the deal cut before the regional peace talks, Israel released 150 Lebanese Shi'ites from its prisons. Although the hostages from western countries were released, none of Israel's hostages (or more likely, their corpses) were. Hizballah, now beefed up, immediately increased its murderous attacks on Israeli soldiers.

That is not to say the cynicism is undeserved – 1984 is a good departure point. An election was called that all the polls claimed Labour couldn't lose. The Likud had a miserable period bringing 450% inflation to the country and involving the nation in the bloody quagmire of Lebanon. The popular Menachem Begin had resigned and the bland Shamir had to fill his shoes, not an easy task for the five-foot-two-inch man who wears a size six-boys. Of Shamir's height, there is a story of him entering a restaurant and asking the head waiter if they serve shrimps. 'Sure,' he replied. 'We'll serve anyone.'

But the polls also revealed that a Yitzhak Navon-led Labour Party would not only win an election but possibly a parliamentary majority for the first time in the country's history. Navon, an ex-Ben Gurion compatriot, was appointed by Begin as the first Sephardi president of the state. It was too wise a choice for Begin's own good. Navon was the most popular president in the country's history and the fact that he speaks Arabic beautifully was an important reason why the Egyptian people accepted the Camp David Accords without open rebellion.

His wife Ophra was a former beauty queen reportedly unpopular with Golda Meir, who privately accused her of unseemly behaviour. As First Lady she turned out to be gutsy and admirable. A victim of breast cancer, she refused a masectomy, asking an overly inquisitive reporter, 'How would you like your balls cut off?'

While Navon's popularity increased, Peres was causing a rash of television explosions as viewers across the nation kicked in their sets when he appeared on the screen. During the 1981 campaign, his public appearances had to be curtailed drastically as a result of eggs and tomatoes being tossed at him the moment he showed his face on a podium. The television kickers and tomato throwers were almost always Sephardic. There is something about a Sephardi that doesn't like Peres. He lost his party two straight elections because Likud had captured the Sephardic vote. Then in 1984, Labour finally had a solution – run a Sephardi, Navon, for Prime Minister and watch the proud Sephardim vote for Labour. A draft Navon campaign took fire throughout the party and into the streets.

Peres was forced to acknowledge that a more popular figure had emerged and agreed to meet Navon at the President's house for consultations. The whole country awaited the results of the meeting and wondered if Shimon would put his party and the country ahead of his personal ambitions or if Shimon would be Shimon and shunt Navon aside. Well, of course, Shimon stayed

Shimon. Navon was given the number two position on Labour's list, an empty gesture as he eventually was appointed the lowly post of Education Minister and Peres would run again for Prime Minister. Throughout the country, Israelis speculated on how Peres got Navon, with the alleged promiscuity of Ophra a widespread subject of speculation.

And, in the end, Shimon led his party from a sure-fire victory to an embarrassing tie, leading to the first unity government with the Likud. As stated previously, Shimon was Prime Minister first with Shamir his Foreign Minister and then after two years they swapped positions.

So, besides the Navon episode, how did Shimon blow an election? He did so by insulting Sephardim. He appointed the leftist Yossi Sarid to run the campaign and he hired a comedy troupe, two-thirds Ashkenazi, to mock Likud and Begin in thick, stereotyped Moroccan accents. Sarid is such an élitist that he had no idea he might actually be insulting Sephardim by using black-faced minstrel-show imitations in political ads.

A similar incident sealed Peres's fate. In an attempt to hip up his image, other popular entertainers were employed. At a huge Labour Party rally on the very eve of the election, Israel's favourite stand-up comic (now a mere game-show host) addressed the assembled saying, 'At least there are no *chakhchakhim* here.' That long, difficult-to-pronounce word is the Israeli term for Sephardim, no different than nigger is to black. The audience loved the racial sneer and laughed. Unfortunately, instead of declaring his indignation for the insult, Shimon sniggered along with the crowd and sniggered away his election chances to boot.

Peres's apologists insist that his two years as Prime Minister were immensely successful, crediting him with reducing inflation to 20%, extricating the country from the mire of Lebanon and generally raising morale. What is conveniently forgotten is that he was, in good part, responsible for two of the biggest scandals in Israel's history. The first was Iran-Contra. Peres sent his personal advisor on terrorism, Amiram Nir, to Washington with a proposal to buy hostages from Iran with Israeli-transferred arms shipments.

The second, the Pollard spy case, was far more damaging to Israel; an American Jew working for Navy Intelligence sold sensitive information to Israel. In both cases Peres assured the Americans that Israel would investigate its responsibility and report back honestly. The promises were not kept, precipitating deep distrust between the two governments.*

The Israeli public demanded the truth about Pollard and, caving in, the government appointed a supposedly non-partisan commission to investigate the affair. The commission head, Abba Eben, agreed to cast the most responsibility on Peres. For a solid week Peres called the commission's report a lie, denied all involvement and finally Eben was removed from his party's electoral list, a typical reward for integrity.

At the end of his term as Prime Minister, Peres did everything in his power to stop Shamir taking over. Nothing worked, though Peres still had enough time left to leave a lasting stain. Only one Sinai issue was left to be resolved in the Camp David Accords. Israel gave Egypt 36,000 square miles of land, three times its own territory, the remains of half a dozen villages and towns, as well as the sites of military bases and oil fields. But the Egyptians weren't satisfied. They demanded a hundred-yard strip of beach south of Eilat called Taba. Israel was in no hurry to hand over the beach, partly because it believed it had an excellent land claim but mostly because a $32-million hotel was built on the sand. Egypt could easily have been a good sport and just let Israel keep its hotel but it demanded the return of every single grain of holy Egyptian soil.

Peres flew to Cairo and promised Mubarak that the Taba issue would be decided by international arbitration. Israelis were furious. Their country had seldom ever had a good day in an international forum (witness its string of successes at the UN). It also had everything to lose and Egypt a hotel to gain. In 1989, the issue was resolved by international arbitration: Israel gave up Taba, hotel and all.

Peres, now the new Foreign Minister, had still another and bigger fish to fry. He decided that the whole Arab/Israeli issue could be decided at an international peace conference. This cockamamie idea had been around since the 1970s when Peres, then a right-wing Defence Minister, called it a danger to the country.

The concept worked like this: all five members of the Security

---

* A third incident almost had equal repercussions. By 1985 Syria had closed down Iraq's oil pipeline to the Mediterranean and Iran was blockading the Persian Gulf. Iraq wanted to build an alternative pipeline to Aqaba, Jordan's Red Sea port, and the American corporation Bechtel agreed to construct this multi-billion dollar project, but only if it received assurances that Israel would never blow it up, even in war-time. American Attorney-General Edwin Meese approached Peres who agreed in return for $70 million a year for a decade, to be transferred to the Israeli Labour Party. When word of the bribe leaked, Meese was forced out of office but, as usual, scandal escaped Peres.

Council, all of Israel's neighbours as well as selected Palestinians, would meet for a conference which would provide an umbrella for secret but direct meetings between Arabs and Israelis.

The objections were obvious from the beginning. Two members of the Security Council, China and the Soviet Union, didn't even have relations with Israel – to which Peres answered they would have to as a precondition to the conference. Two other members, Britain and France, had been embargoing arms to Israel while supplying her enemies. Even this fact did not deter Peres, who answered that all Security Council members would be there just for show anyway, giving legitimacy to Arab discussions with Israel.

Israeli reaction to this convoluted and impractical scheme was negative in the extreme, but Peres flew around the world promoting the plan. He had secret meetings with King Hussein in London and got his backing, and later met with the Soviet representative at an international socialist convention in Rome in order to get his country's approval.

All this showed great initiative but Peres was fighting his own government. A high-level meeting with a Soviet official requires cabinet backing which Peres didn't have. In fact, the cabinet voted in a special session not to have any more talk about this international peace conference. But government approval meant nothing to the determined Foreign Minister. He flew to Washington to get Secretary of State Schultz's approval and promise of American participation. He got it, much to the chagrin of Shamir who sent Moshe Arens to Washington the next week to clarify the issue and cancel Peres's finaglings. Arens reported that Peres was representing himself, not his government. A justifiably confused Schultz inquired how a Foreign Minister can't be representing his government. A good question if there ever was one, the answer known only to Peres.

Meanwhile, back at home, Peres had found new ways to surrender Jewish state land. The Druze, a secret Moslem sect, had set up an illegal tent encampment on a nature reserve beloved by Israelis for its lush vegetation and rare wildlife. The Druze claimed the reserve was actually on the rightful property of the village of Beit Jann. When park rangers and police arrived to evict the protesters, the Druze rioted, overturning jeeps, burning them and beating up 23 rangers and police. The media described the whole incident as a pogrom.

Peres decided to personally intervene to settle the dispute. He had a little *sulha* with village elders and by the time he finished negotiating, the Druze rioters were freed from prosecution and kept most of the land they coveted on the nature reserve. It looked to all Jewish observers that Peres would give away land to anyone, just to make them like him. And such a view cost him the 1988 elections.

DOWN FOR THE FOURTH TIME

Peres, accepting the advice of his American image-experts, ran the 1988 campaign on the issue of peace and his idea of an international conference. His television advertisements included generals giving their vision of what happens when the territories are returned. The most absurd scheme involved building an electric fence around the Jordan Valley.

The issue of settlements is hypocritical as told by Labour, for it was Labour, way back in 1967, who began settling the territories with a string of kibbutzim in the Jordan Valley. Absurdity aside, Peres led his party to disaster for a fourth time because he was out of touch with the mood of the country. A poll conducted by the Jaffee Centre for Strategic Studies on the changes in security attitudes from 1987 to 1989 showed that Labour voters in the 1988 election were the only group that experienced a moderation of views in respect to the Arab-Israeli conflict. This same study centre conducted the 1988 poll that showed 51% of Israelis accepting expulsion of Arabs as a legitimate solution to the conflict with them.

In May 1989, the Guttman Institute of Applied Social Research offered Israelis nine options for solving the Israeli-Palestinian dispute and once again, 51% favoured the choice, 'Israel should cause the Arabs to leave, offering compensation'. By April 1990, 59% of respondents chose that option. The report stated that Labour could win an election, 'if it re-ordered the national agenda by focusing on socio-economic issues rather than the Palestinian one'.

Labour's election campaign resulted in another loss and Likud chose them as a coalition partner in still another unity government. Peres accepted on condition that he become Finance Minister and everyone in the country knew why. Labour-affiliated kibbutzim, health clinics and industries were deeply in debt and on the verge of total collapse. As Finance Minister it was expected that he would use his power to bail them out.

Peres lived up to these expectations and more. The kibbutzim were $4 billion in debt because of mismanagement and failed expansion. The situation was so drastic that over half of its young people were moving to the cities or abroad, and land was sold, even to Arabs, to stay afloat. After Peres threatened the banks in an all-night session, an agreement was reached. A third of all debts were waived and the rest were to be repaid at low interest over 25 years. A similar waiving of debt was arranged on behalf of the huge Koor Industries, Labour's manufacturing arm.

Of course the public, just as deeply in trouble from personal debt of over $15,000 per person, the highest such debt in the world by far, was not accorded equal treatment. The banks recouped their losses to the kibbutzim and Koor by raising the interest rates on bank overdrafts and loans, leading to a devaluation of the shekel. One day, Peres was asked if a devaluation was coming and said no (such practices, it is understood, are not confined only to Israeli Finance Ministers, but occur worldwide). The next day the shekel was devalued and anyone who trusted Peres's word lost money. Needless to say, the banks which bailed out Peres's friends, gained at the expense of the public.

Peres then set about breaking up the government in contravention of the coalition agreement which explicitly forbids any attempt to form a new coalition. As MK Uriel Lynn observed: 'Never before has the country witnessed such a flagrant display of disloyalty and self-seeking adventurism manifested by elected representatives.'[3]

In trying to form a Labour-Religious coalition, Peres proved himself willing to betray both the country and his party, more so than Shamir finally did. His proposed agreement to Agudat Yisrael included a pledge to stop a national bill of rights and to enact legislation banning the sale of pork within six months. He went even further than the Likud which promised to ban obscene billboard advertising. Peres was willing to ban 'obscenties' in the press, books and other media.

Uriel Lynn adds: 'Peres is guilty of brazen falsehoods when he contends that his party promised Aguda less than the Likud had. Maybe Peres is not deliberately lying; it's possible that he doesn't read the documents he signs.'

As recounted in detail previously, Peres did not succeed in forming a coalition. Labour Party reaction against him for his failed coup was quick. A majority of the Central Committee demanded the ousting of Peres as party leader and his replacement by Rabin. An internal party election was held and Peres was re-elected leader, mostly because he had appointed so many of the voting members of the Central Committee.

But there is another reason Peres survived the vote. According to a report from *Ha'aretz*:

A confrontation in the Labour Central Committee is a case in point. When polled, about two-thirds of Labour voters sided with Rabin. In the Central Committee, the party apparatus ruled in favour of Peres. Party elections are typically accompanied by allegations of forged results, members being denied their right to vote or deprived of their membership cards, attempts to bring newly registered members to the polls and so on.

In other words, the whole thing was rigged.

Peres led his party to unprecedented lows. By the spring of 1991, according to a poll conducted on behalf of the leftist daily, *Davar*, no more than 21% of the electorate will vote Labour. And the whole left-wing bloc of Labour and its allies has only 33% of public support. More frightening to Labour, of the first-time voters in 1992 (students and immigrants), only 9% will vote for the party, while 69% will support Likud and its right-wing allies. Even Labour's traditional supporters, third-generation Ashkenazi Israelis, will vote by 52% for Likud, compared to only 29% for Labour. All of Labour's main power-bases were eroded under Peres's stewardship, yet so powerful was his hold on the party that it took four election failures, before he was ousted, and then only by a strange set of circumstances. In February of 1992, Rabin once again challenged Peres for the party chairmanship. As usual, Rabin was portrayed as the hawk and Peres the dove. Unfortunately for Shimon, another dove, Israel Kessar, head of the Histadrut, also threw his hat in the ring. After two terms as Histadrut chairman, Kessar had handed out so many favours that he picked up 19% of the central committee's votes. This cut into Peres's lead just enough to allow Rabin to sneak out a victory..

So what is Labour doing to get back on top? It may skip the direct appointment of Central Committee by party members in favour of primaries. That might be nice. Two younger MKs, Yossi Beilin and Haim Ramon, proposed changing the name of Labour to the Democratic Party and suggested getting rid of the red flag, the *Internationale* and May Day parades which alienate new Soviet immigrants immediately, but Peres decided he liked the symbols. The same two MKs also suggested a separation between the party and its dying national union, the Histadrut and its deteriorating system of health clinics. But other old-timers rejected the proposal.

Meanwhile Beilin, the progressive or as Rabin calls him, 'Peres's poodle', has managed to prove that the new generation of Labourites is just as out of touch as the old. As Deputy Finance Minister he was asked his reaction to a new statistic showing 40% of Israelis are under the poverty line. In Marie Antoinette-style he answered, 'At least no one is starving.' Perhaps not, but many weren't well nourished or sheltered.

Beilin, who allegedly allowed Deri to rob the public coffers under his nose, has recently taken to travelling around the world, à la Peres, to defame the government. In 1991 he flew to Cairo to present Mubarak with his plan for turning the Gaza Strip into a Palestinian state. The Labour Party Secretary-General warned him not to do so in a five-page letter that took him to task for 'obsessive preoccupation with the PLO and the Palestinian state, which has damaged Labour's standing in public opinion',[4] and for selling out to the religious parties, a reference perhaps to his role in the Deri affair.

The Labour Party suffered disaster during Peres's 15 years. And that was enough time to assure that the next generation of Labourites are no great improvement over the current one.

As Joel Bainerman writes in his article, 'Labour Party's days are finished':[5] 'The Labour Party leadership's tired faces remind Israelis: of everything that is wrong in Israel: bureaucracy, the Histadrut, political patronage, socialism, Koor, the kibbutzim and a crumbling healthcare system.'

CHAPTER SEVEN

How Secure, Israel?

From 1984 to the governmental collapse of 1990, Yitzhak Rabin was the Minister of Defence, approved by both the Likud and Labour. His approval by the Likud is inexplicable in light of his role in the sinking of the *Altalena*. As mentioned in Chapter 6, the *Altalena* was an arms ship bought and filled by the Irgun, the Likud-supporting underground fighting force. Ben Gurion ordered the ship sunk and presumably the crew killed under the pretext of preventing a *coup d'état*. The pretext, as history has shown, was totally false and the lives of Jewish sailors were squandered mercilessly in nothing more than a show of power by Ben Gurion. And for his part in the senseless slaughter, the Likud somehow approved the appointment of Rabin as Defence Minister in 1984.

But the *Altalena* incident was not merely inhumane, it was unmilitary. Had the arms landed safely, the armoury of Israel would have almost doubled, leading to a shorter war in 1948 and quite possibly to victories in East Jerusalem and the West Bank which could have prevented the *intifada* of Rabin notoriety 40 years later.

In 1964 Rabin was appointed Army Chief-of-Staff and can be credited with building the fighting force that won the swift and splendid battles of the Six Day War. But just before the war began, Rabin suffered a breakdown and was close to resigning his post, thus generating a vacuum that would have effectively called off the war. According to Ezer Weizman,[1] Rabin was convinced he had entangled the country in a war that would be a fiasco and wanted out. The official version of events is that Rabin, who was smoking almost three packs of cigarettes a day at the time and not much less today, fell victim to nicotine poisoning. Rabin, himself, claims he was just overtired.

Becoming Prime Minister on Golda Meir's resignation in 1974, Rabin's tenure was characterised first by a failure to prevent horrifying terrorism and later by a number of scandals. The scandals began in September 1976 when, just two weeks after Rabin had appointed him to be Governor of the Bank of Israel, Asher Yadlin was charged with bribery and fraud. Rabin should have undertaken a perfunctory security report on Yadlin before placing him at the till of the nation's central coffer and his appointment severely undermined public trust in the Labour Party—but that in itself would not have brought down the government.

After the F-16 sabbath landings and the vote of no-confidence introduced by the ten-member National Religious Party, Rabin fired the NRP from the coalition leaving his government with less than a majority. Elections were called for 1977. He might have led his party to still another victory except that someone tipped off an Israeli journalist[2] in New York that Rabin would be depositing money into an illegal account while visiting the city. The reporter caught Rabin's wife green-handed depositing hundreds of dollars into the account. The prescribed punishment for this offence was three years in prison and a fine of three times the money illegally deposited abroad. This meant Rabin would have to stand trial during his election campaign but, in fact, he never went to the police station or the courtroom. He resigned his post as leader of the Labour Party to Shimon Peres, so instead of being punished himself, the whole nation took the rap.

But old Israeli generals covered in scandal do not fade away. They are given new and exciting opportunities to create further scandal. In 1984, Rabin was appointed Defence Minister in the new unity government led for its first two years by Shimon Peres, who intensely despises Rabin. Together, the dynamic duo conspired to involve Israel in one security disaster after another.

FREEING MURDERERS

It has always been a cornerstone of Israeli policy that they would not negotiate with terrorists for hostages. But freeing soldiers who had fallen into enemy hands while fighting in Lebanon was deemed another matter. It is essential for army morale that POWs know that their government will take all measures to secure their release. Nine such soldiers were held by the PLO faction controlled by Ahmed Jibril, a most bloodthirsty foe of Israel. To secure the soldiers' release, the Shamir government in 1984 approved negotiations with Jibril and upped the stakes by capturing Jibril's nephew. This is an effective strategy and was used five years later when a Shi'ite *mukhtar*, Sheikh Obeid, was kidnapped from his home as a bargaining chip for an anticipated exchange of Israeli soldiers held by the Hizballah, the radical Shi'ite militia. By the spring of 1991, Hizballah announced it would begin exchange proceedings.

The Shamir-Jibril exchange was ridiculously one-sided: six Israeli soldiers, five from the Nahal Brigade, were exchanged for 4,880 mostly Palestinian prisoners plus the PLO archives acquired by Israel in the Lebanon War. However, 4,700 of the prisoners were held in Lebanese detention camps, with the remainder being terrorists who had been captured before promulgating massive bloodshed. The price paid by Israel was high but it was estimated the country's security would not be affected profoundly since the prisoners were expelled from the country. Others say that the moral victory claimed by the Palestinians, as illustrated by the widespread celebrations in the territories after the exchange, planted the first seeds of the *intifada*.

If seeds were planted after the first exchange, the flowers came to full blossom after the next one, sanctioned by Rabin as Defence Minister. Three more Nahal soldiers were to be recovered. Nahal, for those unacquainted with IDF brigades, is the Labourite infantry unit of the army. In this exchange, the price paid by Israel was not detainees in Lebanon, most of whom were released in the first exchange without thought to future negotiations. Instead, this time around Israel emptied its prisons of vicious and committed terrorists. Fifteen of the 1,150 released were considered the most dangerous criminals held by Israel. Their names are a *Who's Who* of mass murder, their victims a sad geographical testimony to terrorism having fallen on the Coastal Road, Maalot, Bet Hadassah and Lod Airport. The surviving perpetrator of Lod was Kuzo Okamoto, a Japanese Red Army terrorist and killer of over a dozen visiting nuns from Puerto Rico. There was a grand total of 380 life sentences among the terrorists released, and many had only served a few years of their sentences.

Perhaps some compensation for the release of the three Israelis could have been garnered by the fact that over a thousand murderers had been sent far away from Israeli soil. But Rabin allowed more than half the criminals, over 600 of them, to return to their homes in the territories of pre-1967 Israel. These men became the vanguard of the *intifada*. By January 1990, 420 of the 600 released (65%) had been re-arrested for crimes ranging from murder to terrorist activity. By 1991 that number was estimated to have risen to 80%. One can only guess at the true figure since Rabin would not allow further re-arrests to be made public, each one being a source of deadly embarrassment to him.

Criticism was extremely high at the time of the exchange. On the day following the exchange, a military source told the *Ma'ariv* newspaper[3] that the influx of hardened terrorists would create an organisational and ideological infrastructure that would lead to increased terrorist attacks. Yuval Ne'eman,* now Minister for Science and Technology, charged Rabin with 'arranging the most stupid act of any Israeli government: three soldiers for 1,150 senior terrorists. Anyone who has dealt with intelligence and espionage knows how much effort has to be exerted in planting a network of four or five activists in enemy territory. Rabin has planted Jibril's network with his own hands. Five hundred hardened and experienced activists were spread throughout the territories. We have met them and their students—the masked terrorists of the *intifada*.'[4]

The present Agriculture Minister, Raful Eitan, also added to the public slamming of Rabin in a *Ma'ariv* article:[5] 'The Defence Minister has failed and he must resign. He should have resigned ages ago but the partisan system allows him to continue failing without giving a personal account. His immediate resignation is required as a result of his failures, which in any normal country would have brought about the conclusion of personal consequences.'

What was Rabin's reply to his critics? He said he had put himself in the place of the parents of the Israeli prisoners and taken a humanitarian step. Later he admitted that the parents themselves, mostly if not all Labourites, had put the squeeze on him. But his official reasoning for releasing over 600 terrorists into Israeli-controlled territory was that it would be easier to 'keep an eye on them'. Using the same warped logic, it would be even smarter to invite the entire PLO to Israel to keep a closer watch on their activities.

In the end three soldiers were released and far more Israelis eventually died as a result of the exchange. One of the Arab prisoners sent home was Sheikh Ahmed Yassin, the leader of the Islamic fundamentalist movement, Hamas. His organisation alone is responsible for dozens of Israeli casualties.

The exchange might never have taken place if the soldiers weren't from Nahal. In fact, an equal number of non-Nahal soldiers still languish in Arab hands and no irrational prisoner exchange is taking place to save them. So what is Nahal and how could it have such an effect on Rabin?

* Ne'eman quit the government in February 1992 in protest of the peace process.

THE FIGHTING FARMERS

Nahal is a unique fighting brigade. Soldiers spend half their service in military training and duties, the other half being farmers, usually on a kibbutz, where military discipline is mostly forgotten in favour of picking fruit, singing songs around the campfire and chatting up young foreign kibbutz volunteers.

The concept of the fighting farmer had noble beginnings. The early Zionists were dedicated to changing the image of the European ghetto Jew who seldom farmed or fought, mostly because he was forbidden to do either. The ideology of the early Zionists included reclaiming the land with hard work and building the first Jewish fighting force since biblical times. Somehow, these two not necessarily similar goals were melded into the legend of what a Zionist was meant to be once a dash of socialism was added to the recipe. And the formula had its effects. Many of the élite Palmach Brigade which fought so bravely in the early days of statehood were from the kibbutzim and they later sent a disproportionally large number of representatives to the Knesset, including Moshe Dayan and the lapsed kibbutznik, Yitzhak Rabin.

Knesset members are asked to fill out a form listing their occupations outside politics. To this day, Rabin still fills in the occupation, 'farmer', though it has been five decades since he's pulled an udder or harnessed a plow. Nonetheless, working the soil of Israel is his chosen field of endeavour and he therefore must have felt a kinship to the missing Nahal fighters – despite how they were captured, and it certainly wasn't in battle. The official IDF report claims that a lone terrorist approached the front-line Nahal post. He called to the Israeli soldiers to follow him and, without his firing a shot, they obeyed. A few minutes later they were captive behind Syrian lines. The officer who investigated the capture could not comprehend why the soldiers, outnumbering the captor eight to one, were such lambs led to slaughter. 'Why the soldiers did not resist,' he wrote, 'is beyond my understanding.'

In a further report Brigadier-General Yossiu Eldar said that soldiers should not rely on IDF efforts to free them when taking the decision to surrender or not.[6]

According to the unofficial account widely known throughout the country, the lone terrorist posed as a grateful villager who brought the soldiers tea every day for a week and gained their trust. On the day of the capture he served drugged tea and led the soldiers, doped, into enemy hands. This version fits the personality portrait of the typical Nahal soldier.

The kibbutz today is a society unto its own in Israel. Once the rugged pioneer breaking new soil, the kibbutzniks of today are the landed gentry of the country, surrounding themselves with the toys of any aristocracy: swimming pools, tennis courts and horses.

Nearby to the kibbutz is invariably an overcrowded development town filled with the proletariat bitterly wondering what the kibbutzim did to deserve vast acres of prime untaxed land while they must pay huge sums to purchase pathetically small plots of rocky soil to build upon. If this legitimate grudge alone hasn't divided the kibbutzim from the teeming cities, the attitude of élitist snobbery elicited by too many kibbutzniks has exacerbated the chasm.

Much has changed since the early years of work on the kibbutzim. It was a fair deal for everyone. The volunteers exchanged work for a free holiday in Israel and the kibbutz got cheap labour. Although a few were so taken with the egalitarian lifestyle that they stayed and became kibbutzniks, most returned home after a few months' washing dishes or picking avocados.

But in the 1980s Europe suffered high unemployment and thousands of youths had little hope of ever finding work. The kibbutz offered an alternative to welfare and hopelessness. Thousands of Europeans volunteered for the kibbutzim but they didn't return home in a matter of months. They stayed for years of kibbutz-hopping interspersed with long sojourns on the beaches of the Red or Mediterranean seas. Far from being motivated idealists, many became taken with their laid-back lifestyle, seemingly one without worry or responsibility. Today many adolescent kibbutzniks are long-haired and leftist. Where once the young kibbutznik joined the officer corps of the IDF, now he wants to get his army duty over as painlessly as possible. And of course, the kibbutzim are broke.[7] In fact, they are $4 billion in debt and would mostly be insolvent if Shimon Peres, as Finance Minister, hadn't made the banks accept a bail-out.

And this is the source which supplies Nahal with a good proportion of its soldiers. Many arrive at the recruiting camp with their hair still long, earrings in place and quickly earn the reputation as *astronautim* or spaced-out idealists who normally would have no place in any army. And this is just the type of soldier who would accept drugged tea from an Arab a mile or two from a battle-front. Even if the tea story is untrue, it certainly sounds plausible and was accepted by the Israeli public. Had the prisoner exchange been the last Nahal snafu, the brigade's reputation might have escaped being permanently tarnished. But Nahal is commonly blamed for giving the *intifada* its first taste of blood and courage.

Approximately a week before the uprising was ignited by a traffic accident, a lone PLO terrorist hang-glided into Israel from Lebanese territory. By sheer chance he landed near a Nahal army post and shot a few rounds in the direction of it. The courageous guard at the gate ran for the hills without firing a shot, leaving the terrorist to kill six soldiers and wound seven others before finally being killed himself.*

The guard was mostly to blame but the IDF was itself lax, having been alerted to the attack[8] half an hour before it took place. The operations officer of the post was later relieved of his command for not properly preparing his soldiers for the impending attack (many were either unarmed or sleeping) and the colonel in charge of the batallion was relieved for overseeing such a pathetic fighting machine.

Demands for the disbanding of Nahal were heard throughout the land, with one man, Dr Yonathan Badar, claiming the failure of Nahal was the result of having two masters, the farmer and the soldier. He added that such a division of loyalties was not to be found in any army in the world, not even that of Maoist China.[9] Others attributed the failings of Nahal to the style of life on the kibbutz. Apathy reins supreme and there is always someone else to rely on, be they harder working members or political rescue in the case of debt. By 1990 Nahal recruitment had fallen to only 40% of its requirements but Defence Minister Rabin would not listen to the calls for the regiment to be disbanded. Labour's brigade would carry on defending Israel.

I'VE BEEN EVERYWHERE BUT I'VE NEVER BEEN IN TAFADA OR OOH ROCKIN' RABIN, WE'RE REALLY GONNA ROCK TONIGHT

As his first major policy decision after becoming Minister of Defence in 1984, Rabin removed Israeli troops from all of Lebanon except for a security enclave in the south of the country along Israel's border. He is credited with extirpating Israel from a madhouse country and hopeless war. But through the eyes of the Arabs this was no victory. In fact, from their point of view, for the first time,

* In February 1992, terrorists armed only with knives and a pitchfork infiltrated a Nahal base and killed three armed soldiers. The deputy commander of this base was also the deputy commander of the base infiltrated by the hang-glider terrorist. The more things change in the IDF command structure, the more they stay the same.

Israel was forced to withdraw from a war, her tail between her legs, because of terrorism.

The enemy felt it had learned well the lessons of Lebanon: concoct a mixture of snipers and car bombs and Israeli soldiers will withdraw. It was a lesson considered relevant to the situation in the disputed territories and fired hope in the hearts of the youth of Nablus, Gaza and Hebron.

In 1986 the government's deep military cutbacks resulted in 6,000 officers losing their jobs at the same time. Rabin held on to a good proportion of the older, more senior men, the ranks of the junior officers being hardest hit. This purge spread such insecurity amongst their class that many who survived the sackings simply quit the military for a safer future in the civilian market-place. Thus when the *intifada* broke out in December 1987, many of the fresh, young military minds, so vital when responding to young and innovative enemy rebels, were not in the field, leaving the older officers steeped in set-piece tactics in charge.

When the uprising broke out Rabin was abroad and missed its significance so completely that he refused to cut short his trip. By the time he returned, the enemy had gained the initiative, especially in the hearts and minds of the foreign public. The IDF was crucified by the world media all the time it was in Lebanon and the military returns for, say, the seige of Beirut could well have been offset by the loss of support for Israel in world opinion. The enemy used crude image-making tactics, like having Arafat filmed kissing babies; that had a strong effect because the IDF was not explaining itself very well at all.

Part of the problem was the criteria used to choose IDF press officers. Instead of selecting multilingual veterans of combat units who understood the hows and whys of fighting, the IDF spokesman's office was and still is filled with typists and translators, occasionally given desk-jobs for health or psychological reasons or just as a favour for well placed parents. After the media onslaught regarding Lebanon, there were demands in the Israeli press for a more professional and well-spoken army spokesman's corps but needless to say, the calls went unheeded.

Rabin treated the uprisers in the streets as soldiers in the field and live ammunition was used originally to quell riots. There may have been no choice since the IDF was not trained in riot-control techniques and possessed no armoury of crowd-control equipment or experience.

The rioters, whether for lack of an armoury or sophisticated PR knowledge, initiated IDF retaliation with supposedly more benign weapons such as the infamous rocks (hence the nickname Rockin' Rabin), sharpened projectiles and slingshots. In any filmed confrontation, the better armed soldiers hardly appeared the underdogs.

The deaths of rioters were graphically recorded by the media who played down Israeli civilian casualties. It was now up to Rabin and the IDF to explain their case, which wasn't all that difficult. Maintaining public order is messy and Israel's record was far better than that of other democracies who face the same trouble. When riots rocked America in the 1960s, the local police and National Guard responded with far more firepower, killing, for instance, three dozen rioters in a few terrible days in Detroit, more than Israeli troops killed in three months of unrelenting attacks in dozens of locations.

Other vital issues were woefully underplayed by the world media, perhaps for lack of information, more likely for lack of sympathy, and they included the use of children as shields in the front lines of riots, the maiming and killing of pacifistic opponents of the uprising and the aim of the rioters which, as was often admitted, was the destruction of Israel. In short, Israel had an excellent case for quelling the uprising with vigour but the outside world barely got the message, especially when delivered by Rabin or some IDF spokesman.

It was up to the IDF to understand the media and gain the expertise to deal with it. But the rioters had the upper hand, sometimes leading the cameras to beatings taking place, other times luring the troops into a confrontation. The money offered by the networks for further violence led at least one Israeli cameraman to stage-direct a group of Arab teenagers in a phoney display of rebellion. According to one sound engineer, such set-ups were not uncommon.

The media forgot all pretence of evenhandedness and, exploiting Israel's hospitality and freedom, reported events in a manner absolutely forbidden to them in any Arab country. When they flew into Jerusalem to cover the uprising, almost all stayed in the Arab part of town at the tacky American Colony Hotel, which soon became a press headquarters for PLO leaders and almost off-limits to Israelis slightly to the right of Jesse Jackson.

The adverse world reaction had its effect on Rabin, who issued orders cancelling the use of live ammunition in all but life and death situations. Intense American pressure predicated against the deterrent use of deportation, probably the most effective riot queller of all.

Rabin's next tactic was to fine rock-throwers rather than shoot them. Rocks do kill and in one particularly sad incident an Israeli Olympic athlete on reserve duty was killed by a rock in the casbah of Nablus. Rocks are lethal weapons and the intent of the throwers is murder. And for such a motive the perpetrator was expected to be deterred by a $1,100 fine.

By December 1990, in just three years of the uprising, nearly 4,000 Jews, civilians and soldiers, had been wounded by Arab attacks. Twenty had died, including a mother and her three young children in a fire-bombing of a bus outside Jericho. The army reported over 120,000 incidents of stone-throwing, nearly 2,500 molotov cocktail attacks, 157 sniper incidents using live ammunition, 58 grenade attacks and 1,004 arson attacks, a few hundred against cars in Jerusalem.

In the same month, an IDF officer writing under a pen-name, declared he had had enough:

> ... Even more strange than all of this are the orders for opening fire, a complex maze of rules and regulations governing the use of different types of firearms under varying circumstances and conditions. Unfortunately, by the time a soldier or police officer decides whether he's legally entitled to use rubber bullets, plastic bullets, live bullets or just run away, he might well be dead.[10]

Rabin's policies of live ammunition and deportation were halted by the media and world opinion and the replacements of fines and relatively harmless rubber bullets were having no deterrent effect. Out of sheer frustration, he 'informally' instituted a roughing-up policy telling senior command officers, 'You must catch them and break their arms and legs.'

But when officers and soldiers did just that, they were tried for brutality. A number of soldiers have already been convicted of causing bodily harm to Arabs. They include two colonels as well as junior officers and soldiers. There are also investigations underway against another colonel, a brigadier general and the biggest fish of all, O/C Southern Command, Major General Mordechai. In all the trials to date, the accused have claimed that they were carrying out orders given to them by Rabin and his top officers, Dan Shomron and Amram Mitzna. The military courts have dismissed the claims of all the convicted soldiers despite evidence of other senior officers confirming that the three had authorised beating as punishment in army briefings.

The officers convicted were all firmly convinced they were following official guidelines. Major Yitzhak Levite said after his conviction, 'I am not sorry for the orders I gave; they accurately reflected the orders of my superiors.' Another company commander testified that Mitzna had perjured himself when he told the court that no orders had been issued at the Command level, 'to beat with intent to punish'. Levite concluded, 'The only difference between Rabin and his senior officers and myself was that I did not lie through my teeth and deny giving orders that I issued.'[11]

So with still another policy having little effect, Rabin's army set up large detention camps, today holding some 12,000 detainees: 7,000 in the Ketziot (Ansar) Camp in the Negev, while the bulk of the remainder are held in the north of the country at Megiddo Prison. Ketziot was set up just before Land Day, a PLO holiday, in 1987. It was intended as a cheap and transitory camp for activists planning trouble and caught in a one-time round-up. Four years and $35 million later, it is a five-block sprawling complex run by over 500 people, mostly reserve soldiers.

Most prisoners are held under a British law called administrative detention. They are suspected of planning violent acts and are held for six months without trial. The prisoners each cost Israelis some $3 a day to feed and are provided with free toiletries, bedding, medical and dental care. So far, in an era of deep military budget cuts that cancel new projects and training exercises, detaining the prisoners has cost over $200 million.

The inmates are not subjected to cruelty or serious deprivation as Ketziot is inspected daily by the Red Cross under POW provisions, though the detainees are hardly soldiers captured in a war. They are released after half a year and the only danger they face is the possibility of internal, factional violence. (So far 26 detainees have been murdered in their lock-ups by other Arabs.) Once released the inmates return to uprising activities, undeterred by their experience in the detention camp.

Thus it seems, none of Rabin's policies for controlling the *intifada* or its effect on world opinion have worked very well. Worse, Rabin seems to be shirking responsibility for giving the beatings order at the beginning of the uprising. There was nothing wrong with a soldier giving such orders under the circumstances but much wrong with his later refusal to back it up.

WHAT HAST BECOMETH OF THEE, IDF?
In the wake of Rabin, the IDF has been left a confused, demoralised

army. One hundred and fifteen soldiers have refused to serve in the territories since the start of the uprising and most have been jailed for taking this stand. Though over a hundred cases of treason is certainly a cause for worry, it does not signify a real breakdown. There are far more serious signs. In 1990 Israeli soldiers were killed in a most 'un-IDF' fashion by the enemy. Three serious incidents will illustrate what appears to be a breakdown in fighting reaction:

(1.) With the rise of Islamic fundamentalism in Jordan, attacks had reached serious proportions on the traditionally quiescent Jordanian border. In one incident an IDF post was attacked by a lone Jordanian, resulting in the death of one Israeli soldier and the non-reaction of his comrades. A later investigation showed that despite the rising danger on the border, only one soldier at the post had over four months' regular army training, the rest being immigrants who had received a most perfunctory and superficial training in soldiery. What this band of amateurs was doing manning such an explosive post was the source of controversy that has not yet led to a change of posting policy.

(2.) A platoon of the rugged Givati Brigade suffered fatalities in an ambush by terrorists in southern Lebanon. The command to fire was issued at 60 metres distance from the intruders – far, far too soon – and the platoon was out of ammunition after the first bursts of gunfire. This allowed a surviving terrorist to lob a grenade which felled five soldiers who were positioned much too close to each other. Two basic errors, close positioning and premature fire, led to the tragedy.

(3.) In November 1990, an Egyptian soldier crossed the border and for 21 minutes fired at vehicles, including a bus full of soldiers, killing four Israelis and wounding 26.

According to MK Uriel Lynn, these mistakes: '. . . show clearly that the IDF does not know how to defend its soldiers and that its level of preparedness for sudden attacks is indeed very low. We must draw the painful conclusion that too many soldiers do not receive proper military training and are not taught how to react to sudden attack.'[12]

Even more deadly were accidents throughout 1990 and into 1991, only explicable in terms of operational and functional breakdown:

(1.) On 23 April, two Sikorsky C-54s collided in the Jordan Valley killing seven crew members. Eyewitnesses reported that one helicopter simply strayed off course into the other, hardly the flight of a disciplined pilot.

(2.) Six months later, a Cessna light aircraft crashed, killing the five passengers on board. The plane took off in perfect weather. A later report claimed the cause of the crash to be negligence and violation of procedure on the night before the accident.

(3.) In April 1991, in full view of holiday-makers, a fighter aircraft crashed into the Sea of Galilee killing both the pilot and navigator. The plane was recovered in 120 metres of water and no technical explanation of the crash has yet been issued.

(4.) But the most documented accident[13] occurred on 19 July 1991 when five soldiers died and ten were wounded, after a shell fired by an artillery unit fell on a paratrooper unit during a training exercise at Tze'elim in the Negev. The unavoidable excuse of human error was compounded by criminal negligence and total disregard for existing safety orders. According to General Amos Yaron's inquiry, this was a case of the entire chain of command collapsing. Six officers were later relieved from duty for gross and deadly negligence.[14]

The saddest feature of the spate of accidents from 1990 is that they could have been prevented had the IDF implemented the recommendations of the Lapidot Committee, which in April 1989 was predicting impending disaster. The Committee's report criticised the army's duplication of effort, overlapping of authority and shortcomings of its safety system. It also noted under-reporting of near tragedies, delayed and incomplete accident investigations and a cover-up of actual accidents. The report recommended harsher sentences for criminal negligence and a new command covering safety only. The IDF ignored the report and its recommendations and such arrogance may have led to the loss of some of its finest personnel through foolish and avoidable accidents.

If battle foul-ups and avoidable accidents are an indication that all is not perfect in the IDF, the suicide rate is a more debatable piece of evidence. A spate of suicides broke out in the spring of 1990 and the world media jumped on the story, claiming this was the result of demoralisation in the aftermath of the *intifada*. As flawed as this theory was, the fact remains that for the first time in six years, the IDF suffered over 35 suicides in one year.

Still another report by Major General Amos Lapidot[15] did note that the IDF may be responsible in part, by not delving into an inductee's psychological history deeply enough, by the humiliation of soldiers during training and by the generally low level of basic training.

However, the factors that lead to suicide could also be economic and personal, and the uprising itself would hardly lead a soldier to take his own life. Bank debts, an inability to purchase housing and general financial pressure, endemic to the country might, especially when a soldier is alone with his thoughts, rifle in hand at a depressing and dark outpost far from family support.

Taken together, the rise in suicides, accidents and battle blunders indicates deep malaise and creeping apathy. Such is the legacy of the Rabin years. But the red, red Rabin is no longer bob, bob, bobbin' along as Defence Minister. Since the government restructuring of 1990, Moshe Arens has taken hold of the reins, in what surely must change for the better, however slightly. Or are we being too kind to the new Minister of Defence?

SCUD MARKS

The IDF has not had a significant military victory since the early days of the Lebanon War. After being car-bombed out of the country, the IDF had to concentrate on the thankless task of putting down a large-scale revolt closer to home or even at home. The Gulf War was the opportunity to protect Israelis with planning and courage resulting in some spectacular operation like Entebbe or the bombing of the Osirak nuclear reactor. But in the end, the IDF stood by while 39 Iraqi-launched Scud missiles landed in or near Israel.

In anticipation of chemical warfare, the IDF had distributed gas masks to everyone in Israel and offered instructions as to how best prepare a gas-proof sealed room. But according to the State Comptroller,[16] the masks were often defective or ineffective and the citizens were victims of a huge deception. The government refused to reply to her charges but the army implicitly admitted some grain of truth by replying it had only a $25 million budget to work with. Only when the Scuds started falling was army advice called into question by the public. The size of warhead allowed by a long-range Scud severely limited the likelihood of a chemical attack; most of the damage was caused by an explosive head plus the impact of the missile itself. And sealed rooms offered minimal protection against explosives – only bomb shelters served this purpose.

But the IDF refused to change its strategy in mid-stream. As the number of dwellings destroyed increased by thousands, and casualties in the rubble by hundreds, the IDF still insisted that sealed rooms were the best protection. Only an enraged citizenry forced the admission that shelters quickly reached were indeed the best protection in this war.

It was nothing short of a miracle that Israeli casualties were so low. The public expected a response from the IDF on the first night of the missiles and indeed, Arens was initially in favour of an IDF mission to take out the Scud sites. But the IDF did not react and the full story of this embarrassing restraint is only just beginning to come out.

The Americans were convinced that Israeli action against Iraq would somehow break up their coalition of allies against Iraq. According to this line of thinking, Saudi Arabia, Kuwait and the Gulf States would all tell America to pack up its gear and go home because Israel was in the same fight. The scenario is simply impossible. But to preserve the coalition, the US implored Israel not to retaliate against a nation firing deadly missiles at her. The allies would knock out the Scud sites and supply Israel with the miraculous Patriot anti-missile system.

But, as an Israeli intelligence officer noted: 'The Americans didn't tell us the truth about missile take-outs. Their pilots were bombing from too high up and a little damage was counted as a take-out. The British dared to fly low and get confirmed hits but there weren't enough of them. If we had been allowed to strike, we would have been a lot more effective than the Americans and had a lot more planes than the British. We could have knocked out the missiles in days.'

The full tale of the Patriots has not been told. With a missile attack impending and Israeli anti-aircraft soldiers already four months into their Patriot training, why weren't batteries in place before the Scuds were launched? The truth, which was never told during the attacks, is that the Patriots didn't knock down Scuds so much as deflect them off their course somewhat. In Saudi Arabia this was sufficient most of the time, for a deflection into the wastes of the desert saved Riyadh endless damage. In the crowded coastal region of Israel, however, a deflection meant a missile falling on an unintended populated target.

Yet this was the only protection the Israeli population was offered. The IDF had Jericho missiles that could have been used in retaliation for Scuds, the finest air force in the region and a plan to parachute infantry units into the launching areas to put an end to the aerial terror. But the IDF did nothing. Instead the public kept up its morale by telling jokes. (Why isn't bingo played in Baghdad? Because when they call B-52, everyone runs to the shelter) and depended on Patriot missiles, in no small part operated by American troops for the first time in Israel's history.

The government expected big dividends in return for restraint.

But, as the Baker failure and subsequent finger-pointing at Israel proved, the dividends didn't come through. Everyday life in Israel was totally disrupted by missile attacks and the government forced the IDF to stand aside and let it happen. If the IDF earned brownie points in the American public-opinion polls, it did nothing to prove to Israelis that the army has what it takes to protect them from a shower of Scuds. The Syrians took note and purchased a large consignment of North Korean Scuds after the Gulf War battles had subsided.

The post-Gulf War army is back to normal, reflecting the ills of the society at large. Some ultra-Orthodox men are trying to enlist to gain better family-allowance payments and the army has mostly refused the new inductees. Nonetheless, when Soviet immigrant soldiers were invited to a Passover meal, prayer books in Russian were banned because the American Conservative movement had published them and the Orthodox of Israel prevailed upon army chaplains to ban them. The Russians, naturally, were the losers, unable to follow the ceremony at their first celebration of the Exodus in their chosen land.

On the political front, Shamir had had enough of Rabin's high-level appointments after O/C Central Command Major General Mordechai was investigated for approving brutality under orders given by Chief of Staff Shomron. The public row led to the appointment of Lt. General Ehud Barak as the new Chief.

Barak wasted no time repeating the mistakes of Rabin, ordering widespread staff dismissals in the name of budget restraints. He retired the IDF's Chief of Training, claiming he was replacing old soldiers with young ones, then hired a replacement who was older and four years retired. Naturally, the budget cuts are guaranteed to further reduce IDF readiness. As writer Bradley Burston noted, 'Though the majority of fighting units will be spared forced resignations, training, border patrol duty, equipment and arms development projects will all feel the force of the budget squeeze.'[17]

The IDF prides itself on its distance from Israeli politics, preferring to paint a picture of an independent fighting force representing Israelis of all political persuasions. But somehow, through means not documented in this study, retired IDF officers are being offered highly munificent government positions. Former Security Chief, Nahum Atzmoni is now the head of Mekorot, Israel's water company. Former Northern Commander, Ori Or, now heads the Keren Kayemet, Israel's forest service, and General

Moshe Bar Kochba is in charge of the dilapidated Israel Railways.

The ties between loyal army service and later public service appointments is symptomatic of all that is enmeshing the country's soldiery with the corruption scandals of the government, irresponsibly melding the essential defence of a beseiged little country with the official deceit foisted upon an unwilling public. Since 1984, Israel has suffered one fiasco after another, mixing vital security issues with ill-gotten political and financial gains, all originally justified by the protection of the state.

CHAPTER EIGHT

The Insecurity Complex: Now Look What a Mess You've Got the Country Into

Always in a battle for its survival, Israel has made some bad security decisions in the past, but very few until the 1980s turned into full-blown national scandals. The Lavon Affair, in which Jewish Egyptians planned the bombing of American sites in Cairo, ended the career of Ben Gurion. Public outrage over the unpreparedness before the Yom Kippur War convinced Golda Meir to resign as Prime Minister. Besides being few and far between, these security scandals resulted in resignations at the top. What distinguishes the scandals of the past decade are the rapid-fire occurences and the refusal of the nation's leaders to accept responsibility for gross misperformance of duty.

The following summaries of the most costly security affairs reveal a disturbing pattern of incompetence and greed that has damaged both Israel's friendship with America* and the trust Israelis rely on in the professionalism of their intelligence services and high-ranking military officers.

NEVER TRUST AN ISRAELI: THE TRIALS OF
JONATHAN JAY POLLARD

Pollard was an American Zionist working for the Anti-Terror Unit of Navy Intelligence and was thus privy to reams of extremely sensitive documents. In his first year at the job he became highly indignant upon discovering that intelligence promised to Israel in high-level agreements was being withheld because of what he believed was anti-semitism in American intelligence circles.

His original indignation later became the core of his defence and, when examined without bias, was a legitimate justification for his decision to pass on information that was probably being withheld in contravention of understandings between the American and Israeli

---

* Since this was written, a Pentagon official was charged with accepting a $2 million bribe from two Israeli officers trying to sell an unmanned reconnaissance aircraft called the Mazlat.

intelligence services. Israel had kept its part of the deal, supplying
America with some $50 billion worth of data and even shipping to
the US an intact Mig 21 fighter jet and T-72 tank, still the most
up-to-date piece of Soviet armour.

While on a study sabbatical in New York, Aviem Sela was
introduced to Pollard and was recruited into a branch of the
Israeli Secret Services (quite unconnected to the kind of mission
Pollard would be undertaking), the Liaison Office for Science, which
normally devotes itself to searching through technical journals for
hints of scientific advances in nuclear and high-tech defence.

Sela, himself, was an active colonel in the air force and was in
America to study computer science, not on an active espionage
campaign. For whatever reason, he recruited Pollard, and his
decision involved the air force in the grimy episode that ensued.

Sela referred his new recruit to Raphi Eitan (not the Agriculture
Minister) who was then Prime Minister Begin's personal advisor
on terrorism. From that moment on Pollard was unknowingly
victimised by a web of personal animosities that beset the highest
levels of Israeli Intelligence. Born on a kibbutz, Eitan distinguished
himself as a Palmach soldier in the War of Independence. He caught
the eye of the head of the Mossad and was recruited. He later played
a key role in the kidnapping of Eichmann and the uncovering of the
first major Soviet spy in the Israeli government, Yisrael Beer.

Feeling his talent was unrecognised, Eitan left the Mossad in the
late 1960s to study and enter the world of business, but returned
to security work after a most unsuccessful venture into private
enterprise. By 1977 he had risen to the rank of terrorism advisor
to the Prime Minister, a position later filled by Amiram Nir with
devastating consequences for Ronald Reagan.

Eitan now felt he was ripe for the role of Chief of Mossad, a job
he had coveted for years. But it was not to be. When Pollard was
recruited he had made a lateral climb through the bureaucracy to
become head of the Science Liaison Office. When Eitan realised
just how well placed Pollard was, instead of transferring his file to a
more suitable branch of intelligence, he kept it for himself, bypassing
the correct channels sending Pollard's data directly to the Defence
Ministry. He took most of the credit for the impressive intelligence
hoping he would leapfrog into the Mossad Chief's chair. Pollard's
documents were about as good as any spy's who ever worked for
Israel. Wolf Blitzer, who wrote a book on Pollard, called him a
'super mole'. The full extent of what Pollard sent to Israel will never
be revealed, unless by Pollard himself, but it is reliably reported

that included among the material passed to Israel were detailed reports on Iraq's armoury of non-conventional weapons and the exact location of PLO sites in Tunisia, including Arafat's house. The latter was immensely valuable in the fight against terrorism. After three Israelis were murdered in Cyprus by the PLO, Israel retaliated with a highly effective air strike on the PLO in Tunisia. The PLO got the message and the number of attacks on Israelis abroad has dropped considerably since 1985. But terrorism within Israel continued. After three Israelis were killed in a bus attack in the Negev, and intelligence revealed an upcoming assassination attempt on Rabin himself, Israeli troops landed in Tunisia and killed the planner of both attacks, the PLO's second-in-command, Abu Jihad. Both incidents were mighty blows against terrorism, resulting in the saving of untold lives and were accomplished thanks to Pollard.[1] But gratitude was hardly forthcoming. Alerted that the FBI were on to him, Pollard drove to the Israeli Embassy in Washington and requested sanctuary. Indeed, his Israeli contact had promised him sanctuary in the event of discovery, and was presented in 1985 with an Israeli passport in the name of Danny Cohen, a gesture of the kind of protection accorded to a top spy. However, when the moment of truth arrived, Pollard was ejected from the embassy and thrown right into the arms of the FBI waiting in the street outside.

From here on, the Israeli cover-up began in earnest. Foreign Minister Shamir denied knowledge of Pollard, as did the head of the Mossad, who was undoubtedly telling the truth. Eitan's personal rivalry with the Mossad had led to the Chief's exclusion from the Pollard data. But Pollard's intelligence file landed on the desks of the Defence Minister Rabin and Prime Minister Peres. If both ministers had been unaware of Pollard's activities, it is most unlikely they would have approved an air force attack against Tunisian sites, given the excellent chance of success based on Pollard's information. If, in the unlikely case both were unaware of Pollard himself, they must have known that someone was shifting top-grade American intelligence to Israel.

If the Israeli leadership thought denials would make the Pollard case go away, they severely underestimated the wrath of the Americans or more specifically, the wrath of the Secretary of Defence at the time, Caspar Weinberger. Two facts made him obsessed with Pollard: he was one-quarter Jewish, stuck with his Jewish grandfather's name and was openly ashamed of both tricks of fate; and he was in charge of Defence when the far more serious Walker family spy case erupted, which involved selling out the American navy and its communication codes to the Soviets. The Pollard case was much more mild, involving the passing of intelligence to an ally who used the data for the common good. The Pollard affair was just the case to get public outrage steered away from the Walker fiasco.

In a case such as Pollard's, Israel could have expected a hush-up. In the aftermath of Pollard, it was revealed that an American spy had risen through the ranks of the IDF and was sending back highly sensitive material about the Lebanon War to America. (There are contradictory reports about the fate of this officer; some say he was quietly sent back to the US while others claim he is still in an Israeli prison, ready to be bartered for Pollard.) Further press reports stated that American intelligence had slipped moles into the Gadna, a military training programme for teenage Jews, many of them American. And an Egyptian spy in America was caught passing secrets to Cairo and was quietly returned home. Without Weinberger, the Pollard case might have been a hush-up with Israel's leaders unaffected.

But with America determined to embarrass Israel over the affair, Israel took the cover-up route. First the Science Attaché and his assistant were flown from Washington to Israel. Then a three-man delegation comprised of the head of the General Security Services, the director of the Ministry of Foreign Affairs and one civilian, arrived in Washington to 'put out the fires that had been lit by Pollard'.

The Americans demanded the right to question the two science attachés and their boss, Eitan. The Israelis agreed, if they were immune from prosecution. The Americans were as yet unaware of Pollard's recruiter, Sela, so the Israelis decided not to remind them. When Pollard later revealed who his recruiter was and Sela was indicted, he had no immunity from prosecution, a natural result of the delegation's deceit eventually catching up.

Peres had to approve the delegation's negotiations and eventually agreed to disband the Science Liaison, return material sent by Pollard and punish the guilty, which was like agreeing to self-flagellation. He also guided the cabinet to issue the following public apology:

> The government of Israel is determined not to spare any effort in its fundamental and extensive investigation to the last detail. . . .
> The government of Israel promises the government of the United States of America that in the event of suspicions being verified, conclusions will be drawn against those responsible.

Our relations with the USA are based on a firm foundation of
deep friendship, close affinity and mutual trust. Spying against the
US is against our policy. Actions like this, if they indeed took place,
were misguided and the government of Israel apologises.

Such a load of guilt-ridden, sanctimonious hogwash has no
place in the diplomatic relations between allies. There was no
investigation taking place at the time of this apology. In fact, the two
investigations that finally did make some effort at uncovering the
facts were initiated by public outrage, after Pollard was convicted
in 1987. Spying against the US was not against policy, despite the
hollow proclamations about mutual trust and affinity. And apart
from Thomas Pickering, the American Ambassador to Israel –
hardly a popular figure in Tel Aviv, who nonetheless called the
apology 'excellent' – no American in the know was fooled.

Pollard was promised a reduced sentence if he made a full
disclosure. But Weinberger had other ideas, insisting that Pollard
receive the maximum penalty and never again 'see the light of day'.
And, since his life sentence began, he hasn't.

Back in Israel, the injustice of the sentence was plain and Pollard
was slowly attaining martyr's status. The two official investigations
were whitewashes, drawing the conclusion that the Pollard morass
was the result of a rogue operation initiated by Eitan and Sela.
The second commission, chaired by Labourite Abba Eben, made
an important distinction. Rabin, as Defence Minister, had to take
responsibility but the ultimate blame belonged to Peres, who by
inference, must have known that spying against the US was taking
place, but let it go on and covered it up once the operation
was blown.

Peres spent a good week calling the Eben report a lie and when he
caught his breath, he had Eben removed from the party's electoral
list. His political career effectively over, Eben may have been the
only victim of the Pollard affair, other than the spy himself.

The actual fomentors of the whole business, Eitan and Sela, did
very well for themselves. Presumably as a reward for public service
and sealed lips, Eitan was made head of the government-owned
industrial complex, Israel Chemicals. He received an enormous
salary in return for his managerial expertise gained as a business
failure in the early 1960s.

Sela was promoted to Brigadier General by Rabin and given
command of the country's biggest air force base, Tel Nof. The
American government loudly protested the appointment, correctly

viewing it as a reward for dedication and silence. Rabin reacted by removing Sela's new rank but not his base command.

The Israeli public, once again badly misled by its leaders who apparently chose to pay off subordinates who knew too much, were not amused, and the press reflected the disgust. Yosef Harif writing in *Ma'ariv* observed: 'At the time when the political echelon should have been trying to find fires and put them out, they lost control and allowed the fire to ruin Israel's standing with American Jews, the media and Congress.'[2]

No incident had ever divided Israeli and American Jews so completely as the Pollard affair. The American Jews are terrified of charges of dual loyalty and not one Jewish organisation of any significance took the correct stance that Pollard's sentence was far too stiff. No Jew of standing admitted he was outraged. And, in fact, most were frightened of an anti-semitic backlash.

Israelis were repelled by their government's actions but no less so than by American Jewry's inaction. Israelis came to view American Jews as cowering diaspora chickens, genuinely insecure of their place in US society. Editorials lambasting American Jews, 'at their cocktail parties', far from the front but pompous and brave, popped up in the Israeli press together with resentment against the wealth and materialism of American Jews.

With a great deal of righteous justification, Americans retaliated against Israel for putting them in such an embarrassing position. Jews there were appalled by the way Pollard was abandoned by the Israeli secret services, embassy staff and cabinet. As Rabbi Eli Rosenzweig of South Bend, Indiana said in the *Jerusalem Post*, 'For a few soldiers, Israel was prepared to release thousands of terrorists. But for one American Jew, who is also a soldier fighting for Israel, the government of Israel is not prepared to do anything.'

If it were not for the actions of two MKs, Geulah Cohen and Edna Solodar, this statement would be completely accurate. These two backbenchers have led a campaign for Pollard's release since 1987. And they certainly have the support of the majority of Israelis who, in their hundreds of thousands, have signed petitions to free Pollard.

The Israeli public reaction is finally having its effect on American Jews. By 1991 many Jewish organisations in the US, including the powerful American Jewish Congress, finally found the courage to speak out and are lobbying for Pollard's release. They have at last recognised that the over-the-hill misfits running the Israeli government are not the people of Israel and that

Pollard is as much a victim of the government as is the Israeli public itself.

IRAN-CONTRA AND ISRAELIS IN LATIN AMERICA

During the 1989 Columbian national elections, the leading opposition candidate, a staunch opponent of the drug cartel, was assassinated. His killer was trained by Israelis and possessed Israeli weaponry. The trainer, Yair Klein, a colonel in the IDF reserves, fled Columbia leaving behind half a dozen of his employees who were, shortly after, secreted out of the country. On his return to Israel, Klein became the focus of intense media attention.[3] Who had hired him to train the killer and, more to the point, was this Israeli training other members of the cocaine cartel in advanced commando tactics?

Klein insisted that in reality he had been hired by ranchers of the Cattle Growers Association and sodbusting members of the Farmers Association to protect them from the hired guns of the cocaine kingpins. As noble as this story sounded, no one in Israel bought it. He was investigated by the police and charged with a variety of gunslinging offences, the most serious being the export of night-fighting equipment, ammunition belts, and aircraft detection devices in violation of a 1986 law forbidding such transfers of Israeli equipment without a license.

Eventually Klein and another officer, Lt. Colonel Yitzhak Shoshani,* were charged with illegal export of Israeli arms. Klein's primary defence was that the alleged crimes took place in Columbia, a country clearly not within the jurisdiction of Israeli courts, but he was found guilty. The question begging to be answered was how Klein acquired the arms in the first place. Who in Israel approved the sale of sophisticated weaponry to a hired gun with a lot of army connections?

Columbia was not the only venue for Klein's talents. He was also accused of running weapons through, and trying to set up a training base on the Caribbean island of Antigua. Rather than reveal the details of this deal, he asked to be charged without a further trial, and his suppliers escaped the embarrassment. He was apparently a lone wolf, selling IDF knowledge for his own profit.

For decades Israel has offered Latin American régimes military training and equipment in return for trade and diplomatic support.

---

* Shoshani was one of the officers accused of bribing a Pentagon official to help procure sales of the Mazlat.

By 1986, however, this simple but deadly game had expanded to encompass CIA-trained militias, hostages far away and drugs in a scandal that almost ended the Reagan Presidency: Iran-Contra.

In 1985, while Shimon Peres was Prime Minister, three Israelis with high-level contacts in Iran interceded on behalf of the US. They were to arrange the exchange of American hostages held by Iranian-controlled Shi'ite militias in Lebanon for the sale of American military equipment through Israel. The three were: Yaacov Nimrodi, a former Israeli military attaché in Teheran, Al Schwimmer, the American-born founder of Israeli Aircraft Industries and David Kimche, director of the Foreign Ministry. Naturally Peres has denied appointing this talented triumvirate.

By the next year, the Israelis, having made the match between buyer and seller, were deemed unnecessary and the three men were in the process of being phased out of the dealing. Perhaps too, they had been sufficiently rewarded, for by the spring of 1991, Nimrodi and Schwimmer were being investigated by the police for a missing $2 million in the transactions. Peres replaced them with his terrorism advisor, Amiram Nir.*

Once Nir took over, the operation spun madly out of control. It became not a straightforward arms-for-hostages deal but a mechanism to take the Iranian cash and use it to fund the Nicaraguan Contras and other covert operations. Very little of the plan went smoothly. Only one hostage, Benjamin Weir, was released in exchange for the sale of 500 anti-tank TOW missiles. Another shipment of arms, this time Hawk missiles, was returned by the Iranians for being incompatible with their launchers – and also because the Hebrew lettering had not been removed, much to the sanctimonious outrage of anti-aircraft officers who didn't realise their government was accepting equipment from the devil Jews. Another shipment was held up in the port of Eilat while the wily Persians, desperate for arms to stave off the Iraqis, dithered on the price.

One must stress again that this was an official Israeli operation. Israel does not fly planes from its airfields to Teheran or offer the use of its only southern port to Pollard-style 'rogue operators'. If further proof of the officiality is needed it can be found on a piece of White House stationery sent to Peres by Reagan on 3 October 1986. On it the President writes, 'I want you to know of my personal gratitude

* Recent investigative reporting, especially into the 'October Surprise', see p.108, place the first sales of weapons to Iran five years previously in 1980. The 1985 date reflects the official version of matters.

and that of the people of the US for the extraordinary efforts being undertaken on our mutual behalf by Mr Amiram Nir. As you are aware, he is participating in an endeavour of great importance to both our nations and peoples.' Unless someone took the great trouble of forging this item of correspondence, Peres was aware of what Nir was up to. And if Reagan knew Peres like Israelis know Peres, his gratitude should have been tempered with great trepidation.[4]

And if Reagan knew Nir like the Mossad knew Nir, alarms would have sounded well before the damning note was sent. Although Nir had achieved the rank of Lt. colonel and commanded an armoured brigade, the Mossad were reportedly horrified by his political appointment because of his reputation as a blabbermouth and braggart. His penchant for telling all to boost his importance led to his claim that he had written the secret agreement concerning Iranian money transfers to fund covert operations that was later initialled by both Reagan and Peres.

One man who could not risk any more of Nir's slips of the tongue was George Bush. On 29 July 1986, Nir met the vice-President in his room at Jerusalem's King David Hotel and briefed him on the progress of the whole operation. According to the Fuller memorandum included in the Tower Commission's Report on Iran-Contra, Nir admitted that Iranian moderates were no longer the negotiating partners. 'We are dealing with the most radical elements,' Nir admitted to Bush.

The administration attempted to quash this inclusion in the report. One of the central justifications for the operation was the establishment of ties to Iranian moderates with the long-term goal of a less anti-American Iranian régime. If Bush was informed that his government had been drawn into negotiations with the kidnappers of American Embassy staff with the intent of helping them win their war with Iraq, then the moral imperative of the operation was lost and Bush should have made a supreme effort to bring down the whole house of cards.

Bush did not deny meeting with Nir, adding flimsily that he 'couldn't remember much about the briefing', nor did he, 'fully understand what Nir was saying at the time'.

As Yossi Melman and Dan Raviv wrote in their book, *The Imperfect Spies–The History of Israeli Intelligence*, 'the only person who could perhaps have buried Bush politically died in a plane-crash just three weeks after he was elected.'

When Irangate turned into a major scandal, Nir was set up as the fall-guy . . . His American co-conspirator and fellow colonel, Oliver North, testified that Nir first suggested overcharging the Iranians for TOW missiles and diverting the excess money to the Contras. Admiral Poindexter corroborated the allegation that the whole operation began with Nir's initiative. North further claimed that Nir opened and maintained the Swiss bank account used for funnelling the money to the Contras.

And the high-level accusations did not desist. The former American Attorney-General, Edwin Meese, declared that 'representatives of Israel' had been responsible for selling US arms to Iran and transferring the profits to the Contras. And General Richard Secord, who organised the Contra supply network, testified to the congressional committee investigating the affair that he knew of Israelis who had deposited $800,000 into the Swiss account that was the Contras' lifeline.

But despite all the self-serving finger-pointing one still has to wonder why the Contras should have been of any concern to Nir or Israel. Ideologically, it made far more sense for the Americans to be behind the scheme. The congressional committee demanded a full disclosure by the Israelis but, as was the case with Pollard, Peres promised an honest report and provided next to nothing. Nir wanted to testify in Washington to clear his name but Peres confiscated his notes and papers, forbade him and all the principals from testifying to the Tower Commission and instead issued a superficial chronology of Israel's involvement in the affair. Once again, Peres entangled Israel in a huge American scandal of which he was a principal protagonist and once more, he besmirched Israel's good name by transparently covering up his true involvement.

But not everyone was satisfied with Israel's explanation, and reports hinting at Nir's deep involvement began leaking out. In March 1989 a German arms seller told *The Middle East Insider* that Nir 'was killed because he knew too much'. He claimed Nir had not only the facts on Iran-Contra but also on Bush's connections to Noriega with all the drug implications. He also claimed Nir kept records of the millions of dollars that went to the Contras.

Before Nir's death, Michael Ledeen in his book, *Perilous Statecraft*, wrote: 'Of the central figures in the Iran-Contra affair, only he has remained totally silent. Insofar as anyone may have something new to add to our knowledge of Iran-Contra, it is likely to be Amiram Nir.'

An Iranian arms dealer fighting extradition in London, Javid

Nagdi, bargained with the police to exchange a visa for inside information on 'the death in Mexico of Amiram Nir'.

Bob Woodward of the *Washington Post* published an account of his 13-hour interview session with Nir in London. Nir claimed 'only half the Iran-Contra affair has been made public' and that 'only half of the story of secret arms transactions with Iran was publicly known'. And in this interview Nir made his devastating claim that he drew up the secret agreement initialled by Peres and Reagan which authorised the whole arms-profits-to-Contras operation.

A fair guess is that by now Nir's death would have been beneficial to leaders and former leaders in America, Israel and Central America, and he should have gone into hiding. But the events leading to his death were even more bizarre than what preceded them.

There is no solid proof of what exactly Nir was up to but there are dark suggestions that still another Israeli, this time a close aide of Shimon Peres, was caught up in the seamy world of Latin American arms and drug smuggling.

Nir left government service shortly after the rotation of 1986, which saw Shamir take over as Prime Minister from Peres. In March 1986 he flew to Geneva and met with Manucher Ghorbanifar, the Iranian arms merchant, Adnan Khashoggi, the Saudi billionaire who financed previous arms sales to Iran and Albert Hakim, General Secord's business partner. Nir held an account at the Crédit Suisse Bank as did North, Secord, Hakim and Ghorbanifar, but it is not known if money changed hands after the meeting, nor is it known what was discussed by the four comrades in arms. What is known is that shortly after this get-together, Nir opened an office in London, which, needless to say, one source claimed was an agency for an unidentified Israeli security firm.

Nir flew to Mexico city from Madrid on 28 November 1988 and immediately hopped on a connecting flight to the central Mexican city of Uruapan, famous in the region for avocados and drugs. And, unbelievably, it was reported that avocados may have been the reason for his trip and/or the cause of his departure from the land of living.

An August 1989 article in *Newsweek* called 'Death, Intrigue and Avocados' claims Nir visited a company called Nucal de Mexico which had just bought an avocado-packing plant in Uruapan. The head of the company was an Israeli named Avraham Cohen who admitted that Nir had interviewed him for his job.

Local exporters claimed that in a short time Nucal had control of the shipping of a third of the region's avocado output and the company was a front for Israel to control the avocado market of the world. A preposterous claim perhaps, but one of the owners of Nucal was Nissim Gaon, one of the richest Jews in Europe, whose influence on Israeli economics and policy through his leadership of the World Sephardic Union was profound. It is strange, indeed, that this industrialist would choose to purchase a large chunk of an avocado plant in the boondocks of Mexico.

If Nir's sudden interest in salad fruits challenges credibility too much, there is also the possibility that the business was an elaborate front. According to *Newsday*, US intelligence sources believed Nir was a middleman for a large arms deal of Israeli weapons coming in through Vera Cruz, a port on Mexico's east coast. The paper quoted American Drug Enforcement Agency officials as saying there had been a steep rise in the efforts of cocaine smugglers to ferry drugs from the region to the US. Their efforts coincided with a large shipment of Israeli weapons transferred from Vera Cruz to unknown sources in Mexico City.

Arms for drugs? This would certainly be in line with Nir's expertise and background. And it would go a long way towards explaining the $700,000 reported found in Nir's suitcase at the crash site by the magazine *Ha Olam Hazeh* in May 1989.

By a less than odd coincidence, on the very day Nir's light Cessna crashed in Mexico, Oliver North was standing trial on charges of conspiracy to defraud the American government and lying to Congress. Nir was to testify at the trial and no one can say with certainty if he would have complied willingly. But one can be sure that he was in no fit shape to do so after the crash.

One conclusion in a recent article[5] suggests a clear motive for wanting Nir out of the way: 'He was possibly the only non-American [including Peres] who knew the entire history of money transfers from Swiss bank accounts to Contra rebels against the Nicaraguan government, those that originated from arms sales to Iran and perhaps even others which began as drug money before being laundered through Swiss banks.' Whatever the truth, the Labour Party did not abandon their fallen member. When Nir was buried at a military funeral in Tel Aviv, Rabin delivered a eulogy which spoke of Nir's 'mission to as yet unrevealed destinations on secret assignments and to secrets which he kept locked in the heart.'

One may surmise that, at least since the mid-1980s, the highest political leaders have sanctioned profitable operations in Latin

America which have entangled Israel in crime and blackened its reputation. The operations were copied by mercenary IDF officers who took the government's lead in seeking profit in a world of revolutions, assassinations and drugs. One strange case seems to fit into this pattern but is leading in some very sinister directions.

An Israeli, Ari Ben Menashe, stood trial in New York on charges of criminal conspiracy to sell military transport planes to Iran. He was caught in a 1989 sting operation planned by the US Customs Service. He was recorded while arranging the sale of three C-130E transport planes to Iran for $36 million. Ben Menashe claimed to be working for the Israeli government, which Israel denied vehemently. Ben Menashe was cleared of all charges in the end but the publicity added to Israel's image of a vigilante on the loose.

Ben Menashe spent a year in prison awaiting trial and that is hardly the preventative rule of the American Customs Service. They obviously felt they had a big fish and if what Ben Menashe has been telling reporters and politicians is correct, he may turn out to be the man who lifted the cover on Iran-Contra.[6]

According to Ben Menashe, a former Mossad agent, he was Shamir's Amiram Nir, sent by the Prime Minister to procure arms for covert operations. Menashe claims that the seemingly preposterous figure of $82 billion in arms had been sold by Israel to Iran over the past decade and the profits were held in a slush fund controlled by three men in South America of which he was one. He was set up in a 'sting' after refusing to transfer money out of the fund.[7]

His is only one man's tale and must be regarded with great scepticism until confirmed. The decision to sell Iran arms dates back to 1980 and was initiated by CIA chief William Casey, George Bush and his assistant Donald Gregg. Israel's involvement began with Menachem Begin and was confirmed in a signed memorandum, called the 'October Surprise', with the upcoming American President, Ronald Reagan.

Begin had stacked Mossad appointments with agents loyal to him and the Likud, and the Mossad took directives from Begin and then Shamir.

When Peres became Prime Minister he discovered the Iran arms deals and the slush fund, fired the three principal conspirators and replaced them with Amiram Nir. Peres gave at least tacit approval of the whole operation for he attempted to continue in the same direction but with his own loyalist as a middleman.

But the Likud loyalists in the Mossad had different ideas and sabotaged Peres at every opportunity. Ben Menashe cites the Baram incident as an example.

In 1986, still another IDF officer, Avraham Baram, was arrested along with 17 other people in Bermuda while in the midst of an arms deal with Iran. He was extradited to New York and eventually sentenced.

The Baram episode sabotaged a Peres deal, as did the arrival in Iran of the rejected Hawk missiles, their Hebrew lettering unremoved. The IDF and Mossad are far too experienced as arms merchants to have sent such a delivery unless there was a purpose behind it.

Ben Menashe's scenario paints Shamir as the real power in the Mossad who carried his bitter rivalry with Peres into the corridors of Israel's intelligence services. As for Amiram Nir, he was a hapless victim of the rivalry, given minor banking duties but basically exploited.

In this scenario the real arms trader was the retired General Secord, now a private businessman who was one of an élite five men contracted by the CIA to procure arms for Iran. Nir knew of some of his transactions but was a bit-player in the deals.

Even if the whole truth never comes out, it is very clear that Israel was deeply involved in a massive scandal that came within a hair's breadth of bringing down the American government. But Israel escaped Scot-free, no doubt as a reward for acting as proxy for secret American interests.

When America is forbidden to interfere in foreign conflicts, Israel has stepped in. Israel is known to have trained Sri Lankan forces to fight Tamils, Kurdish rebels to fight Iraqis and Chadian soldiers to fight Libyans. African dictators from Mobuto of Zaire to Mengiste of Ethiopia have benefited from Israeli expertise and in return have given Israel diplomatic relations and Jews for immigration. And by acting as a proxy for American interests throughout the Third World, Israel has become invaluable to powerful figures in the CIA. It is one of the unspoken reasons why American loyalty to Israel is basically unshakeable despite bitter disagreements over the future of peace in the region.

But there is a long-term price for its policies. Throughout Latin America, peasants associate the Uzi and Galil automatic weapons with dictatorial repression and have come to hate Israel for helping prop up cruel régimes. Israel's role in Nicaragua was more than just transferring funds from Iranian arms sales. The Sandinistas were pro-PLO to an extreme and co-operated with the organisation in arms training. With the fear of a PLO base in Central America emerging, Israel supported the Contras in ways forbidden for a time by the American Congress.

Iran-Contra threatened to blow the lid on the full extent of Israel's involvement in Central America and possibly other adventures in the Third World. That Peres mismanaged the operation is undoubtedly the case, but it is possible that his strings were pulled in the wrong direction by agents in the Mossad who didn't appreciate him being Prime Minister.

Whatever the truth, Iran-Contra revealed an Israel up to its neck in international skulduggery, putting misguided military objectives far from home ahead of the immediate good of the too long-suffering people of Israel.

NU, NU VANUNU

By the summer of 1986 the Intelligence services of Israel were functioning under extreme duress. The Shin Bet, or civilian secret counter intelligence, which controls the country's internal security, had barely escaped a scandal that could have ripped it asunder.

Briefly referred to previously, it was called either the Bus 300 or Shin Bet Affair. Four terrorists, who had attacked an inter-urban bus were reported killed in a shoot-out. Unfortunately for the Shin Bet, one was photographed being taken away from the shooting very much alive. A media investigation revealed that two terrorists were taken away by the Shin Bet, interrogated and beaten to death. Amnon Shahak, who was the head of Aman (military intelligence) was consulted in an official inquiry. The head of Shin Bet, Avraham Shalom, who was responsible for framing his junior colleagues and covering it up, was later pardoned together with others on his staff.

Bus 300 exploded on Peres's doorstep, an inheritance from the previous administration. But the cover-up and pardons were his own era's snafu – and far from the only one. The Pollard affair and Peres's involvement were barely contained and by the summer of '86, Iran-Contra was about to blow up in his face. If all this containment and deceit was wearying Peres and the intelligence agencies, still another scandal, maybe the biggest of all, loomed large on the horizon: the Mossad learned that an ex-nuclear technician named Mordechai Vanunu was about to reveal Israel's atomic bomb programme to a London newspaper, *The Sunday Times*.

By July 1986, the security agencies were totally wrapped up in irresponsible in-fighting. The two intelligence services, Mossad and

Shin Bet, were headed by political rivals and were locked in a battle for supremacy. The Shin Bet was headed by Avraham Shalom, a close Peres associate, while the Mossad was led by a bland bureaucrat, Nahum Admoni, a Shamir appointee. Shalom wanted Admoni's more prestigious post and devoted much energy – which would have been better spent on the nation's internal security – to undercutting his Mossad counterpart.

But Admoni was no great boon to Mossad morale. He was a mousy and meek non-activist who rejected planned Mossad operations, including an Iranian coup to be launched from Sudanese airfields, and cut agents' activities to the bare essentials. He is blamed in Israel for allowing Peres to proceed with Iran-Contra against the advice of many of his own better qualified people, although the negligence may yet prove to have been planned.

The Mossad had also been badly exposed by Peres's policy. In July 1984, customs officers in Stansted Airport outside London inspected two large shipping crates and found in one former Nigerian government minister, Umaru Dikko, drugged unconscious. Beside him was an anaesthetist holding an intravenous drip and looking very white, possibly from the fear of discovery. Two more white men were discovered in the other crate and all three were later revealed as Mossad agents. The trio were tried and jailed but this did little to appease the British public, appalled at Israel's use of drugging and kidnapping to curry favour with Nigeria as part of its foreign-aid programme. Britain suspended relations with Nigeria for violating British law but Israel escaped such a penalty – and wouldn't the curious reporter just have loved to have been a fly on the wall in the Foreign Secretary's office when Israel pleaded its case for exemption from Nigeria's diplomatic punishment?

Altogether, the years 1984 to 1986 had not been vintage ones for either the Mossad or the Shin Bet as one scandal after another rocked the intelligence establishment while the chiefs acted more as politicians than spies. And both shared the blame for the fiasco of Vanunu, leaving Peres with just enough room to transform a traitor into a worldwide symbol of Israeli oppression.

In 1976 Vanunu was hired as a technician in the Dimona nuclear reactor located in the Negev Desert. All employees go through a strict security examination by the Shin Bet and are required to sign an equally strict secrecy pledge. Suspected enemies of the state are not hired but Vanunu was no such thing when he started work.

But by 1982 he had become a student at Ben Gurion University and adopted a dual life: by night a lowly nuclear technician in the most secret facility in the country but by light of day, he transformed miraculously into super-student radical.

Vanunu embraced any radical cause he could comprehend as well as others beyond his experience. He founded a branch of Campus, a leftist student movement, and represented Israel at a 1984 conference in Paris. He had so alienated himself from the conservative Jews of his university that his only friends were Arabs.

Vanunu continued to challenge the university administration's tolerance. He took a leading role in the defence of Arabs arrested for bringing PLO propaganda on to the campus, was elected to a student leftist/Arab council and got his picture in the papers by being photographed at a demonstration in favour of a Palestinian state.

Lest the reader view such activities as a citizen's right in a democracy, please understand that in Israel, very few Jews actively demonstrate for Palestinian statehood and those that do are confined to the fringes of the academic/artistic communities. They would not wish to work in a bomb factory or be permitted to. Yet somehow for his first two years of radical activity, Vanunu escaped the notice of the Shin Bet despite the fact that his university is filled with informers. More surprising was the fact that Vanunu had attended meetings of the Communist Party, which is totally infiltrated by the Shin Bet, but no one raised an eyebrow. In short, the Shin Bet was guilty of an extraordinary oversight in the case of Vanunu.

But Dimona plant security was to blame as well. In 1983 Vanunu flew to the US and was told to take a direct flight to avoid the possibility of a hijacking. He flaunted this basic security precaution, flying by charter from Shannon, Ireland. Though deluged with reports about his radical activities and investigating his suspicious flight arrangements, still plant security allowed Vanunu to keep his job provided he stayed out of radical student politics. Yet in December 1984, Vanunu stood for re-election to his leftist student organisation council. He was grilled by Dimona security again, which by now should have got the idea that Vanunu was a genuine and intolerable risk but still he remained unreported to the Shin Bet.

The Shin Bet were given Vanunu on a silver platter in the same year when he actually applied for a job as an agent with the secret service. He was rejected after a background check that revealed his activities. Yet he was somehow deemed suitable for work at the country's most sensitive security installation.

Security around Dimona is serious business. Stragglers are advised not to attempt to cross the network of barbed wire, dogs, guards and minefields. Hawk and Chapparel missiles protect the site from air-attack as does the air force which has twice downed planes that strayed too close to Dimona airspace. In one incident over a hundred people in a Libyan passenger plane died and in another an Israeli Air Force jet was downed for flying too close to the reactor.

These fears are justified. Terrorists have threatened to crash a passenger plane into Israel and such an attack on Dimona would become the country's Chernobyl, spreading radiation throughout the tiny area of the Jewish state. By the same token, a bomb inside the plant could wreak devastating damage and Vanunu was a prime candidate for planting it. Still, somehow this confused and bitter student radical slipped through all the layers of protection around Dimona.

Luckily, Vanunu came armed only with a camera. But he managed to take 57 photos detailing the inner workings of the bomb factory. Although he was forbidden entry into the top-secret area where the bombs were assembled, he discovered that the supervisor left his key on an open shelf when he left work for the day and no one guarded the most sensitive area at night. Vanunu photographed the bomb-assembly labs and conceivably, could have stolen a nuclear bomb out of the plant had he intended to hold the nation to ransom.

In 1985 Vanunu's behaviour left him one of the victims of a government budget cutback. He was fired but did not blame his own attitude or public displays of pro-Arab sympathies. Instead, in the tradition of Shas, he blamed anti-Sephardic discrimination. He took his case vehemently to the plant union and was reinstated. The reader must try to imagine a country where, defying normal logic, the centre of atomic secrets is run by union decisions.

It seemed that no matter what Vanunu did, his job was secure. But in October 1985 he unfurled a PLO flag at a rally and Dimona finally had enough and let the axe fall. Yet knowing the secrets he carried and where his sympathies lay, no one prevented his flight from Israel in 1986.

This is when the Shin Bet screw-ups end and Mossad's begin. Vanunu met a common bunko artist named Oscar Guerrero who, claiming to be a journalist in Australia, convinced him to sell his story to the highest bidder. Vanunu appointed the man as his literary agent and handed over 12 of the Dimona photos as part of his sales pitch. Guerrero, wanting to make a buck from both ends, contacted the Israeli consulate in Sydney to report a traitor, while simultaneously conducting negotiations with *Newsweek* to sell the traitor's story.

The consulate reported this to the Mossad which confirmed Vanunu's employment at Dimona but not his leftist activities. The Mossad, thoroughly missing the danger Vanunu posed, initially shrugged off the report but later changed its mind when Guerrero presented four of Vanunu's photos to the consulate. Finally, the Mossad was convinced and hustled seven agents to Sydney to take care of this security disaster in the making.

This was the moment to nip the Vanunu affair in the bud. He had not yet spoken to any reporter willing to take on his story and had he disappeared he would have taken his story with him, with no one the wiser. But the agents received no instructions because their meek chief waited a week before informing Peres. By then Vanunu's story was in the hands of *The Sunday Times*.

Peres, more than anyone in the country, understood the significance of what Vanunu was up to. Peres was the architect of Dimona and the long cover-up to keep its activities a secret. As far back as the mid-1950s, it was Peres who negotiated with France for the construction of the reactor and it was Peres who founded the Science Liaison Bureau (of Pollard fame), to supply the reactor with fuel and data. And it was Peres who began the policy of cover-up, initially not even informing his own security agencies of the true purpose of Dimona.[8]

In his long career of deceit, Peres's Dimona hush-up made the most sense. If it became known that Israel possessed a nuclear arsenal, the Arabs would demand their own as protection and someone, perhaps the Soviet Union or China, might provide it. Israel had no interest in a Middle East nuclear race. So Peres set the precedent denying the existence of Israel's nuclear capabilities with the catch-all lie, 'Israel will not be the first to introduce nuclear weapons to the Middle East', which all government leaders have echoed since. Vanunu would expose the years of deception and blatant lies and, at the least, deeply embarrass Israel. At worst, he could take the photos to the nearest Arab or Soviet embassy and endanger the whole reactor.

In matters of grave security issues or covert operations there is no democracy in Israel, no Knesset and no citizenry. There is just the Prime Minister and whoever he chooses to share policy with him on any given issue. Such select individuals belong to what is known as the Prime Minister's Club. For Vanunu, Peres sought the advice of Rabin and Shamir, the latter possibly to share responsibility for a failure.

According to Louis Toscano, author of a highly readable account of the Vanunu affair called *Triple Cross*, Shamir suggested killing Vanunu but Peres rejected the solution, ending their first meeting without having chosen a course of action and thus allowing Vanunu more time to spill the beans to the press. But as Toscano notes, 'In reality the solution to the Vanunu problem was strictly Peres's call. The Prime Minister had sole authority over the intelligence agencies. And he had made up his mind.'

After taking charge of Pollard and Iran-Contra, Peres took control of the Vanunu situation and cleverly decided to do nothing, believing that even if Israel were exposed as a liar, at least the Arabs would think twice before causing any serious trouble.[9]

Using that calculation as the basis for his policy, Peres ordered that no effort be expended to prevent Vanunu from going public with his story and photos. Afterwards he would be brought back to Israel, obviously against his will, to stand trial in secret.

When the story was released by *The Sunday Times*, Peres alerted none of the government to what was coming and manned the controls from his command-post in New York. This strategy of appearing to be caught helplessly offguard was terribly embarrassing to the intelligence services as a *Newsweek* summation in October 1986 illustrates: 'The case had been called Israel's worst security lapse; though he made no secret of his Palestinian sympathies, Vanunu was allowed to leave the country after being laid off from his job at Israel's Dimona atomic facility last November.'

Even the leftist press of Israel was aghast at the handling of the affair as illustrated by this editorial in *Davar*: 'If Mordechai Vanunu in fact wanted to signal the Shin Bet that he was no longer fit to be employed in a sensitive position, he chose every conceivable means of doing so, the most public ways possible. Did those responsible indeed not see these blatant signals, which were the topic of the day in Vanunu's own surroundings? If so, this would appear to be an instance of a severe security breach . . .'

The affair had, as Toscano writes, 'badly strained relations between the Mossad and Shin Bet . . . Admoni did not believe the Shin Bet had been infiltrated but he shared the fears of the right wing that something was amiss at Shin Bet.' Admoni demanded an investigation of military intelligence, but Peres, already exhausted from covering up his role in Iran-Contra and Pollard and bailing out the Shin Bet after the Bus 300 incident, wanted no part of further public outrage.

Despite shock in Israel, Vanunu's revelations had elicited barely a ripple abroad where Israel's nuclear capabilities, even those concerning the nuclear bomb, drew little attention. Vanunu might have quietly faded away, a minor footnote suspected of being a fraud, had Peres not decided to revive the issue by kidnapping the traitor and bringing him back to Israel.

He phoned Margaret Thatcher and warned her that Vanunu would be leaving England hastily but not strictly illegally. Thatcher accepted Peres's promises of a clean operation and Vanunu, always desperate for any woman who might be persuaded to sleep with him, was easy prey for a female American-born Mossad agent, who seduced him to join her on a quick romp through Rome, from where he was whisked back to Israel.

His disappearance whetted the appetite of an intrigue-starved world public and revived the atomic issue just as it had faded away into obscurity. Surely, people reasoned, if someone, clearly Israeli, took the trouble of kidnapping this man he must have been telling the truth all along. Vanunu did not gain fame or notoriety abroad until he was reported missing by *The Sunday Times*. After that, Peres managed to enmesh still another ally in an Israeli scandal. The British press and parliament demanded to know if an illegal act had been committed on British soil with the compliance of Margaret Thatcher. Since it had, Thatcher was forced to lie to save her career. The prolonged disappearance was turning Vanunu into a *cause célèbre* worldwide, threatening the British Prime Minister. Israel had no choice but to admit Vanunu was in custody and say that he was not kidnapped from England.

The Vanunu affair haunted Israeli officials wherever they went. President Herzog, a former Military Intelligence Chief, suffered on a trip to New Zealand – intended as a friendly trip – when reporters in this nuclear-obsessed country dogged him with Vanunu inquiries at every opportunity. And Herzog lied to them all responding, 'We've made it very clear that we will not be the first to introduce nuclear weapons in the Middle East.' The statement had been reduced by now to untruthful party line and groups around the world were siding with Vanunu over his government.

Nine Australian senators joined 36 British Members of Parliament in nominating Vanunu for the Nobel Peace Prize. He may not have won this honour, but he did receive a share of the Right Livelihood Award, presented by the Swedish parliament the day before the Nobel Prizes are announced. Twenty scientists, including 12 Nobel Laureates and one astronomer, Carl Sagan, signed an appeal on behalf of Vanunu, calling him 'a man of conscience'.

And even as his trial progressed, Vanunu found the initiative to further embroil the government in diplomatic scandal. Despite the supposedly strict security around him, Vanunu managed to find a pen and write a message on the palm of his hand. Surrounded by press photographers he placed his hand on the inexplicably clear window of the car transporting him and told the world he was kidnapped in Rome. Now it was Italy's turn to have a government crisis over Vanunu and Israel's handling of the affair.

Vanunu's message caused a furore in Italy and placed its Prime Minister, Bettino Craxi, in a thankless position. If the Mossad had worked without its counterpart's connivance, then Israel had broken Italian law and this would demand an official reaction. Israel took the usual step of not telling the truth. Peres denied anything had been done to infringe on Italian sovereignty. The Italian government launched its own whitewash investigation managing to wriggle out of a potentially embarrassing position by concluding that Vanunu himself was a Mossad operative and not an innocent tourist.

Back in Jerusalem, Israel's leaders had devised a plan to cover up their involvement in the whole protracted, humiliating mess. For reasons of national security, Defence Minister Rabin ordered Vanunu's trial closed to the public and restricted testimony to one issue only – whether Vanunu had broken his security pledge. Evidence regarding the veracity of his information, beliefs or motives would be quashed from testimony. There would be no chance to investigate either the Mossad agents who kidnapped Vanunu or Peres who ordered the action, since the illegality of his abduction was not an issue in the charges against him.

But Vanunu's attorney challenged the ruling and won a concession that forced Peres to be questioned. He arrived in court armed with an order from Prime Minister Shamir barring him from testifying to anything but the most general observations concerning national security. For 90 minutes Vanunu's lawyer tried to implicate Peres in the wider espionage story but each time specifics were required he turned to Shamir's order for protection.

Once again Peres had mishandled a huge security breach and manipulated Israeli law to weasel out of responsibility. The grand plan had failed. Although the Arab nations are better acquainted with Israel's nuclear potential, their reaction was not to seek accommodation. Instead new weapons were added to their arsenals, chemical and biological. One of Saddam Hussein's prime excuses for the extent of his non-conventional weapons programme was that they offset Israel's bombs. Libya, Egypt, Syria and presumably post-war Iraq, have active chemical and biological programmes and Arab nations are scrambling to buy long-range missile-delivery systems for such weapons. Vanunu and Peres were wrong: revealing Israel's atomic potential did not lead to a calmer Middle East. Only peace will bring peace.

Vanunu, Pollard, Bus 300 and Iran-Contra . . . all security disasters since 1984. All successful in demoralising the Intelligence agencies and the Israeli people who depend on them. All prolonged affairs that deflected attention away from the vital tasks of attending to immigration, reforming a political system and saving a deteriorating economy. But they were not the last of their kind in this brief period, not by far.

MONEY LOST IN THE SECURITY MARKET

Diaspora Jews apologise for Israel's flimsy economy claiming the country spends so much on defence that it has little left over for civilian uses. In fact, Israel spends some $6 billion of its $30 billion annual budget on defence or 20% of which almost $2 billion is covered by American aid. The cost to the public drops by an undisclosed figure when the profits from the sales of old and captured equipment to the Third World enter the equation and drop further when sales of new equipment developed by IDF-run industries are calculated. The actual percentage of the government budget devoted to defence is kept secret but reliably estimated at about 7% or approximately the American taxpayer's burden.

The arms industry is a necessary offshoot of the energy Israel must expend on raw survival. Arms are now Israel's leading source of revenue, ahead of agriculture and tourism. Unfortunately, it seems that whenever Israelis and money are in close proximity, money convinces the Israelis to lose all objectivity and not a few personal codes of ethics.

According to Israel Dranov, a military marketing director, Israel's military industries are butchering each other, without ethics, rules or norms, in order to carve out a place for their similar products in the international marketplace. Among the tactics employed are defamation of competitors and unrealistic price slashing. The result of the undercutting is company losses. The Defence Ministry has tried to put a lid on the in-fighting without much success but then who is the Defence Ministry to talk about the calm spending of public and foreign aid monies after the Lavi scandal?

In the sizzling summer days of 1987, a loud public controversy erupted over the decision to build or cancel a fighter jet called the Lavi (meaning lion cub in Hebrew, hardly an animal that gets off the ground much). Never before had a security issue been debated so openly.

Israel had previously managed to build a successful second-line fighter, the Kfir, thanks to a Swiss engineer who illegally transferred the blueprints of the French Mirage to the Israeli Air Force. So elated was the Air Force by the Kfir that in 1974 it approached the Minister of Defence, Shimon Peres, with a request to build a super Kfir, later called the Lavi. Peres turned down the request but in 1980 the Air Force Commander, David Ivri, approached another defence minister, Ezer Weizman, a former Air Force Commander, with the same proposal and it was pushed through the cabinet for approval.

A few months later, Weizman resigned and Menachem Begin took over his post, though retaining the Prime Ministership. This time Ivri upped the stakes. The plane approved by the cabinet was too small for future needs. Instead the Air Force would like to build a front-line fighter. Ivri admitted that the new plane would cost some $2 billion more to develop and far fewer would be built, but Begin approved the change anyway without informing the cabinet. Or putting things into sharper focus, Israel had a defence budget then of $7 billion annually and Begin approved an additional $2 billion to build a plane, without seeking government approval.

Only after this decision was taken was official research into the project's true feasibility undertaken. Research, taken as an afterthought and thus deliberately self-justifying, estimated that the 15-year cost of building the new plane would be $12.3 billion or the same as procuring an equal number of American F-16s. Of this figure, $2.7 billion would go to initial research and development. The study implied that since the cost was the same, the Lavi was money better spent since it stayed within the Israeli economy. The issue then, was not whether a better plane would join the air force armoury, but employment.

This was no small issue back in 1981 and it isn't today. The fear of unemployment was acute at the beginning of the 1980s as jobless Israelis began leaving the country in hordes. In fact, more Israelis were leaving the country than were being replaced by immigrants. Besides the nightmare of the spiralling Arab birth-rate haunting the country, expensively trained engineers were seeking opportunities abroad, taking their locally acquired skills with them. The Lavi would employ thousands of talented designers and engineers and help stem the tide of emigration.

Still, there was a big snag: American approval. The Americans would not be thrilled that Israel was building a rival to the F-16, just as they had not been thrilled when the Kfir entered the marketplace challenging their own interceptors at a cheaper price. They blocked sales to Ecuador and Taiwan using diplomatic muscle at the time and were not likely to support still another competitor in the skies now.

Enter Moshe Arens, a long-time supporter of the Lavi, whose commitment to the project dated back to 1977 when he was the chairman of the Foreign Affairs Committee of the Knesset. Now he was Israeli Ambassador to Washington and he approached the Americans with a request to allow $150 million in American aid to be exchanged for shekels in order to develop the Lavi. The request was turned down initially but Arens planted the seeds well. By November 1983, just as he was becoming the new Defence Minister, America approved $330 million to be spent in Israel on the plane. This was the result of a bitter debate in Washington which had not previously allowed military aid to be used for anyting but American goods.

So, with $330 million in hand plus what could be taken out of Arens's own budget, development of the Lavi began in earnest. Thousands of engineers were hired and factories were fitted out to manufacture the fruits of the engineering. A significant chunk of the economy was committed to the manufacture of the new plane and Arens became personally and indelibly associated with the Lavi – which is why he led the battle to save the plane when the Americans, fearful of what they had wrought, officially requested the cancellation of the project. Israelis opposed to the plane for political or economic reasons joined the fray, beginning with the Governor of the Bank of Israel who presented the government with a memorandum explaining his objections. The Lavi, he claimed, was deeply cutting into other, more immediate development programmes in the IDF and eating away at the military budget. Cutbacks were affecting IDF readiness and all in the name of a plane no one was certain would be a success. To offset the losses, taxes would have to be raised and however the Lavi was fuelling the economy with employment would be negated by less public spending power. Other objections were raised by military experts.

Since the Lavi engine and most components were American, the plane would not be a protection against a future embargo. It was just as wise to buy the proven F–16s and add Israeli aeronautics.

These were noble arguments but they ignored two facts: to date over $1.5 billion had been invested in the Lavi and the first prototype had flown brilliantly. To end the project in mid-stream would disrupt the lives of thousands (even tens of thousands according to some estimates) of workers committed to the project. Factories would close and Israel's finest engineers would be jobless, sending many of them abroad in search of work.

In the end it all came down to a partisan cabinet vote. Since this was a Likud project and elections were scheduled for the next year, Labour voted against the Lavi in a bid to wound its electoral rivals. One Labour MK, Shoshana Arbeli-Almozlino, supported the Lavi on employment grounds. Just before the cabinet vote she was surrounded by Labour leaders trying to persuade her to change her mind. She resisted at first, saying, 'You cannot pressure me at the last moment.' But Peres would not allow her to 'bring about a Likud victory', and did pressure her somehow. Almozlino left the meeting in tears and could not be consoled. The Lavi was cancelled in a 12-11 cabinet vote thanks to her last-minute change of heart. And thanks to the government's handling of the whole affair, thousands of people were fired and hundreds of engineers left the country. And $1.5 billion, mostly public money, bought a rare flightless white elephant.

DOTIN' ON DOTAN

There have been reports of misappropriations of security funds. In one proven outrage, the Defence Ministry sent unqualified personnel on trips abroad as a reward for faithful service to the bureaucratic cause. There is reportedly an atmosphere of waste and greed in arms-purchasing circles but nothing quite so seamy as the Dotan scandal of 1990 ever came to light.

In October 1990, Israelis were forced to endure still another security scandal. Brigadier General Rami Dotan, Chief of the air force's Equipment Branch, had been arrested on charges of bribery, theft, fraud and conspiring to commit a felony (murder). As many as a dozen senior Defence Ministry and air force personnel were expected to join him in the ranks of the arrested.

Dotan's crimes began in the mid-1980s when he was stationed in New York as a purchasing officer for the air force. Working in concert with Yoram Ingbir, the owner of an engineering firm, he would approach companies and agree to purchase equipment for large sums of money on condition that the company then made smaller purchases from Ingbir's firm. To further cover the trail of bribes, Dotan and Ingbir set up a number of dummy companies to channel the under-the-table funds.

The new companies came to serve a secondary and very profitable scam. As Chief Equipment Officer of the Air Force, he would order goods from the fictitious companies which, of course, would never be sent but with creative paperwork, delivery would be confirmed. And somehow no one in the Air Force noticed that millions of dollars' worth of equipment was ordered but never arrived.

Dotan had managed to swindle some $12 million and was building an empire of fictitious companies which invested the money through Swiss banks. It was a perfect scam and may have worked forever but for one Ophir Pa'il, an accountant who worked for Dotan for a time in the New York office and then struck out on his own representing American arms firms to the air force. According to *Ma'ariv*,[10] when Dotan excluded Pa'il from the benefits of his scam, Pa'il decided to blow the whistle on him. He sent a letter detailing Dotan's crimes to the IDF in the spring of '89 that resulted in a commission of inquiry into Dotan, which met twice; the first time Dotan wasn't even called as a witness, and the second time, he and his accomplices lied to the commission. In a huge breach of conduct, the Commander of the Air Force, Major General Bin Nun, transferred a copy of the commission's findings to Dotan, allowing him to shore up his testimony. Bin Nun was later rebuked for his, 'error in judgment'.

Dotan came to the conclusion that the only thing standing between his discovery and increased wealth was Pa'il, so he hired Sergeant Major Yaacov Frank to 'silence' Pa'il for $50,000. Frank was in charge of the budget of the Propulsion Department of the Air Force and apparently privy to Dotan's schemes. Certainly, $50,000 would have propulsed his lifestyle and he accepted the hit assignment.

If Frank was willing to co-operate with Dotan, another, as yet unnamed Air Force officer discovered the scam in 1986 and was threatened so effectively that he emigrated from Israel.

Dotan's methods cast suspicion on his second marriage to the former wife of his closest friend. Press reports hinted that he might have pushed his friend into granting a divorce with an alleged murder attempt. As one of the conditions for full disclosure later on, Dotan asked that his wife be excluded from any criminal investigation and whatever it was he was protecting her from will never be revealed.[11]

A smiling Shimon Peres and Margaret Thatcher at a Dedication Ceremony in Ashkelon. Both were involved in the Vanunu scandal.

Rabbi Meir Kahane became a threat to the Likud and was thrown out of the Knesset on charges of racism.

Rabbi Yitzhak Peretz, the Minister of Immigration, is a fish out of water in that post. He has turned the lives of countless immigrants into a bureaucratic nightmare.

Ethiopians in a synagogue in Beersheva. Jewish Agency policies have led to the destruction of the social and spiritual fabric of Ethiopian Jewry and the creation of black ghettos within a number of Israeli cities.

Russian immigrants at Ben Gurion Airport. Within three years, the wave of Russian immigration has dwindled to 4000 a month — less than 10% of the numbers expected.

כאן שבתת
רעב

תנו ממשלה
חכמה ?
קחו ממשלה
מתחכמה

Doctors on hunger strike at Haddassah Hospital, Jerusalem. A very sick health system where striking doctors leave patients to their own devices.

Yitzhak Rabin resigned in disgrace in 1974, but eighteen years later was appointed leader of the Labour Party.

Prime Minister Yitzhak Shamir.

Arye Deri, Minister of the Interior, has sat in the Israeli cabinet for two years while under investigation for embezzlement.

Menachem Porush, Deputy Minister of Labour, sent gentile troopers to seek out those 'illegally' conducting business during the Sabbath.

Zevulun Hammer, Education Minister. Over 25% of Israelis by the fifth grade are functionally illiterate.

Rehavam (Ghandi) Zeevi, who is known to have consorted with murderers, got four years in the Knesset (instead of jail).

Health Minister Ehud Olmert.

Housing Minister Ariel Sharon. He was responsible for constructing 45,000 apartments in 1990. By 1991, 30,000 remained unsold.

David Levy, the first Israeli Foreign Minister never to have graduated from high school, and unable to speak English.

Moshe Arens, Defence Minister since 1990, 'father' of the Lavi and 'Bus 300' affair.

Rabin's legacy — Palestinians on top of the Al Aqsa mosque in Jerusalem.

Tent dwellers, Valley of the Cross, Jerusalem. The housing crisis in 1990 forced thousands of Israelis to seek alternative shelter.

After the first two investigations cleared Dotan, he continued his crimes with a new and higher rank. It was only after evidence was presented from a disgruntled foreigner in August 1990, that Dotan was finally investigated by the police.

The dozen officers expected to be implicated in the embezzlement conspiracy never emerged but two prominent personalities did. One was Colonel Yitzhak Sar, chief of the Air Force Quartermaster Branch, who received over $100,000 in hush money from Dotan. The other was an American-Israeli attorney, Harold Katz, a courier for the ill-gotten funds. Katz was known to followers of the Pollard case, for Pollard had used his home to copy secret documents. He was also suspected by the US Justice Department of acting as a financial liaison to Pollard. Katz was arrested trying to leave Israel and was the first to crack in jail. Dotan entered hospital a free man but his room was bugged and by the time he left, the game was up.

He plea-bargained only a 13-year sentence in return for full disclosure of his operation and remunerating stolen money to the Air Force. Not every officer was happy with the light sentence. Benny Peled suggested leaving him alone in a room with a loaded gun, while Ezer Weizman more mercifully declared he should be tarred and feathered.[12]

There is no doubt that the supervision system in the Air Force collapsed completely and allowed Dotan to embezzle funds for over five years. An ex-manager of the Ministry of Defence delegation in New York explained that their system of purchasing is useless with regard to the supplying of orders from the different arms services branch. What is of interest is cost-control, not honesty.

One high-ranking officer exploited the sloppy acquisition bureaucracy in the IDF to his great but temporary benefit. There have been reports of other officers taking kickbacks from companies or taking bribes to exclude soldiers from reserve duty. Israelis expect a different standard from the IDF than from the politicians it is responsible to. In the past decade security funds have been squandered and stolen and the full extent of all losses will never be known because of military censorship. But those revealed have been bad enough to lower the morale of the 400,000 men taken away from their families and jobs for at least 40 days a year to do reserve duty. However, the enemies of Israel's security network have been busily undermining morale in other insidious ways.

ON TOP OF MOUNT TEMPLE, ALL COVERED WITH BLOOD
The pattern of security lapses just described seemed destined to culminate in some incident that would thoroughly humiliate Israel worldwide. Each year since 1983, a big foul-up was followed by a bigger one the next year. Not wishing to break precedent, 1990 was the year of the most impressive PR disaster Israel had suffered since the Sabra and Shatilla massacres seven years previously. Israelis had not fired a deadly shot at Sabra and Shatilla; the same could not be said of the Temple Mount riot on 8 October 1990.

On that day, over 20,000 Jews gathered at the Western Wall to celebrate one of the holy days of *Sukkot*. Above them on the Temple Mount, some 4,000 Arabs gathered to disrupt the Jews' celebration with violence, and hopefully cause an international incident. They succeeded magnificently but at the cost of 19 Arab dead. A small price for the humiliation of Israel.

The PLO organised the proceedings skilfully and Israeli police accommodated them with outstanding ineptitude. The pretext for the PLO demonstration was a rumour that a small organisation, the Temple Mount Faithful, had planned to lay the cornerstone for the Third Temple on the Mount that holiday. In fact, the Supreme Court of Israel had rejected this organisation's petition for entry into the Temple Mount for a cornerstone-laying ceremony on 3 October, and shortly afterwards the commander of the Temple Mount police station informed the Waqf (Moslem authority) of the decision. The fact that the Temple Mount Faithful would be barred from the Mount itself was well understood by the Moslem guardians of the Mount compound, but the riot took place nonetheless. It was too powerful a pretext to be disbanded by Israeli law.

Atop the Temple Mount stand two mosques, Al Aqsa and the Mosque of Omar. Beneath them lie the ruins of both Solomon's and Herod's Temples which stood as the capital of Israel from 1200 BCE until the destruction of the Second Temple in AD 70. Even in exile, the Temple remained the spiritual capital of the Jews. Altogether the site has been Judaism's most holy place for 3,200 years.

In 638 AD, the newly emergent Moslems attacked and captured Jerusalem. The Jews were forcibly converted to Islam and by 652, mosque construction had begun on the holy Mount. The Moslems clearly could have built on any number of alternative sites, even a block away from the grounds. But they chose to assert hegemony over the city by squatting permanently on the foundations of Jewish pride and centrality.

According to Moslem legend, the conquerer Omar sought the highest point in the city to build a mosque in his name and was directed to a garbage pit above the Western Wall. The story is hardly convincing. Higher points, including Mount Zion, exist in the city and the faithful Jews would hardly have permitted their holiest site to be used as a refuse dump.

To justify the desecration of the Jewish Temple site, more powerful myths were invented. The Al Aqsa mosque became the site where Muhammed rode his white stallion, Barak, to heaven. This convenient jumping off spot is not mentioned in the Koran. In fact, the prophet took his heavenly journey from a northern city undisclosed by the Koran. Whether one accepts the flying horse tale as factual or legendary is a separate and unrelated issue. Muhammed, himself, unlike Solomon, had never been within 500 miles of Jerusalem and had directed his followers to pray facing Mecca and not Jerusalem.

Since the founding of Israel, Jerusalem has become Islam's third holiest site according to rhetoric. But for the 1,047 years it was in Arab or Turkish hands, it was nothing but a neglected provincial backwater. It was not a site for pilgrimage as were the two genuine holy cities of Medina and Mecca. By the 19th century, dozens of travel writers including Mark Twain noted how totally forlorn a city Jerusalem had become.

Since the reunification of Jerusalem in 1967, the city has become an enormously important political symbol for the Islamic people, but their religious justifications for returning the city to Moslem hands are built on sand. And when Israeli archaeologists request permission to dig into the sands to recover the remains of the Temples, they are rebuffed each time by the Moslem authorities determined not to be undermined by any historical facts which might be uncovered.

The Jews have every right to uncover their heritage or even to build a new Temple alongside the mosques and certainly if the will was there, both would be accomplished. But Israel has tacitly sanctified Moslem control of the Mount for entirely political considerations. Arab protest is not worth the price of national assertion in the field of Temple real estate.

In the aftermath of the Six Day War, Israel could have instituted a policy of sharing the Mount. The Arabs were too weak and divided to mount a protest and they had not yet learned how to apply oil threats to the world. But by 1990 it was too late. The world had accepted Islamic claims on the Jewish Temple site as predominant, and historical arguments would never win the day, no matter how accurate.

But that does not stop many Israelis from resenting the Moslem presence on the Temple site and dreaming of a day when the Third Temple would sit in its rightful place. Arabs are deeply aware of the Jewish dream and the intrinsic weakness of their own claims to the Mount. A rumour that the Third Temple was being constructed was a powerful weapon in the hands of the leadership of the uprising. This was just the type of gossip that could turn hotheaded protesters into martyrs.

The organisers spread the rumour through the usual information channels of mosques and leaflets. And Israeli intelligence was aware that on the Friday before the incident, the *muezzin* and preachers of the Mount were calling for a protest to stop the cornerstone-laying, that handbills were distributed calling for a demonstration and that activists were calling on the homes of at least one Jerusalem neighbourhood the night before the riot, urging people to gather in protest at the Temple Mount. Yet all the warnings fell on deaf ears as the Israelis in charge did nothing to disrupt the assembly of protesters on 8 October, another Black Monday.

The Israeli command that controls Temple Mount security is divided three ways: the local police handle day-to-day protection, the General Security Services (GSS) takes care of overall intelligence, while the Border Guards of the Military Police stand by to quell large disturbances. The communication amongst these elements broke down on the day of the riot.

More unforgiveable was the fact that the security forces had expected trouble long before the riot broke out. On 21 August 1990 National Police Headquarters issued the following warning:

> Jewish festivals are the time preferred by the terrorist organisations and local groups for staging attacks intended to cause many casualties . . . on the assumption that such festivals offer convenient opportunities for attacking large public gatherings in known sites on defined dates.
>
> . . . In the Temple Mount area in particular, there is special sensitivity . . . as a result of the large congregations of worshippers. In our estimation there is a high likelihood of a wide variety of attacks in Jerusalem.

Could a warning possibly be any clearer without spelling out danger in bold letters? Acting on the possibility of trouble on 23 September, a meeting was held in the office of the head of

Israel Police's Intelligence Department. According to the Zamir Commission's report, issued in the aftermath of the massacre, 'At this meeting the possibility was raised that during . . . *Sukkot*, Arab activity on the Temple Mount was liable to cause the situation to deteriorate.'

Two days later another meeting was held by the Jerusalem Security Committee at the office of the Commissioner of Police. At this meeting, 'it was reported that there was information concerning the possibility of riots and disturbances on the Temple Mount during *Sukkot* . . .'

By the morning of the riot, Israeli police had recorded the fact that the Temple Mount loudspeaker had called for a gathering of young men three days before, and many had a leaflet in their hands with the same message. On the very morning of the riot two newspapers predicted the upcoming trouble. According to *Yediot Achronot*, 'the Supreme Moslem Council and religious leaders in East Jerusalem have called on the residents of the city and territories to come to the Temple Mount today in order to guard the place and prevent the entry of the Temple Mount Faithful.'

Even the press knew what was coming yet on the fateful and bloody day only 13 policemen and 44 Border Guards protected over 20,000 Jews gathered at their holiest site on one of their holiest days.

But this force could have been more effective if simple signs were read properly. For days, boulders and projectiles were piled up supposedly for use at a construction site on the Mount. The weaponry was there for all trained eyes to spy. By six in the morning there were already 200 individuals gathered on the site, a fact the Zamir Commission calls, 'a number quite inexplicable on a normal day'. The individuals were mostly *shabab*, or young thugs, who as a rule are not devoted mosque-goers at any hour of the day, let alone before dawn.

By 8.10 a.m. innocent pilgrims trying to enter the Mount were pushed back by the *shabab* and forced to leave for their own protection. A half-hour later over 2,000 mostly teenage Arabs had gathered on the Mount, now free of unwanted tourists. They had already begun chanting the usual 'slaughter the Jews' nationalistic slogans and this was reported to the Jerusalem Police Headquarters. This report and other equally disturbing ones were not made known to the proper authorities for over half an hour, more than enough time for the professional organisers to swing into action.

At precisely nine o'clock, Faisal Husseini entered the Temple

Mount providing the expertise that had so far been lacking. Husseini is astoundingly portrayed by the international media as a Palestinian moderate, the kind Israelis can do business with safely. He is anything but. In actual fact he is the PLO liaison for the Israel district and his arrival should have been the tip-off that something big was in the air.

Israeli Intelligence was acutely aware of the PLO-Saddam Hussein alliance and the possibility that the PLO would arrange an event so spectacular that focus would move from Hussein's invasion of Kuwait back to Israel where it rightfully belonged. Why Husseini was allowed in the Temple compound is well beyond explanation, but things really heated up once he was inside.

Within 15 minutes the Arab schools adjacent to the Mount were emptied of students who were sent scurrying along to the impending bloodbath. By ten o'clock the provocative sermons began, rocks were piled up and knives were at the ready. By 10.45 a.m. the rioters were sufficiently fired up, sermonised and armed to attack the small force of police on the Mount. They forced the main body to retreat outside the compound, locked the gates behind them and succeeded in trapping two policeman at their post inside the compound.

By now a serious incident was in the making. The rioters had turned their attention to the Jewish worshippers below them and for the first time since the recovery of the Western Wall in 1967, Jews ran away from their holiest site to escape the barrage of projectiles.

Despite the significance of the rout of worshippers, there was a more immediately worrying fact to be dealt with. The police post within the compound, now guarded by only two policemen was likely be overrun, leaving an armoury of 53 pistols and three Uzis to the rioters.

The police mounting their charge were unsupervised by higher command. The Commissioner arrived 90 minutes after the riot was quelled. And the policemen were undoubtedly enraged by the site of the Western Wall cleared of its joyous festivities by a rabble of trouble-makers. Nevertheless, when they finally broke through, the police fired tear gas, rubber bullets and warning shots. When the emboldened rioters, fuelled on fleeting victory, refused to back down, the police decided their lives were in immediate danger and shot live ammunition, lots of it, killing 19 people, wounding scores more and landing Israel in the world doghouse.

The whole incident was a massive security failure. To underscore the obvious, what follows are some of the conclusions of the Zamir Commission:

The danger facing the worshippers at the Western Wall and the special sensitivity of the entire site should have alerted the command centres and headquarters that exceptional events were taking place and should have caused the commanders to rush to the Mount . . . to take the requisite measures.

Of the breakdown of intelligence previous to the riot, the Commission concludes:

The commanders . . . failed to take account of . . . the calls for incitement by the *muezzin* and the preachers on the Temple Mount on the Friday before the events, the calls in Arab neighbourhoods to congregate on the Temple Mount, the leaflets disseminated on this theme and additional phenomena . . . Neither had the police system devised contingency plans . . .

And so on until a grisly picture of intelligence, command and field breakdowns emerges. As usual, the price Israel paid for the miserable lack of preparation that led to the bloodshed was international rebuke. And naturally Israel lost the PR battle miserably. This is par for the course even when a military action is a total success. After years of being maligned and impugned, the country will not learn the PR game.

Of many striking examples of image-building incompetence, the strike on Iraq's nuclear reactor in 1981 is a classic. Israeli jets were ordered by Menachem Begin to destroy the bomb machine of Saddam Hussein and in one of the greatest air stories in history, two squadrons of F-15s and F-16s flew 1,600 miles over enemy territory, flattened an almost impregnable installation – yet killing only one worker – and returned without the loss of even one plane or pilot.

The world media reacted by flattening Begin. It is not certain that the media could have been persuaded to paint a true picture of this glorious mission but the government barely made an effort to convince them. Even after Iraq dumped chemical weapons on the Kurds and Iranians, the wisdom of Begin's mission was never acknowledged. Finally, during the Gulf War it dawned on a very few journalists that Begin had saved American troops and Israeli missile victims from a nuclear war.

The inability to portray the true face of the PLO is a prolonged result of Israel's media incompetence. In vivid contrast the British media, almost to a person, expects the Israelis to sit down with the PLO to discuss the future of Palestine, yet only a hardy few would suggest the British government should sit down with the IRA to discuss the future of Northern Ireland. The hypocrisy is crystal clear yet the British have mastered the PR game and when their soldiers kill in Ulster, the UN doesn't make plans to condemn them the next morning.

The Temple Mount tragedy was a PR exercise more than anything else and the timing of the Arab riot was aimed for maximum exposure. Well before the actual riot itself the PLO had prepared a UN resolution condemning Israel for 'attacks on Moslem holy places' and if there was no immediate justification for the resolution, they would cook one up.

As Gerald M. Steinberg, a senior lecturer in political studies at Bar Ilan University, writes in the *Jerusalem Post*:

> The Palestinian leadership planned this media event to perfection; they had news releases ready before the first casualties were taken to the hospitals. The major networks around the world broadcast the Arab reports verbatim. Every hour the BBC World Service told its listeners that the violence began spontaneously when, 'Israelis sought to lay a corner-stone for the Third Temple on one of Islam's holiest sites' . . . After 12 hours, when the BBC finally acknowledged that the Arab attacks may not, as initially reported, have occurred spontaneously, and that the riots may have been planned to provoke a massive police response, it was too late.[13]

The ineptitude of the Israeli politicians has consistently allowed the Palestinians to outflank them. There may not be a general alive who in an honest moment wouldn't admit that Israel giving up the West Bank would be committing suicide. The maps show Israel retreating to an undefendable border and PLO killing-sprees would lead most juries to agree they would be a most unreliable neighbour. Yet Israel has not the talent or organisation to get the message across in the forum of world opinion.

In Part One of this book, the reader has been introduced to a governmental system so flawed to the core that only the snakes survive in this man-made wilderness. The political system itself would not necessarily portend the fall of Israel for, given enough time, it might be forced to straighten itself out by an enraged citizenry.

However, time is a luxury in Israel where survival is a day-by-day affair. The vultures are hovering and the sharks are circling, prepared to attack at the first smell of blood. For the time being, only a dependable and strong security system keeps Israel alive and it has in the past several years been showing deep cracks. The wrong men in government have been telling the wrong men in the defence establishment to do patently the wrong things. And until a few trustworthy people assume positions of power, we can expect no end to wrong decisions.

Israel depends on just a few nations for its survival. These select nations, a few in Europe, one in North America, have chosen objective morality over oil-stained ethics in their decision to stand by an embattled ally. But if the ally doesn't start behaving with intelligence and competence, Israel may find itself very much alone.

Israel's fight is just, her people decent and moral, mostly. Their government is letting them down and, far more worrying, their defence establishment is following suit. But it is economics, if anything, that will ultimately destroy Israel unless the entire economy is overhauled soon.

Most Israelis lead an awful existence of deprivation, harassment and debt. Life in Israel should be immensely rewarding. The people have an ideological reason to exist, the climate is cheerful, the population colourful, the landscape lovely. But an entrenched bureaucracy is sucking the spirit out of a brave and fine people.

Israelis are cheated constantly: cheated at the bank, in the market, by the tax department, at the health clinic. They overpay on every item but are underpaid unless they cheat back. The system is nasty and not a few people have become nasty in turn. Life has become a runaround of overdrafts, conniving for basics, rude clerks in grim offices and endless unnecessary tension in the name of bare survival.

In recent years the brutality of life in Israel has taken a drastic turn for the worse. In Part Two we shall learn the real reason Israelis may have to sacrifice all they have given for nationhood; their lives have become unendurable in a system that is unbearable.

PART TWO

Suffer the Poor Israeli

CHAPTER NINE

To Your Bad Health

While the first part of this book has dealt with just how crooked the Israeli political system is, the second part will illustrate the immense suffering inflicted on the people of Israel. The reader is forewarned: you're going to find it difficult to believe all of it. The systems Israelis must live under will seem like practical jokes devised by the devil himself. And where better to begin Lucifer's travels than in the world of health, sanitation, hygiene, the environment and anything connected to the physical well-being of a people.

POLITICS, CLINICS AND INSURANCE

The Histadrut was founded over 70 years ago as the national labour union. In time it expanded to encompass industry, real estate, recreation, transportation, banking, sports, and on and on until its tentacles reached into the lives of every Israeli. The Histadrut created, then dominated, the national health plan called Kupat Cholim Clalit (shortened for our purposes to Clalit) and thereby politicised health to this day. Employing the majority of the country's doctors and nurses, Clalit runs 1,200 regional clinics (80% of the total) and controls 40% of Israel's hospital beds.[1]

Although Histadrut elections are open to all parties, Labour has yet to be challenged in any leadership contest. By controlling the upper echelons of the Histadrut bureaucracy, Labour has moulded the union in its own image. Every government worker (55% of the population) is a Histadrut member and every month a proportion of his salary is deducted to pay for his membership in the Clalit health plan. So how does the dominant health plan of Israel operate if its ultimate ownership is a political party? It operates as badly as the Labour Party.

When a member is unwell, he must show up at his own local clinic where havoc awaits him. He is not allowed to choose his own doctor; if hospitalisation is required, he is not allowed to choose which hospital or surgeon; should drugs be prescribed, he must purchase them at the clinic pharmacy or lose his insurance medicine reduction; if the member has a job, he must lose a morning's pay for he cannot choose when an appointment suits him. He must show up between 7.30 and 8.00 a.m. and register for a place in line.

A reporter from *Ha'aretz* arrived at a clinic at 7.30 a.m. to register a sick relative. There was a note on the regular doctor's door telling patients that the doctor would not be in the office that day and urgent cases were advised to register with the clinic clerk to see another doctor. But the office opened only at 8.00 a.m., or half an hour after registration closed. And in this bureaucracy as in others, there was no bending of the rules. The replacement doctor could not be seen unless his patients were registered before 8.00.

But that wasn't the end of the reporter's problems. In order to make an appointment for the next day, the clerk had to decide whether the case was urgent or not, though a clerk is hardly a medical expert. Once the patient gets a place in the queue, the agony just begins. He might have a raging fever but will still be delayed up to five hours in the clinic waiting-room. If the doctor diagnoses a serious problem, there are two options. He will send the patient to a specialist of his choice no matter where his office is located and that means going back to the clerk to make the appointment. There is no seeing a specialist directly. Even if the patient has chronic asthma and knows it, he cannot simply make an appointment with his usual ear, nose and throat specialist. That is against the rules. If the clinic doctor senses the possible need for hospitalisation, he does not simply send the patient to a hospital for tests. First he sends him to a Clalit laboratory where he must undergo tests, which are totally unnecessary for, if the results prove serious, the patient will be sent to a hospital to repeat the same tests. Professor Chiro Servidio describes the clinics as 'bordering on molestation'.[2]

Politics are the only reason Clalit exists or is allowed to, for it has accrued debts of over half a billion dollars. The government covers the debts reluctantly. Clalit is financed three ways: a third through government subsidies, a third through government-arranged bank loans and a third through membership dues. A nice arrangement that doesn't work.

Membership dues do not begin to cover a third of Clalit's costs, and so loans are based on budget sheets prepared up to two years after they should have been presented.[3] The government subsidy is calculated at the end of the year instead of the beginning like everyone else. According to *Ha'aretz*, the suspicious accounting measures are there to prevent the government from knowing the exact nature of the financial disaster, which if exposed, would hamper subsidies and preferential loans. But the public must pay: every employer is forced by law to pay a tax distributed to the country's four health plans. Clalit receives 70% and the rest is divided between the smaller health plans.

Two of the other health plans allow members to visit private doctors at their convenience. They are infinitely more humane and, in recent years, anyone who can escape the grip of the Histadrut has turned to them. In one year, from 1986 to 1987 the number of members in the two plans rose from 17% to 23%. The fact that Israelis who are non-union members are choosing alternatives terrifies Clalit, which has been draining the government for decades with its notion of health hegemony. In 1989 a census was conducted by the National Insurance Institute to discover what percentage of Israelis belong to what health plan. Clalit petitioned the High Court of Justice for a restraining order barring publication of the results of the census, claiming them to be 'incomplete and misleading'.[4]

The public was not fooled by Clalit's motivation for the petition. Government leaks claimed that because of the public shift in health services, the Histadrut plan would lose $4.5 million a month in allocations, with $2.25 million going to one of the other plans.

Clalit is desperate for members and has taken extreme measures to lure them in. Untold new immigrants still unaware of the horrors that await them (or of the alternatives) are registered into Clalit by Histadrut Absorption Ministry clerks. It has become the forced refuge of the underpaid and elderly who are placed on Clalit as part of their old-age pensions. Those who can afford it join the private health plans even though that means paying about $150 a month for a family of four. The other plans pay their doctors better salaries, so Clalit has also been suffering a serious outflow of physicians. To compensate them, the Histadrut provides free apartments to select doctors. Clalit owns a thousand apartments in the country which the doctors mostly rent out to subsidise the mortgages on the homes they actually live in.[5]

Other employees of a higher stature are pure political appointments. Well-paid clinic directors have no need for a medical background, just clout in the Labour Party. In fact, the current National Director of Clalit is not a physician.[6] The real reason for Clalit's existence is less the health of the public than the failing health of the Labour Party. With the Histadrut empire crumbling, the health network is the last piece of property that can attract and keep people in the Histadrut, whether against their will or not.

If Clalit is an unpopular Labour Party organisation, why didn't Likud break it up and encourage the establishment of private health insurance plans? One reason is that with 75% of the population tied to the one health plan, forced to utilise its clinics and unable to escape its network, slaying the beast would mean killing a lot of patients in the battle. This fact keeps Clalit operating despite the public revulsion to its existence. No matter how badly run it is, the government cannot stop the supply of money without a massive public upheaval. Knowing that the government must bail out the system gives Clalit the confidence to buy properties, like a huge private hospital in Jerusalem as well as agricultural land, all of which it cannot realistically afford.

Professor Arthur Eidelman, Chairman of the Neonatology Advisory Committee of the Israel Medical Association says of Clalit: '. . . it does not represent a health insurer whose objective is to organise medical care. Its decisions and priorities are influenced . . . by outside factors concerning political and ideological interests of the Histadrut.'[7]

Such political influences blind Clalit to reality. The Labour Party seeks allies in buttressing its collapsing health system so offers several religious parties cheap membership in the plan. A 1977 government recommendation to scrap Clalit was torpedoed by the National Religious Party because 15,000 of their members were on the plan. And in 1990 a major government commission recommended the separation of the Histadrut from Clalit and a national insurance scheme in the style of Britain's, thus cutting Clalit from the source of its funds. The Histadrut rejected the commission's findings and as for the government acting on them, Dr Sohar realistically says, 'Not a chance. They won't get it past the Knesset.'

The politicisation of Clalit results in a jealous guarding of its doctors that has spread to the smaller plans. This means if a patient has a unique ailment and the doctor best trained to treat it is working for a different plan, he cannot be consulted with compensation.

ISRAELI HOSPITALITY

Clalit controls 30% of the country's hospitals and 40% of its beds. Most of the rest are in the hands of the government. The competition between the two bureaucracies has led to endless strikes and sanctions, bankruptcy, blatant corruption and human anguish. Let us begin with strikes.

Whenever Clalit staff get a raise, the government hospital workers demand equal consideration. The result is great disquiet on the hospital scene. The seeds of discontent have long been planted. Doctors in almost all Israeli hospitals receive the same pay determined by seniority, not skill. Thus an open-heart surgeon and a pediatrist both receive the same salary, which may be as low as $5 an hour. To emphasise the point, an Israeli open-heart surgeon is often paid less than a messenger boy in New York, about $900 per month.

But even these paltry salaries cannot solve the debt problem so even more heartless cutbacks are instigated. Doctors and staff are banned from working a second shift, which would incur overtime pay. So (and any Israeli will swear it's true) X-Ray labs, CAT scans, ultrasound machines, tomography testing, and so on, all close down by afternoon in Israeli hospitals. Billions of dollars in medical equipment lies idle because the Histadrut and government don't want to pay staff extra to utilise them. One rather obvious result is that patients stay in hospital longer waiting for tests. But that's okay too because the hospitals receive their money by the number of beds filled. It doesn't matter if one patient has tonsilitis and the next leukemia, it costs the same to treat them.

Doctors, nurses and hospital workers are very unhappy about their conditions and grumbling often turns into outright rebellion. More than 12% of the workdays lost to strikes in the past decade have been in the medical sector and that means a lot of ill people left untreated.

In March 1983 8,500 doctors went on strike paralysing every hospital in the country. They demanded a 200% increase in salary, understandable since the average basic pay then was $435 a month. Despite being a labour union, the Histadrut opposed their own doctors, believing such a raise would be a bad example to their other workers.

The government agreed to a 150% pay increase for the notoriously exploited junior doctors but did not match the offer for senior positions. So the senior physicians rejected the offer to the great chagrin of the younger ones, who were forced to continue the strike.

For two months hospitals were run on reduced staffs, cancelling all but life-or-death operations. Then the doctors staged a mass walk-out leaving behind a skeleton staff to mind the emergency

rooms. When this failed they tried a new strategy. The doctors of
Israel went on a mass hunger-strike and since the hospitals were
close to empty, most of those treated were the malnourished doctors
themselves. Stories of public suffering were rife. Patients awaiting
surgery were returned home, a few reportedly for good, others to
repeat their tests and worries after the strike ended. And it took
118 days of striking before the doctors returned to work.

Prof. Zvi Bentowitz of Kaplan Hospital in Rehovot didn't support
the strike, explaining the doctors 'had lost their human consciences
by abandoning the hospitals'.[8] Despite their miserable lot, Israel's
doctors defied all norms in medical ethics and paved the way for
all the other breaches of humane conduct that followed.

An all-out strike by Israel's nurses began on 23 June 1986.
Again the issue was a pay raise and when their demands weren't
met, there was another hunger strike. Unlike the doctors, the
nurses had no sympathy from the public because they struck *en
masse*, leaving behind not a single nurse to care for the ill. The
government ordered soldiers to take over the nurses' posts and
volunteers from the citizenry, disgusted by the human suffering
left in the nurses' wake, joined them. But surgery was cancelled
and life-saving equipment left unattended. The reader only need
imagine a hospital without a nurse to realise the impossibility of
the situation. All but life-and-death cases were sent home to relieve
the pressure and hospitals again turned into madhouses with lives
recklessly endangered.

The nurses failed to attain their principal demands but they
made one point. Sometimes, they are more important than doctors
in the maintenance of a hospital. Yet, still another group of
underappreciated workers made the same point.

1987 was the year hospital workers went on strike leaving
behind uncooked food, unemptied bedpans, unwashed laundry
and untyped clerical work. This time the patients suffered more
miserably than ever. Their most basic needs, like clean sheets and
food disappeared. For a week television news presented a horrific
picture of children lying on soiled linen, geriatric patients deprived
of medicine and even water, and overworked volunteers trying to
make order of unmitigated chaos. The strike took place for the usual
reason: Clalit workers got a raise, government workers didn't.

In 1988 doctors at government hospitals went on strike after
Clalit doctors were allowed to take on second shifts and thus earn
extra pay. In the end Clalit, under government pressure, cancelled
the second shift. The government doctors gained nothing and the

public lost eight more hours a day of physicians' care. But at least the doctors of Clalit didn't gain an advantage over the government's doctors.

Worse than any of these strikes, however, was the one undertaken by the private hospitals for the chronically ill in 1985. After the government withheld payments to these institutions, the patients, old and dying, were removed against their will from their beds and deposited on the doorsteps of government hospitals. Humanity had never sunk so low in Israel. Jewish medicine, the pride of the people, mocks all norms of decency in Israel's hospitals.

THAT OLD BLACK MEDICINE

Because of the ban on overtime, patients always have a long wait for surgery. The bitterness of the strike of 1983 created an attitude of callousness among hospital surgeons that surpasses criminality. Feeling undercompensated for their work, a few high-ranking surgeons decided that a patient on the waiting-list could jump the queue and have his operation performed without further delay – if he paid the doctor a substantial bribe under the table. If caught demanding a bribe, Israeli doctors can be prosecuted for fraud and non-declaration of income. But since it reduces doctors' wage demands, the practice is usually secretly approved of.

The head of the neuro-surgery department of a major hospital went too far when a woman's family refused to pay the bribe and the surgeon held up the operation long enough to cause the patient permanent paralysis. Israeli prosecutors investigated the doctor, Yechiel Heilbronn, and discovered the bribes he demanded were far in excess of standard black medicine norms, some in the $5,000 range. Heilbronn travelled to the US in 1989 and refused to return to Israel for trial. He was arrested in Michigan while awaiting extradition. In jail he told American reporters that he was being turned into 'a sacrificial lamb' for all the graft taking place in Israeli hospitals.[9]

DECAY, OKAY?

According to a recent State Comptroller report patients must wait many months for elective surgery, 'causing irreparable damage . . . Many patients die before reaching the operation.' The same report notes that the Ministry of Health has not established criteria for mammography examinations, which is just as well since much of the equipment is malfunctioning, releasing far too much radiation.

Finance Minister Yitzhak Modai meanwhile, has trimmed the

budget of the new Health Minister, Ehud Olmert, who informed the universities that far fewer doctors may be trained because the country can't afford them.[10] And he announced that the majority of immigrant doctors, mostly from the Soviet Union, would not be allowed to practise in Israel for fear of causing an income loss to established and not necessarily talented, Israeli doctors. Prof. Yaron Ezrahi, a scientist at Hebrew University, sums up the situation: 'In the health sector, not only may research be declining but services are simply awful. Diagnostic methodology is not good either . . . Israeli science has dropped on the international scale . . .'[11]

And this assessment is glorious news compared to the state of Israel's public health.

CHAPTER TEN

Sanitation, Hygiene, Pollution, Health

While the health service is in chaos, government failures in other areas are costing Israelis their health. Recent reports show that people swallow massive doses of chemicals and germs each time they eat. Some have already died and many are destined to follow if they continue to seek nourishment from Israeli food and drink.

DINING OUT

Over a decade ago Dr Ilan Reshef of the Jerusalem Health Authority led an investigation of the city's restaurants. Germ counts were taken from plates and utensils and most of the city's worst offending eateries were serving as many germs as it takes to make a customer ill.

Today Dr Reshef is a most disappointed man. 'Nothing was done after the report was published,' he says. 'No one prosecuted the offending restaurants and they have continued to operate in the same unhealthy way'. Reshef resigned his post in disgust and since then only one other official germ count has been compiled in Israel.

Alma Avni, former Director of the Ministry of Health is appalled by the situation and by 'the incredible apathy of the Israeli public who will eat at any restaurant even if the washrooms are filthy and the tables wiped with a rancid rag.' She believes the government must maintain health standards in public eating-places but only a complete change in the bureaucracy will defend Israelis from their own lack of finickiness. Each city or town with a city hall or town council has a local health office and it has the right to grant or rescind licences to eateries. It is the municipal councils that send out the inspectors to do the checking but will only take action if an actual poisoning is reported due to an Israeli law that protects restaurateurs from closure before trial. It is the inspectors' duty to gather the biological evidence for prosecution.

But not many inspectors are qualified to examine biological

143

evidence and act on it. A draft law demanding at least one trained biologist to be staffed by all local health offices gathers dust in the Health Ministry. There are too many politically appointed inspectors for the law to be passed.

'Because we are trained professionals,' adds Avni, 'and the inspectors often aren't, they are reluctant to co-operate with us. Obviously, the inspectors should come under the Ministry's jurisdiction but that would mean too many firings of incompetent people with political pull. So the government allows the people to be poisoned without protection.'

The legal system as well as the cost, prevents constant germ counts from being conducted. Visual testimony counts for more in Israeli courts than laboratory results. Hence only one report based on germ counts has been undertaken in the past decade and it was never released to the public. However, with much gratitude it was released for publication in this study.

Thirty-five dining establishments in Netanya were tested and only ten were found to be hygienic. In eight of the others, each spoonful of food contained over a million germs, a genuine threat to the eater's life.

In the types of eateries tested, 17% of restaurants were up to the standards of health of the modern world, another half were passable, while a third were unacceptable. But of the quick-serve cafeterias not one was up to scratch and 20% were unfit for human patronage.

The safest dining spots were the hotels; 55% were in good shape while 45% were passable. According to Moshe Drori who prepared the report, 'Israel has a 10 to 15% poisoning rate in our restaurants. The rate in northern Europe is 0.02 to 0.05%. That means we have a standard comparable to many dirt poor African countries.'

How much is a severed finger in your pickle jar or a mouse in your soft drink bottle worth? These were the worst health infringments found by the Health Ministry in packaged foods in 1990 and the biggest fine the companies received was $2500. But at least the crimes were prosecuted. The Justice Ministry in northern Israel threw out 90% of all similar cases brought to it by the Health Ministry for reasons of 'lack of public interest' and 'too great a time lapse'.[1]

SPRAYING OUR LIVES AWAY
Israeli agriculture sprays pesticides with reckless and profitable abandon knowing that there are only three government inspectors

and even if caught by one of them, he will be unable to enforce whatever laws might have been breached. The lack of control has led to incredibly indiscriminate spraying. Israeli farmers use 250 times more parathion per acre than Californians.

Israelis living in rural areas are the first affected by the pesticides. Dr David Rapner of the Emek Hospital in the northern city of Afula has treated hundreds of victims of pesticide poisoning. He claims the components of the pesticides are the same as those of nerve gas and the resulting symptoms include severe headaches, insomnia, vomiting and memory loss.

The overuse of pesticides as a cheap way of increasing crops is encouraged by a total lack of rules governing their use. The Ministries of Health, Agriculture and the Environment each has some responsibility for pesticide control but none has overall authority. Each has conducted tests on the effects of pesticide abuse but because of rivalries between them the test results are not released either to the competing ministries or to the public. In actual fact, no one in any of the ministries is responsible for controlling pesticide poisoning.

Similarly, no one in any official capacity is overseeing the use of raw sewage for fertiliser. And in water-short Israel this practice is widespread and has led to cholera epidemics in the disputed territories.

When fruit or vegetables are exported to Europe all pesticide or sewage residues must be removed or the produce will be rejected. So such potential poisons are assiduously cleansed and the produce constantly tested before shipment to foreign markets. If a shipment is found to be substandard it is returned to Israel and sold in the marketplace. According to Uri Golner, Chief Government Produce Inspector, the two inspectors who used to test fruit and vegetables for the Israeli market were fired in 1991 because of budget cutbacks. That means *no one is testing Israeli produce for poison.*

Nuzhat Katzav of the Histadrut Environmental Board confirms this horrific fact. 'No one is checking our produce and no Israeli knows if he's eating a carcinogen or not.'[2]

What is unsuitable for European palates and stomachs is dumped on the shelves of Israeli supermarkets without regard for the health consequences. According to Dr Jerry Westin, a disgruntled former government scientist, 'The spraying is overseen by farmers of the Agriculture Ministry with a vested interest in farm profits, not by doctors who have an interest in health. Israel is a world-leader in cancer because of the food we eat.'

WATER, WATER, EVERYWHERE BUT NE'ER MORE TO DRINK

Water is not necessarily a scarce resource in Israel but it has been made one. Israel is blessed with three large water sources: the Sea of Galilee (also known as Lake Kinneret), the coastal aquifer (a huge underground storehouse that follows the Mediterranean sands) and the mountain aquifer (underlying the limestone Judean Hills and containing the purest water in the country). Properly utilised, these three sources, all replenished by the winter rainfall, are capable of supplying Israel with enough water to support its needs.

But improperly exploited, these three sources are insufficient and they are being abused by the incompetent Water Commissioner, Tzemach Yishai. After a decade of malice, Yishai was finally fired under extreme duress. If not for Agriculture Minister Eitan's threat to bolt the coalition, Yishai would have stayed on til the Kinneret became a salt sea. Of his tenure, Israeli journalist Menachem Ranat writes: 'In any normal country he would have long ago been fired. He has not learned hydrology, ecology or geography or any subject relevant to water. This self-appointed expert brazenly dismisses all the opinions of scientists.'

The Israeli water utility, Mekorot, recommends the amount of water that can be safely pumped out each year based on scientific studies. In the years 1987–89, Yishai approved quotas between 8 to 14% higher than the experts suggested was safe – and this during drought years.

Overpumping of the coastal aquifer allows seawater to rush in and overwhelm the fresh water, and recently wells have become saline and useless. This is what is currently happening to Lake Kinneret. It is part of the Jordan River Valley which flows from the Golan Heights to the salt wastes of the Dead Sea. The primary reason why the Dead Sea died is the fact of its being surrounded by salty wells. Because this body of water is located in a practically rainless region with very high rates of evaporation, fresh water could never overtake the underground seepage from the salt wells.

The Kinneret is also surrounded by salty wells but it receives ample rainfall and is further fed by the snows and streams of the surrounding Golan Heights. However, if too much water is pumped out, the lake will be overcome by the salt wells. The Dead Sea is the lowest spot on earth, about 1270 feet below sea-level but the Kinneret is still lower than Death Valley. A red line has been established at 213 feet below sea-level. The lake cannot fall below this line or it will become unusably salty. Yishai appears to have ignored all warnings about dropping below the danger-line and has pumped the lake to within inches of it. According to Dr Yosef Amimelech, 'If we fall half a metre below the red line the lake will turn to salt and Yishai is allowing that catastrophe to happen. We're going to lose the Kinneret for generations.'[3]

By the spring of 1991 the salinity of the lake had risen from its normal 210 mg per litre to 240 mg and the disaster was expected to worsen as the red line was breached by the end of the summer. The Sea of Galilee is being killed not just by overpumping but also by the vast quantities of uncontrolled fertiliser, sewage and pesticides which flow into the lake from its many feeder streams.

In June 1991, the Kinneret Limnological Laboratory which monitors the state of the lake was threatened with closure because the Water Commission had stopped its funding. With the lake drying up before their eyes, the scientists worked two months without pay as scientist Dr Yuval Cohen explained, 'This is a national priority and because we are responsible people we have continued the monitoring.'[4]

Israel is filled with responsible people like Dr Cohen who love their country, work for its good and are victimised by its heartless and corrupt government. But standing up to those in power without the means to pay the rent is near impossible. Without scientific monitoring the Sea of Galilee could die without the public being aroused to save it.

LOOK WHAT SEEPED INTO OUR WATER LAST DECADE

The coastal aquifer receives no better treatment than the Sea of Galilee. Israel has only one toxic waste dump and it's located in the Negev Desert, 170 km from Tel Aviv. Industrialists wishing to save a long journey have been dumping illegally along the coast and no one knows where the dump-sites are so no one can clean them up.[5] But one scientist, Dr Leah Mushkat, using German funding, conducted an extensive investigation into the condition of the aquifer. She discovered that below the topsoil of fields irrigated by sewage, the level of organic pollutants was 3,000 times the permissible level. In one drinking-well used by a moshav she found pesticides, industrial waste and chloro-organic solvents. It was closed down but other areas have not been so fortunate. Because chlorine is added to the water in Tel Aviv, when it seeps underground it interacts with other pollutants to form a veritable witch's brew of dangerous compounds which are pumped out of the ground to supply drinking-water to Israel's biggest city.

Tourists to Israel are greeted by a huge garbage dump 60 metres high between Tel Aviv and Ben Gurion Airport. This small mountain sits above an unlined pit above the coastal aquifer. Wells nearby pump out drinking-water. According to the State Comptroller's 1990 report, of 544 wells drilled that year, 211 were found to be highly contaminated, yet the water was not filtered of microbes and chemicals. Israeli water is treated only once it's in the pipes. The comptroller recommended stopping drilling in contaminated areas but she has been ignored; she also recommended nationwide filtration to eliminate most coli bacteria, but to no avail. Hence the spread of amoebic diseases found in 30% of schoolchildren in Jerusalem.[6]

The comptroller's report stated that levels of nitrous oxides in underground water are almost double that permitted internationally, but because of the cost of drilling new wells, the government has refused to eliminate the polluted ones in use. Even bottled water, an alternative only for those who can afford it, is no great solution in Israel: a recent survey showed the local products to be no healthier than tap-water.

The comptroller also examined the drinking-water of the Galilee where there was a dysentery outbreak in 1990. She discovered that not only were the residents drinking from polluted streams, but that the area lacked properly trained personnel necessary for chlorination. In many Galilee towns the residents are drinking their sewage straight.

LIQUID DEATH

A large part of Israel's sewage systems, many built as recently as the 1970s and 1980s, have collapsed. That means pipes carrying sewage are dripping into drinking-water pipes or straight down into the groundwater. Residents of Kiryat Shmoneh, a long-suffering town near the Lebanese border noticed their water was brown one day and dozens took ill. Sewage water was flowing out of the town's taps.

A more serious incident occurred in Haifa in 1985 – 8,000 people were poisoned when sewage seeped into the drinking-water; 95 contracted typhus, resulting in one death. This was *the worst water disaster in the western world for 20 years*.[7]

In March 1989, 1200 more people in the Haifa area were infected with bilharzeous dysentery from drinking tap-water mixed with faeces.

In the summer of 1990, the entire southern coastal region,

including Tel Aviv, had to boil their water or suffer a similar fate as Haifa.

Too many Israelis feel ill too much of the time. Many newcomers report constant low-grade fevers and stomach upsets cured only by a trip out of Israel. And no wonder. A Health Ministry report claims the chances of becoming infected with a contaminous disease in Israel are *18 times higher than in the United States*.[8] To put it another way, Israelis are ill 18 times more often than Americans. And sometimes Israelis become very ill indeed.

In the summer of 1988 Israel suffered a polio epidemic. Twenty people contracted the disease, mostly from the towns of Hadera and Ramle. In the midst of the spreading panic, the sewage water of 74 locations was tested and the polio virus was found in 27. The reason Hadera and Ramle had the majority of the victims was a decision in 1982 to try a new innoculation system that was cheaper than the old one. Previously a combination of Salk and Sabin vaccines worked well, but the two towns were chosen by the Health Ministry as test sites for Sabin vaccinations alone.

Dr Rachelle Fishman, a biologist who studied the epidemic decries the decision to switch vaccination systems: 'The WHO had stopped polio cold in the Gaza Strip with the double vaccination. There was no need to endanger Israelis by changing horses in midstream. A Dutch company convinced the authorities to use a vaccine that was suitable for northern Europe but any scientist could have figured out the combination of heat and poor sanitation in Israel would put too much of a strain on this system. Somehow the Health Ministry didn't understand the obvious.'

In 1989 two dozen children were taken to hospital in the northern city of Nahariya suffering from vomiting, headaches and blurred vision. This was the beginning of a six-month meningitis epidemic which finally killed six children.

According to Professor Gedalia Sherf of Haifa's Technion College, Israel leads the western world in stomach-related diseases,[9] a fact inexplicably not mentioned in tourist brochures. And yet no government body is trying to discover where sewage is leaking into the drinking-water. As Dr Yecheskiel Zakai, former chairman of the water utility says, 'Until people start dying in droves the authorities will not try to understand the poor quality of our drinking water.'

Uri Marinov, Director General of the Environment Ministry, explains how the government is allowing the public to be poisoned: 'The Water Commissioner [has] all the authority to prevent water pollution. He has done nothing. There have been no regulations, no

---

(See below.)

prosecution of polluters or of those overpumping. He was answering the demands of the agricultural community, a community not concerned with the future .... What is very disturbing is that government officials are among the major violators of environmental policy ... they disobey the water and sewage laws daily.'[10]

If those in charge of Israel's water are willing to sacrifice the health of the people to grow a few more avocados, the good people in charge of the air are quite prepared to choke a number of citizens to run their air-conditioners.

A RECEDING AIR LINE

In Tel Aviv the huge Reading Power Station causes untold suffering for residents of a wide area surrounding it. The government Planning Committee was about to ban its construction so the Electric Company came up with a clever ploy. They lobbied the Knesset to withdraw the authority of the Planning Committee to cancel the station.

Cars blacken Israel's air because there are no controls restricting auto emissions. Catalytic convertors are unheard of in the streets of Israel. Haifa, home of water-borne death, has one of the highest levels of air pollution in the modern world because of thermal inversion and petrochemical refineries that obey no anti-pollution laws. Why, the exasperated reader might ask, do they not obey laws? Partly because there are no laws to obey and partly because they are government-owned companies which would not be compelled to stop causing respiratory diseases even if there were laws on the books requiring some abeyance.[11]

KILLING US SOFTLY WITH NEGLECT

A quarter of the magnificent Negev Desert is being destroyed by a huge nuclear complex and by the Ramat Hovav toxic waste dump.[12] This grand dump is not like other dumps in the world. There is no concrete lining to prevent seepage into the ground-water or the nearby valleys, and materials are not separated by toxicity. Radioactive waste is mixed with chemical waste which is mixed with medical detritus. And this scrumptious soup obeys no manmade laws as Dr Fishman explains: 'There are no regulations about dumping the most hazardous substances produced in the country. Who ever heard of a toxic dump without materials separation? The New Jersey mafia dump their toxic waste more responsibly.'

While the Negev is being murdered, a drive up Israel's coastal highway reveals river after river sullied by dumping. The Hadera

River has all the consistency of maple syrup. The Alexander River has the unforgettable fragrance of Evening in Pittsburg. The Kishon River, once a fisherman's paradise, is too filthy today even to support mosquito larvae.

The Pruginin Glass Report documents the sad degradation of Israel's nature and beauty spots: 'The extensive development sweeping all parts of the country has resulted in the serious degradation not only of landscapes but of unique environmental systems, threatening some of them with extirpation. Thus, for example, the coastal dune environment . . . is gradually disappearing; the coral reefs in the Gulf of Eilat have been seriously damaged, placing their future at grave risk.'

The gravity of the destruction of Israel's natural landscape cannot be overstated. If any natural site should be declared an internationally protected historic spot it is the Jordan River. By 1991 irrigation had so reduced the quantity of fresh water entering the lower Jordan that it became a polluted salt channel and little more. Not content with the destruction, a kibbutz began construction of a hydroelectric dam that will finish off the upper Jordan by diverting over a third of its waters through turbines.

Israel may be one of the most beautiful countries on earth but it is in danger of disappearing under garbage. Only 2% of all garbage is recycled, by far the lowest figure of any democracy. The situation is so absurd that Israel actually imports waste paper from New York and aluminium cans from Europe to manufacture new paper and cans which will end up recycled in Israeli dumps.[13]

Everywhere the filth is piling up. A train ride from Tel Aviv to Jerusalem passes through the stunningly beautiful Sorek River canyon. A gas mask makes the trip more pleasant since the Sorek River is a gutter carrying Jerusalem's raw sewage to the Mediterranean.

Of course, that makes swimming in the Mediterranean rather unpleasant. In a once lovely coastline of 200 km, there are no less than 50 locations of polluted beaches. That is, a dump site every 4 kilometres.[14] Up north, the sewage treatment plants are overburdened or have stopped working altogether.

It's not a pleasant story but that's what happens when a political system collapses. When no one is in charge and no one takes responsibility, no decisions are made. So no one takes sewage out of drinking-water and people contract typhus, meningitis, cholera and polio. Then no one allows toxic dumps to seep into the ground-water unsupervised and no one lets hazardous waste run freely into the rivers and wadis. And no one cares that a country of great beauty is turning hideous while its people are exposed to doses of poison unthinkable in any other democracy. Finally, no one loses all concern that the next generation of Israelis may not be around because they're too sick to drink the deadly water or eat the infected food.

CHAPTER ELEVEN

With the Best of Intentions: the Misuse of Foreign Charity

In the fiscal year 1990–91 world Jewry donated well over $2 billion[1] to Israel. This sum includes worldwide donations from Israel Bonds, Hadassah, Friends of various universities and schools, religious contributions and so on. Although much of the money went to private foundations, most was directed to the Jewish Agency by two organisations, the United Jewish Appeal (UJA) of the USA and Keren HaYesod, representing all other Jewish communities. The Jewish Agency also sends money back to world Jewry through the World Zionist Organisation (WZO) but to reduce confusion, references to both will mostly fall under the term favoured by Israelis, the Agency. And most references to diaspora charity fund-raising will refer to America since it has the biggest and wealthiest Jewish community and supplies the bulk of foreign currency that lands in the coffers of the Jewish Agency in Jerusalem. Most of the money is given by private donors in America under the illusion that it's going to help some Israeli emergency, but actually stays in America. In the past fiscal year, 44% was funnelled to Israel, significantly less than most donors know about or would accept if they knew. The Agency is, as one official describes, 'a white elephant with a billion dollar budget'. Most of the cash goes towards immigration while the rest flows in the direction of slum rehabilitation, education, rural settlement and of course, administration and lots of it. Officially only $47 million of foreign largesse pays the clerks and directors who have their fingers in the till. But many other people are hired and many come close to being useless expenditures.

BRING IN THE JEWS
The basic tenet of Zionism is the gathering of Jews in Israel. Without this goal, there really is no particular need for Zionism at all. Without Israel, the UJA would have no focus for its tremendous

fund-raising talents, but without the UJA there would be no need for a Jewish Agency. The Agency was the Jewish government of Palestine before independence. After the state was founded, the government and civil service administration replaced most of the Agency's functions. The Agency should have been disbanded the moment the Israeli flag flew over the new nation but sentimentalists who would have been out of work sought new reasons for the Agency's existence. The role found for it was to collect foreign money and provide parallel services to the government. The justification for the overlapping and redundant functions was to give diaspora Jews a feeling of being part of the building of the new nation without actually working up a sweat or getting shot.

The Israeli Zionists, no matter how hard they try, cannot respect western Jews for refusing to give up their savings, languages, friends and jobs to rush to an overheated sandpit to redeem Jewish soil. They view western Jews as spoiled, frightened and weak, and try to change this state of affairs by luring Jews to Israel. To this end the Jewish Agency sends emissaries, really missionaries (called *shlichim* in Hebrew), out into the Jewish jungle to bring back converts. In 1986 the Agency sent 760 missionaries around the world for periods of two to three years each, including 260 to the United States. Housing, feeding and flying the missionaries cost, on average, $60,000 each. If they actually functioned, the money might be called well spent in the name of Zionism and ingathering, but the missionaries are the usual politically appointed people that run the Agency and Israel.

A missionary job is the plum offered as a favour to political mediocrities, frustrated ex-army officers and the families of party supporters. It means three blessed years away from the Israeli pressure-cooker, a free house and good salary to be spent in cities far more exciting than Haifa, and a chance to earn spare cash as a lecturer or Hebrew teacher in order to load up on goods for the trip back. With such noble motivation, the missionaries have mostly done irreparable damage to Israel's standing among Jews throughout the world. As Charles Hoffman, author of the definitive book on the Agency, *The Smoke Screen*, writes:

> Many *shlichim* could not be effective . . . since they lacked the proper qualifications or personal traits. They often had a poor command of English and knew little about American Jewry. They were sent anyway due to their political connections . . . . The politically appointed *shlichim* had little incentive to master the rules concerning

immigration and explain them to their clients since their performance would not be judged by professional criteria.[2]

The Katz Report, issued in 1987 confirmed what every immigrant knows: the emissaries had little influence on immigration and generated more harm, waste and inefficiency than anything else.[3] Yet world Jewry still pays their bills even when there is no need for missionaries. The author's wife arranged her immigration from the Israeli emissary in Glasgow. With a Jewish population of just 8,000, this emissary, possessor of a two-storey office, might send half a dozen immigrants to Israel a year but inspires none of their decisions. That's over $10,000 an immigrant, all of whom made an independent decision to try life in Israel.

The finest example the typical emissary could offer is to have nothing at all to do with the Jewish community assigned to him. His mentality and personality are usually a total turn-off to diaspora Jews. Far too often he insults the community by insisting diaspora Jewry is doomed to extinction by assimilation and insists that Jewish fulfilment is only conceivable in Israel. All this may be true to an Israeli but is tiresome to foreign ears.

If the emissary keeps to himself, Jews seeking a life in Israel will come to him and be given misinformation. Nowadays, most of the potential immigrants are religious and do wish spiritual fulfilment in their holy land. Others just want to escape from failure or bad memories with a drastic change of scenery. The majority of both categories begin their new lives in Israel in earnest, but homesickness sends a number back while the incredible backwardness of Israeli life is so shocking it claims most of the rest. Every year a meagre 2,000 American Jews of a population of 5.7 million (and dropping fast) immigrate to Israel. That is an average of 10 per $60,000-a-year missionary. Of those who make the move, over 60% return to America, most disgusted by the experience. Had the missionaries truthfully prepared the immigrants for what awaited them in Israel, many would have changed their minds but others would have been more realistic and possibly readier to struggle. But missionaries, the majority of whom are mostly sent away on extended holidays as political favours, seldom have the sophistication to size up their jobs. The cost of these missionaries, however, is a pittance compared with the other political appointments.

POSITION AVAILABLE IN AGENCY FOR FAILED POLITICIAN —
APPLY LABOUR PARTY

A quote from Hoffman: '[The Agency] has, inevitably perhaps, succumbed to the temptations that would afflict any organisation with a guaranteed source of funds and little outside supervision. In everyday language, this process of organisational degeneration is known as corruption.'[4]

A vignette – An ex-general was given a PR position, office and secretary. Over time the secretary, named Yael, and the general succumbed to the daily passions that rise when working in a dingy bureaucracy. The secretary grew dissatisfied at her humble job and made demands on the general for a career advance. Because of her typing and telephone skills he found a position abroad for her as an emissary far from his wife and family.

A fable? If so, repeated and recorded constantly. The Agency is run on favouritism from the top down. According to a recent publication: 'Another long-standing bone of contention is the lack of democracy surrounding Agency appointments . . . the leaders have institutionalised a kind of mutual back-scratching arrangement. This is meant to ensure that the party represented by the chairman maintains a hold on several key positions while the rest are allocated in direct proportion to the strength of Likud and Labour in the Knesset.'[5]

Yes, the Agency is still another 'private' organisation run by the government. That means the heads of those departments with budgets worth tens of millions are appointed by political parties and paid for by world Jewry. Charles Hoffman describes the Agency as 'a dumping ground for third or fourth-rate politicians who did not have the ambition or the skills to carve out a career in the main political arenas . . .'.[6]

Today's Agency chairman, Simcha Dinitz, is a Labourite who was once Israel's ambassador to Washington. During the 1984 elections he was on Labour's campaign committee. According to a fellow committee member, 'He showed no intitiative. He only said what would please the party leaders. It became a joke among us.'[7] With no hope of winning a place on the Knesset list, Labour shunted him to the head of the Agency to represent Israel to donors worldwide. Since his appointment, he is convinced he brought hundreds of thousands of Soviet and Ethiopian Jews to Israel. The fact of the Soviet Union opening its gates and America closing hers is merely coincidental to him.

Dinitz earns a six-figure salary. He does not pay for his endless trips abroad (he is out of the country for four months every year) or his vendettas against rivals within the Agency whom he harasses with funds reportedly 'misused [by] the legal department to settle scores with employees.' According to the same source,[8] politicisation has so increased under Dinitz that the atmosphere at the Agency is 'paranoid'.

But Dinitz is mild compared to his predecessor, the late Arye Dulzin, who reigned from 1978 until 1987 as Likud's man in the Agency. Under Dulzin's bland tutelage the Agency lost credibility with Israelis who came to view it as 'a bloated, highly politicised administration', dedicated to squandering foreign donations. In his last year Dulzin spent hundreds of thousands of dollars on a film purportedly about the history of the Agency but since the hero was Dulzin himself, it was viewed as petty self-aggrandisement. The film won very poor reviews from the critics and was never shown publicly.

Undaunted by the poor critical response to his first venture into the arts, Dulzin spent another small fortune of charitable money to produce the classic biography, *In the Service of the Jewish People*, a 500-page scrapbook of his own speeches as well as press clippings spanning the fateful years 1956 to 1982. Gideon Samet, a senior editor at *Ha'aretz*, stopped short of praising the work: 'In the waning days of his career, Dulzin has performed a symbolic act that expresses, as nothing else could, the true nature of the institution he heads: superfluous, wasteful, bloated and cut off from reality.'[9]

The American donors were not totally blind to the kind of organisation to which they were directing vast sums of cash, and, in 1985, Dulzin was presented with a list of changes demanded by the diaspora leaders. One of the changes was that Agency departments be run by professionals, not political hacks, and that the professionals be appointed by merit, not nepotism. When Dulzin was presented with these reasonable requests, he screeched at those present, 'I refuse to consider it. These proposals mean the end of Zionism.'[10]

Dinitz and Dulzin are men driven to egomania by the trappings of power at the Agency. Today's Agency Treasurer, Meir Sheetreet, on the other hand, is a hopeful politician co-opted by the corruption.

Sheetreet was a brilliant mayor who transformed his improverished town into an enviable suburb. He entered the Knesset as a reformer, channelling his energy against government abuses. This Sephardi from the Likud was making too much noise but had no hope of rising through the moribund party hierarchy. So he was given the munificent post of Agency Treasurer to calm the protests. And how it worked!

In 1990 an American contractor from Miami named Joseph Adler offered his prefab-housing technology to solve the shelter needs of Soviet immigrants. He demonstrated this process at a kibbutz near Jerusalem, putting up large two-storey houses in 48 hours each at a cost of $30,000 per home. In the same year, Scuds fell on Israel and American wallets opened. By February of 1991, it was announced that the UJA alone had raised $1.2 billion to settle Soviet Jews. Using Adler's method all Soviet immigrants that year could be housed with money raised by American Jews. But Adler doesn't know Israel. The last thing Israeli contractors want is a cheaper building technology and the last thing the banks want is cheaper mortgages, or no mortgages at all, using foreign donations as capital instead of bank assets.

So in February 1991, Sheetreet announced that Soviet Jews would not be receiving housing grants but rather loans to be taken out at Israeli banks and guaranteed by UJA and Jewish Agency assets. As for cheaper housing technology, it would not be available. The loans could be used to purchase a home at 200% of its true value built by Israeli contractors with government connections.

If American donors knew the money they gave to house Soviets was going to enrich well connected contractors and the banks, they might well withhold their donations to Israel. Sheetreet defended the policy so transparently, he became a minor laughing stock in Israel.

The Soviets were being denied grants, he explained, for their own good. If they were to get easy money they would be resented by other Israelis who cannot afford housing. Simply put, by denying the immigrants money intended for their use by the donors, Israel would be more harmonious. Whatever integrity Sheetreet may once have possessed, he was bought and sold by 1991. But the diaspora Jews had been equally bought. They accepted Sheetreet's reasoning and approved the loan scheme on behalf of all the donors who, mostly, had no idea what was being done with their money.

GIVE 'EM TO THE BIRDS AND BEES — I WANT MONEY

The Agency's bank ties do not end with immigrant loans. Through a sub-division called The Colonial Trust, the Agency actually owns majority shares in Bank Leumi. Thus donation money used to service the Agency's $650 million debt, in part, went straight into the Agency's own bank. A very handy way for some sly bureaucrats to make the Yanks pay twice.

The diaspora leaders found this state of affairs appalling and used their influence to reduce the debt to $450 million by 1988. However, in the first six months of 1991, an additional $50 million was added to the debt[11] and $50 million more was expected that year.

When a goodhearted Jew in Cleveland donates money to the UJA, he undoubtedly feels that most of it will help suffering Jews in Israel. Of the 44% that finally arrives in Israel, some 15% goes towards paying the interest on debt. That leaves just 25 cents in the dollar going to what the donors intended, including the cost of salaries for overpriced political appointees. But waste and misallocations cut further into even this paltry figure. Yet the story is just beginning.

The Agency owns companies worth hundreds of millions of dollars in fields as diverse as canning, wine-making, real estate and transportation. While some companies were legitimate investments, many others were bought as favours to the government or some other public body that needed money. Naturally most of these investments paid for by foreign charity became losses and a drain on Agency resources. The main reason the companies were kept, 'seems to have been that they provided Dulzin with an opportunity to pass out directorships on their boards to his political cronies'.[12]

CURLY, LARRY AND MOSHAV

If foreign, mostly American, funds are buying companies as political favours, they are also buying farms that don't grow much of anything but debts. Back in the 1950s, the Agency decided to settle some new immigrants, mostly from Sephardic lands, in semi-co-operative villages (on similar lines to kibbutzim) called 'moshavim'. Some of the villages were established purely for security considerations on barely arable soil and populated by people who had never even grown a geranium in their lives. By the late 1970s, many moshavim couldn't make a living from the soil but since they were receiving massive aid from the Agency, were able to transfer that money into collateral for loans at commercial banks. 'The money went for new investments on the farm as well as for fancy houses, big cars and trips abroad. Some settlers even stopped farming the land themselves and leased it illegally to Arabs, while continuing to enjoy Jewish Agency support.'[13]

The 1985 budget put an end to the easy living, and by the end of 1986 the moshavim had amassed a debt of over a billion dollars. About 150 of Israel's villages were bankrupt and unless action was taken, the countryside would be depopulated.

It was discovered quickly that two thirds of the bankrupt moshavim were under the care of the Agency while the majority of independent moshavim were solvent. Forty years of bilking foreign donors with glowing reports of rural settlement successes were about to come crashing down. This the Agency could not let happen. The rural settlement budget was $75 million annually and employed 435 workers. So a decision was made to bail out all the moshavim in distress with the exception of some 10% which were beyond recovery. All together the Agency and its mostly American money paid $75 million in 1986 to bail out the moshavim. Needless to say the Agency and its banking connections left the rest of the population to wallow in its debts. Foreign money intended to relieve poverty in Israel had primarily been spent maintaining the huge homes purchased by the hopelessly run farms of the Agency.

Humble homes were also refurbished with foreign money through a huge Agency programme called Project Renewal. Begun in 1977 this programme evolved into a twinning plan. Western Jewish communities adopted poor Israeli districts and funnelled cash towards recreation and cultural facilities but mostly towards rebuilding the crumbling government housing.

What the donors apparently didn't realise was that the Agency had in previous years bought government housing stock and owned 30,000 apartments in impoverished neighbourhoods. Despite its massive budget, the Agency never found enough cash to maintain these apartments and they deteriorated. After 1977, hundreds of millions of foreign dollars were spent to refurbish buildings that had degenerated into large shanty-towns by Agency neglect in the first place. As with the moshavim, diaspora Jews paid a fortune to rescue ill-judged investments by the Agency. And yet, because of a sinister cover-up, western Jews never made the connection.

SCHOOL DAZE

The Agency is responsible for funding educational institutes in a partnership with the government. The abuses here are rife but one, which Charles Hoffman calls 'the shell game', is a classic case, and it worked like this.

American Jews were not prepared to donate directly towards maintaining the costs of the Lebanon War, in contrast to its generous reaction to the Six Day and Yom Kippur Wars. The UJA was asked instead to raise $200 million for higher education since the cost of the war was threatening government allocations to that sector. What the donors were not told was that the Finance Minister, Yoram Aridor, father of modern Israeli hyper-inflation and today Israel's ambassador to the United Nations, had severely cut the allocation the year before. The Americans raised enough money to exceed the official allocation by tens of millions of dollars. The excess cash went into the government's back pocket for other expenses. In other words, Americans who refused to finance the Lebanon War with their donations, were tricked into doing just that.

But they were cheated only mildly compared to the institutes of higher education which suffered a huge cut in their funding while being used as pawns in the ruse. As Hoffman writes: 'Aridor's policy . . . gradually plunged the universities into a fiscal crisis in which they accumulated over $120 million in debts by 1987 . . . . These massive cuts and the decline in teaching and research forced the universities to lower their standards and impaired their hard-won standing in the international scientific community.'14

Most American donors belong to the Conservative and Reform branches of Judaism. Orthodox donors are a small element in UJA fund-raising. Indeed, since a good chunk of the Orthodox are anti-Zionist and don't accept Israel's existence, it would be absurd for them to contribute to a Zionist fund-raising campaign. Yet once the foreign money reaches the Agency, a lot of it is funnelled to Orthodox schools and institutions because, 'over the years, the eagerness of Likud and Labour to please the ultra-Orthodox parties has created a situation where the Agency has become a prime backstairs channel for funding anti-Zionist yeshivas [seminaries]'.15 In fact, far more money from abroad flows to Orthodox schools than Conservative or Reform institutions.

By the mid-1980s the Agency channelled about $7 million a year to about 150 Orthodox institutions. Another 280 yeshivas received funding totalling $3.2 million via other UJA channels. And such Orthodox political parties as Shas and Agudat Yisrael have received direct funding from a slush pile called 'the Constructive Funds', which is an Agency device for giving political parties diaspora money for whatever uses they desire. Every year the Agency sets aside some $2.7 million just to pay off parties for being loyal or in the future hope of loyalty.

Since most Americans are Reform or Conservative, does their money advance their own causes in Israel? Of course not. In immigration centres run by the Agency throughout the country, only Orthodox teaching or services are to be found. Rabbi Charles

Weinberg of the Agency explained the lack of pluralism: 'It would be absurd to confuse [the immigrants] with the Reform and Conservative movements.'[16] As long as the Israeli political scene is held in balance by the Orthodox parties and as long as Israelis hold positions of responsibility in the Agency, Conservative and Reform interest will be shunted aside. Western Jews, mostly non-Orthodox, are paying for the discrimination against their own branches of Judaism in Israel. While Orthodox institutions are regularly granted monies by the Agency, 'Reform and Conservative requests were subjected to a run-around,'[17] hopping from one office to the next until the requesters gave up the fight.

The facts are there. Millions of dollars of diaspora funding intended for universities is diverted to politics. The university infrastructure has collapsed thanks to the inadvertent help of western Jews whose charity was abused by Israeli politicians. Orthodox institutions which teach a hatred of the kind of Judaism most Americans profess receive the lion's share of educational allocations while the branches of Judaism preferred by the donors are victimised by blatant discrimination. So why on earth are western Jews giving even a penny to the charities of the Jewish Agency?

The answer is they don't know any better because the vested interests of world fund-raising, by protecting their own rear ends, have covered up the truth.

WHO NEEDS INFORMATION? JUST HAND OVER YOUR MONEY

The UJA has an armlock on information about Israel reaching the local Jewish communities of America. Those Jewish newspapers not owned outright by the UJA are not about to ask embarrassing questions that will spell the end of UJA advertising or financial support.

With the newspapers firmly in their pockets, the UJA plant stories favourable to their interests or take out advertisements thinly disguised as articles for the same purpose. The UJA pays writers well and it seems virtually every English-language writer in Israel has worked for them at one time or another. But few can stand the deceit and most quit after a short while. One writer gave her reason for giving up the lucrative work: 'I interviewed a poor kid who benefited from an Agency educational programme. I asked him what he wanted to be when he grew up and he said a bus driver. They changed the text to read that he wanted to be a doctor. A doctor is not a bus driver and the change bothered me enough to complain.

I was told it's not so important to write what the kid said but what he should have said. That was it for me.'

When outside reporters dare to report honestly the Agency fights back with all its resources. The author was a victim of Agency spite after reporting on $2.5 million donated by the Jews of a minor Canadian community in Winnipeg to the town of Gan Yavne. Having reported on a dozen similar town projects, the conclusion reached was that something was very wrong here. No town was less deserving of foreign aid. Gan Yavne is a cross between New Rochelle and Golders Green, a suburb of large gardens and private houses.

Also confusing was the appearance of Shimon Peres at the opening ceremony of a luxurious community centre paid for by Canadian donors. This was in March 1990 when Peres was in the midst of failing to form a government after breaking up the coalition. A little investigation proved that the town's mayor and Peres were old friends and this would go some way to explaining how this suburb was approved for rehabilitation funding.

The suspicions of a political favour were deleted from the final article which appeared in the *Jerusalem Post*. But what remained was enough to send the Canadian fund-raisers on a smear campaign against the writer to the point of warning him never to appear in Winnipeg, as if they controlled the city.

Idelle Ross, who was reporting on a Montreal project in a Jerusalem slum for Israel Television's English news had a similar reaction. She and former Jerusalem city councillor Jeff Halperin investigated the project and discovered the project supervisor was receiving a salary of $120,000 annually and that rent alone was eating up $24,000 a year of donor money. Ross took a camera crew to the opening of a sports facility, barely a piece of tarmac, built by the Canadian fund-raisers. The first 15 seconds of her report was a glowing official appraisal while the next 45 seconds was a more critical view taken by local residents who wanted to know where the rest of the money was hiding. When the report was broadcast only the first 15 seconds were seen by viewers. After the official praise ended so did the report due to 'a technical glitch'. Ross lost her job a week later.

Meanwhile western Jews come to Israel on fund-raising 'missions' which are slick and deceptive. The potential donors visit poor neighbourhoods and are greeted by children handing out flowers in gratitude. The mayor will give a speech praising the fund-raisers for saving his town from certain collapse. Then it's on to the bus for lunch where a minor Israeli politician will give a further speech of

praise. After that it's off to a military base for a tour and a speech
on national security by a middle-ranking officer which will leave the
donors convinced they have been privy to a sensitive and exclusive
overview of Israel's security situation. After five days of soldiers, old
people, Ethiopians, greenery in the desert and uplifted Sephardim,
the mission is convinced its money will be well spent.

But the fund-raisers and many of the speakers know better. As
one speaker explained, 'I never mention the Jewish Agency – not
its functions, its departments, nothing.' As for the fund-raisers, they
know better than anyone else what is wrong with the Agency and
they complain amongst themselves. But if an outsider expresses
similar complaints, 'they would spring to its defence – even if this
meant misrepresenting the facts'.

As for the donors themselves – according to one, 'They have
suspended their critical faculties. They can't afford to ask questions.
If they decide that a lot of money has been wasted, what must they
think of themselves? They have convinced others to give. What
about all the time and money they have put in over the years?
They can't face the prospect that much of it is wasted.' They are
the guiltiest party. Because they have a vested interest in keeping
fund-raising a big business, they have deliberately and maliciously
allowed countless naïve Jews to throw away their hard-earned
money.

As Harry Taubenfeld, an American Zionist leader notes, 'They
don't care about Israel or Zionism, only about the 60% that they
take off the top for their own purposes.'

And this is the key; the actual well-paid employees of the
fund-raising organisations connected to the Agency, 'are living
off the back of Israel'.[18] Using Israel's emergencies, be they war,
inflation or Soviet immigration, the UJA and similar organisations
raise money, lots and lots of money. Over $1.2 billion by the UJA
alone in 1990/91. This is not the kind of industry where one can
easily tamper with displays of sincerity. If the Agency is rotten to
the core, then it is no one's business but their own, for to reveal how
misspent funds are in Israel will endanger fund-raising in America.
And since almost 60% of funds stay in America and flow through
the coffers of the fund-raisers, there is too much to lose by open
discussion and truthful revelation.

And the big givers have their own rewards. They fly to Israel
and meet with cabinet ministers, sometimes even the Prime
Minister, and return to America to be debriefed by congressmen
or the media. They become Middle East experts, as if owning

a chain of supermarkets qualifies someone for the diplomatic
corps. Back home, they are the leaders of their Jewish communities and though unelected, they have bought status. They are
in no hurry to sacrifice their positions in the name of reform
though they know well that the money they have given ends
up in good part at an Agency that is 'corrupt and anach-
ronistic'.

All this façade for what? All the funds raised by the Agency
add up to no more than 2% of the Israeli budget. The money
is barely needed and it pays for, according to the courageous
lonely voice of Charles Hoffman, 'inefficiency, waste, duplication, mismanagement, political patronage and corruption, fiscal
irresponsibility, incompetence, distorted priorities', and the list
hasn't ended.

There are other voices in the wilderness. Joel Bainerman, who
lectures twice a year in America, says: 'I tell them the biggest
favour they can do for Israel would be (to) stop giving money.
They're propping up corruption and making the lives of most
Israelis far worse.'

Dr Eliezer Jaffe, a professor of social work at Hebrew University, published an article in *Moment* criticising the Agency as
'highly politicised', and donors as 'fatalistic and passive'. He urged
Americans to boycott donations through the Agency in favour of
'new mechanisms for spending their money in Israel'.

Unfortunately other mechanisms are just as victimised by the
Israeli government. Hadassah, America's biggest Jewish organisation (over 350,000 members) annually donates hundreds of millions
of dollars to its medical facilities in Israel. Unfortunately they do
not exchange donations for reform of the health system, nor do
they set up private hospitals to bypass the government system. The
result is well equipped hospitals whose staff are on constant strike
and whose equipment stands idle two-thirds of the time to satisfy
scandalous government requirements. And since the hospitals get
paid by occupied beds, Israelis must sit in hospital for days on
end for simple operations like hernias to squeeze cash from the
government, while serious operations are put on long waiting lists
because they are uneconomical.

A parallel story occurs in education. The Friends Abroad of
various universities and colleges in Israel raise over $40 million
annually for higher education but this only perpetuates the decline
of learning in Israel once the government plays its shell game with
the Education budget.

If foreign Jews invested in honest industry, Israel would be better off but businessmen are frightened off by red tape, bureaucracy and incompetence. The primary channel for diaspora money to Israel is charity and all the evidence indicates that almost every donation to Israel means participation in corruption.

CHAPTER TWELVE

Save Ethiopian Jews: Win Valuable Prizes

The most serious function of the Agency is to bring endangered Jews to Israel and the most expensive task thereafter, is to house them. The treasurer of the Agency, Meir Sheetreet, is also housed by Agency funds but rather better than any immigrant. (*Yediot Achronot* ran a rather blistering criticism of this formerly modest-living MK who purchased an ostentatious abode with foreign charity intended in no small part for housing immigrants.)

ADDIS ABABA BLUES

In June of 1991, some 15,000 Ethiopian Jews were airlifted to Israel from the clutches of Mengiste's dying régime. The Agency portrayed this as a triumph of co-ordination and proof that American Jews get action for their bucks. Of course, the airlift was dramatic but totally unnecessary – a case of simple incompetence. Back in 1985, virtually the same rescue was taking place under the code name, Operation Moses. While in full swing, the chairman of the Agency, according to press reports of the time, leaked the operation to the media, reportedly with government compliance, in order to raise more money from abroad. The Ethiopian régime which was selling Jews for arms was understandably piqued by the worldwide revelations emanating from the Agency, as was the Arab government of Sudan, which permitted airlifting the refugees from its soil for reasons not yet fully understood but probably involving bribes of one kind or another. Both governments quickly cancelled co-operation in the rescue and only 7,500 Jews made it to Israel.

The others were told to camp nearby the Israeli Embassy in Addis Ababa to await the resumption of the airlift. The Jews agreed and sold their possessions for a pittance in order to rent shacks by the embassy. These shacks became both a slum and graveyard as the promised airlift didn't materialise for six years.

MEANWHILE BACK IN ISRAEL

Those Ethiopians who did make it to Israel in 1985 suffered untold indignities reminiscent of those suffered by North African Jews a generation before:

> The North Africans were lured to Israel by promises of social, political and economic equality and to an end to the oppression they faced from the Moslem majorities who scorned Jews as outsiders. To their dismay, however, the Sephardim soon encountered a remarkably similar pattern of discrimination in Israel . . . . The European Jews created a society that was essentially European in nature and arrogantly stamped out attempts by the Sephardim bewildered by their alien new world, to inject aspects of their own national backgrounds into the developing Israeli culture.[1]

The failure of the North African immigration is now blossoming into disaster in Israel. By 1991, according to the Ministry of Health, there were 40,000 heroin addicts in Israel, almost all Sephardim. Even more disturbing was a report in June 1991 by the same ministry, which stated that 80,000 families in Israel were malnourished, meaning some 240,000 Israeli children, mostly Sephardi, were not receiving the very minimal standards of nutrition, this a generation after their parents arrived in Israel seeking a better life.

With the appalling precedent of the North African immigration well understood, how did the Israeli authorities choose to handle the new East African immigration? About the same damn way as before. In the words of our expert on the Agency, Charles Hoffman, 'the adjustment problems of new immigrants were due not only to the inherent difficulties of learning to live in a new country. They were also the result of the confusing labyrinth of Agency and government officials they were forced to negotiate.'

According to Hoffman, the Agency set up centres to absorb the new Ethiopians but the Immigration Department

> . . . failed to provide proper training for the staff . . . . Center directors were appointed in some cases without proper qualifications . . . . In the absence of proper training, instinct took over, which often brought out the ethnocentric and paternalistic attitudes that had been inflicted on many Middle Eastern immigrants of the 1950s . . . . Teaching them the 'right way' meant insisting they do it the 'Israeli way' which actually meant whatever practices the homemaker herself might follow. Interaction between the immigrants and absorption center staff who had little knowledge of

Ethiopian culture would produce misunderstandings that gradually grew into mutual hostility and mistrust.[2]

A study by two anthropologists, Dr Alex Weingrod and Dr Michael Ashkenazi of Ben Gurion University in 1984 concluded that the absorption centres' 'totalistic environment' created a class of people dependent on functionaries who were unable to cope individually once they left the centres. They made recommendations to restructure the centres which the Agency rejected out of hand.

The absorption centres were exploited by the government which was reluctant to spend any of its tight budget on immigrant housing. Knowing that the Agency would not evict Ethiopians with nowhere to go, the government was in no rush to build new housing. It was far more economical to keep the immigrants in overcrowded temporary quarters than construct new accommodation. Soon after, the Agency surrendered and allowed Ethiopians to stay in the centres, often created out of vacant public housing blocks owned by the Agency. As the centres became the permanent homes to the Ethiopians, Israeli cities began to acquire black ghettos.

The Agency added to the slum atmosphere in an act of defiance against the government. Refusing to be held responsible for government machinations at the Ethiopians' expense, the Agency turned over 15 absorption centres to the government's Housing Ministry free of charge but before doing so they ripped out such public services as playgrounds and pay phones. The government really didn't want to be in charge of these new acquisitions nor to hire staff to take care of them. So the buildings began to fall apart and instant slums were created. Journalist Ran Kislev notes that in recent months no more than 15 Ethiopian families moved out of the absorption centres in the whole country.[3] Other Ethiopians, desiring to be near their kin have been occupying nearby buildings resulting in 'the creation of black ghettos . . .'. This process is be found throughout Israel in such locales as Afula, Ashkelon, Beersheva and Upper Nazareth. The litany of social problems is familiar to anyone living near a black ghetto; 50% of Ethiopians in Ashkelon are on welfare; the divorce rate of Ethiopians is two to three times higher than for other Israelis, and a third of families is headed by a single mother. Of those women living in nuclear families, there is a large percentage who are battered.

The Ethiopian family structure is falling to shreds in Israel. Back in Africa, the Ethiopians turned to their religious leadership and councils of elders to solve social problems. The Israeli

authorities broke up these vital organisations, scattering them to
the four corners of the country, replacing them with government
social services, minor functionaries with BAs in Social Work and
report-writing anthropologists.

Not a few of the social problems can be traced back to 'Blabbermouth' Dulzin and his 1985 news leak that put a lid on the
first large-scale rescue operation. Ethiopians who loaded family
members on one plane, expecting to join them after boarding
an upcoming flight found themselves stranded and separated.
According to journalist Leah Abromovitz: 'Couples who have
been separated by cultures . . . often find themselves on different
'wavelengths'. Some may have made other commitments, thinking
their original spouse dead. Children who have studied in Israeli
institutions are loathe to accept the authority of a parent with whom
they have had little contact during the most significant years of their
development.'[4]

Hasia Levin, Director of the Association for the Advancement of
Ethiopian Family and Child, mentions another source of friction
that exists throughout the Ethiopian community in Israel. In
Ethiopia the Jews were a community divided in two, roughly by
urban and rural backgrounds. The authorities, lumping all blacks
together, don't take into account this long-standing rivalry with the
result all too commonly being knife-fights.

As Ran Kislev writes: 'After the extended family framework was
destroyed by immigration and the dispersal of the immigrants to
different towns, now the nuclear family is being destroyed in the
blink of an eye. Processes that took ten or twenty years for the
immigrants from North Africa and Asia in the '50s and '60s are
now taking place within a few years.'[5]

Getting the fathers respectable jobs (as if all honest work
isn't respectable) was a priority of the authorities, believing that
self-esteem goes hand in hand with labour. Perhaps it does but
in an attempt to prevent Ethiopians from taking only menial
employment, called not coincidentally in Hebrew, black work,
the authorities created a programme of Hebrew-language classes,
followed by vocational training. It doesn't take an academic study
to realise that adults from all nations have trouble grasping a new
language fast enough and well enough to go on to technical courses.
In Ashkelon very few of the targeted immigrants even finished
their year's Hebrew classes and almost none went on to vocational
training. The vast majority quit school to work at 'black' jobs or
sign up for the dole.

Those who actually completed vocational training did not necessarily find welcoming arms in the job market. In April 1990, 35
graduates of the Hadassah Neurim School applied for placements
through the government's Absorption Ministry. A list of eight towns
committed themselves to employing and housing the graduates.
Shortly after and for reasons one can probably surmise, five of the
towns cancelled their commitments and then all of them did so. As
for the graduates, 'Time is passing and the bitterness is building
up. They feel that all they have achieved in three years of study is
vanishing into thin air.'[6]

And these are not the only victims of a wasted education –
85–95% of Ethiopian teenagers are sent by the Agency to one
of their religious boarding-schools. There, separated from their
families and living with all the doubtful amenities of any institution,
they learn little of later practical value. Most of the boys go on to the
army, which may be the finest school of absorption in the country.
But the girls of a religious school are taught to shirk military service
and once released into society, often have nowhere to turn. Sadly
and unbelievably, there are now religious Ethiopian prostitutes in
Netanya, up the coast from Tel Aviv.

But life isn't perfect for the boys once their army service is done.
Single people of any colour in Israel can receive a mortgage of only
$27,000, not enough to buy a share in a bathroom in a bad part
of town. (Couples receive about 50% more and the figure rises
with each child.) This discrimination against the unmarried means
that single Ethiopians, without the family financial support that
most Israelis depend on, are effectively homeless. The problem is
recognised and could be solved with a simple change in the banking
laws. But banks in Israel, which sometimes appear to exist for the
sadistic joy of watching the public squirm, have no interest in
ameliorating social illnesses. Thus other solutions were employed.

One-room apartments in specially built 'hostels' were constructed
for the temporary housing of immigrants. Typically, temporary
housing turned into permanent slum living. An even worse solution
was the renting of down-and-out hotels to house immigrants. The
hoteliers, paid by the immigrants, crowded their establishments to
inhumane levels. In one pathetic case, hotel-owners in Tiberias
banded together and threatened to stop feeding the Ethiopian
guests unless they received more money from the authorities.

In another case, whole families were placed by the Agency in
dilapidated caravans and mobile-homes no larger than 40 square
metres. Many were humiliatingly evicted in June 1991, when,

without warning, Agency officials arrived at the Kadouri Caravan Park in Kfar Tavor and ordered 150 Ethiopians to pack their gear and be ready to move within two hours to absorption centres. According to Kfar Tavor resident Dina Hother, 'When I arrived at the scene, most of those who had been told to move were already aboard the buses. Many were in tears. They looked shaken and their heads were bowed.'[7] Hother went looking for her Ethiopian friend who, it turned out, had run off with her children and hid in a field to prevent being turned out of her home, such as it was. Those Ethiopians who stayed behind and refused to leave their homes were forcibly evicted with or without their meagre possessions.

It had been a bad two days for the immigrants. They had complained before about the low-quality food being forced on them and requested their own cooking facilities. This reasonable request was denied and the day before the forced evictions, a number of immigrants were taken to hospital with stomach ailments. Some had just returned from hospital only to find trucks and buses waiting to transfer them out of their homes.

And if the arrogance of the Jewish Agency has succeeded in stripping a people of its pride, by comparison with the religious establishment, the Agency has been a scion of human dignity.

GOT GOD IF YOU WANT IT

In 1980 Adissu Messele, a new immigrant from Ethiopia was taken to an office. There a bearded examiner extracted a few drops of blood from his penis and immersed him in a ritual bath. Adissu thought the pin in his penis was an innoculation and the bath a friendly religious gesture. Several months later he received a certificate of conversion. He was not considered a Jew in Israel until he had been tricked into a ritual circumcision and purification rite. He ripped the insulting certificate to shreds and wept openly. And Adissu's story is far from unique – it is a typical tale of Ethiopian Jews who arrived in Israel before the big wave of 1985. The Chief Rabbinate of Israel (which is akin in many respects to the Vatican and its relationship to Roman Catholics) did not accept the Ethiopians as true blue Jews, even though the Ethiopian Jewish community may be the truest Jews of all. They arrived in Ethiopia 2,500 years ago and shortly after, found themselves cut off from the rest of world Jewry. Their traditions reflect the original Judaism of animal sacrifices and orally transmitted law.

While the Ethiopians added some local traditions to their religion, the rest of world Jewry evolved very differently. As a result of their dispersal from Israel by the Romans, the law became sanctified in a written *Torah* followed by two books of codified holy regulations, the *Talmud* and *Gemarah*. These governed the day-to-day affairs of a people without a land and did much to prevent wholesale assimilation into foreign cultures. Without the two books, the Ethiopians were not governed by the same complicated rules of the rest of Jewry. To the rabbis who ruled Israel's seat of religious government, this meant the Ethiopians weren't totally kosher. And because the religious political parties of the mostly secular Knesset traditionally controlled the Absorption and Interior Ministries, the Ethiopians could and were denied citizen identity cards unless they underwent ritual conversion.

Unfortunately, the anti-semites of Ethiopia did not concur with the doubts expressed by the Israeli rabbinate and began murdering and vandalising the property of Jews because they were Jews. After the fall of Haile Selassie in the mid-1970s there was a vicious anti-semitic uprising in Ethiopia, in which many Jews died. Israel could not stand by and let a Jewish community be butchered. In 1977 Menachem Begin became the first Prime Minister determined to bring the Ethiopian Jews to Israel. A similar request was made to Golda Meir when she was Prime Minister by a group of American Jews. In her famous reply she asked why they were so concerned about a bunch of *shvartzim* (Hebrew slang for spades). And this from the woman who opened Africa up for Israel with extensive economic, military and technological ties.

The first trickle of Ethiopians were fooled into conversion but by the time of the big rescue in 1985, word was out about rabbinate chicanery. The Ethiopian Jews, who had no doubts about their validity, fought back. In August 1985 they staged a month-long rally outside the Chief Rabbinate in Jerusalem protesting the conversions. They won the overwhelming support of Israelis. For once, the rabbinate caved in to public pressure and made a deal with the Ethiopians promising recognition of their Jewishness and all the rights thereof. The rabbinate also agreed to recognise Ethiopian religious leaders as valid purveyors of the faith. It seemed like the Ethiopians had won. Such naïveté.

The rabbinate thereafter forgot about the agreement and issued the following instruction to official marriage registrars: 'All those who come to register for marriage must undertake to perform the commandments and undergo circumcision and immersion before three rabbis; a woman will be required to accept the commandments and perform immersion. If it be proven that the applicant has been properly circumcised, he will be required only to accept the commandments and undergo immersion.'

So, in order to get married, all Ethiopian men had to unzip their pants and pull out their dicks for three rabbis to examine. And who would perform the marriage? No Ethiopian rabbi, for the rabbinate reneged on its agreement to accept Ethiopian spiritual leaders and offered only to retrain them in auxiliary functions. A bizarre compromise was reached. One ancient rabbi, David Chelouche of Netanya, found it within his conscience to marry unconverted Ethiopian couples and the rabbinate appointed him and rabbis of his court to perform all the marriages in the country. The Ethiopians were shunned by the religious establishment of their new country and to this day, there is not even one Ethiopian synagogue in Israel. The closest approximation is a small apartment in Beersheva. On a recent festival, two dozen worshippers crammed into the apartment, while 500 others prayed in the parking lot below.

The fight to end the forced conversions had a further deteriorating effect on the Ethiopian community. The mostly secular leaders of the protest, suddenly thrust into the limelight, were accepted as the spokesmen of the Ethiopian community by the powers that be, replacing the traditional religious leadership that had stayed intact for centuries in Ethiopia.[8] The former spiritual guides were dispersed throughout the length and breadth of the land, thus isolated from their former flocks. To further erode their authority, the rabbinate collected quislings from their ranks who accepted the coerced conversions and tried to get their followers to fall in line. These guides were viewed with great disdain by the majority of Ethiopians including religious leaders, who prized their own traditions more highly. For 2,500 years the Jews of Ethiopia remained Jews against impossible odds because of the spiritual strength of their leadership. In a decade the Israeli rabbinate shattered the religious core of Ethiopian Jewry, with the collusion of the Jewish Agency.

In 1985, the Agency hired a researcher to determine which group really represented the Ethiopian community in Israel. One organisation was crowned king. 'Thereafter,' writes Ran Kislev, 'and with no further inquiries, UJA funds were allocated to this organisation to the tune of $100,000 a year. Worse still, no one ever checked what happened to the $400,000 it received over four years.'[9]

The Education Ministry is the personal property of the National Religious Party. It decreed that throughout the 1980s all Ethiopian children be educated at religious schools. There was no choice; if an immigrant was Ethiopian and of school-age, he would be shipped to a depressing religious school run by the Jewish Agency. In contrast, Soviet or any other immigrant parents could choose the type of school most suitable for their children. As Shlomo Alkale, chairman of the Ethiopian immigrant organisation, Beta Yisrael, said, 'Maybe they think we just don't know enough or are too primitive to be consulted.'[10]

After the second great rescue of 1991, this paternalism was exposed and became such an embarrassment to the Agency that it changed to a free-choice policy. By the summer of 1991, almost all students of Agency religious schools were black while every student of its secular schools was white. The Agency can hardly be admired for its efforts in the field of integration.

Why the religious establishment wants the Ethiopians is easy to understand in light of its experience with Sephardim. After cutting them off from their leaders, they moulded their students in the image of the eastern European ghetto. Today these ear-locked, black-hatted Sephardim are the political powers and constituencies of three Knesset parties. The Ethiopians are just as malleable as the Sephardim were and, with the disintegration of their former religious traditions, they are putty in the hands of Israel's rabbinic establishment. The graduates of religious schools may well be the next generation of Ethiopians, black-hatted, black-frocked and black-skinned. At best, this new Ethiopian Jew will adjust to his new identity; at worst, he'll be a traffic hazard at night.

Despite studying in state religious schools, the brightest students will never carry on to one of the prestigious yeshivas of the country because the religious establishment is bigoted and does not advance the dark complexioned. They just don't want them turning secular.

After the big rescue of June 1991, the Minister of Absorption, Rabbi Yitzhak Peretz discovered that 700 of the new immigrants were being housed in godless kibbutzim. He let loose a barrage of invective, claiming that a kibbutz education led many Sephardic Jews into lives of drugs, prostitution and crime.

Blaming communal farms for Moroccan prostitutes in Tel Aviv in front of the jeering Knesset and then in an embarrassing TV debate, should have signalled the end of Peretz's career as Absorption Minister. The Citizens' Rights Movement actually called for Shamir to throw Peretz down the steps of the Absorption Ministry building. And that was an official statement. One newspaper editorial noted that 'Peretz seems far more concerned with the immigrants' Jewish pedigree and their religious environment than with the staggering difficulties they face upon arrival.'[11]

Ethiopian Jews graduated from political victims in Africa to political footballs in Israel. They are caught in the middle of the religious/secular war and are paying the price. Instead of just allowing this proud and gracious people the simple courtesy of preserving their heritage intact, Israel is determined to destroy their identity and create a new type of Jew: an African who would have almost have fitted into the life of the Russian *shtetl* (village).

CHAPTER THIRTEEN

Save Soviet Jews: Shower with a Friend

1990 was a watershed for the Zionist enterprise. Israel became such a desirable place that over 200,000 Soviet Jews immigrated to the country. Of course, it helped that the Soviet Union was such an undesirable monster that masses of its people chose to leave. Predictions based on the number of applicants for immigration to Israel strongly suggested that in 1991 between 400–500,000 Soviet Jews would make a permanent move to Israel. However, by the summer of 1991 only 87,000 had arrived and no more than 170,000 were expected for the whole year, a drop of over half the expected arrivals. What went wrong? Simple. The Jews who arrived the year before sent letters back to Mother Russia warning others to stay away from Israel. Life was better under dissolving communism than under hopeless Zionism.

The combination of Gorbachev, perestroika and the demise of Eastern European Marxism led to the opening of the Iron Curtain, mostly for Jews, the only nation of Soviet people without a republic. Israel wanted these Jews but the Jews mostly wanted an American home. In the early 1970s Jewish activism led to American pressure to allow Soviet Jews to rejoin their co-religionists in Israel and 150,000 did arrive. These were the hard-core Zionists, it appears, for by the end of the decade over 80% of Jews who left the Soviet Union under the pretext of moving to Israel, actually had no intention of doing so. They would eventually settle, mostly in America, but would compromise on practically any other country just so long as it wasn't Israel.

Israel felt cheated. These Soviets left their country on Israeli visas and reaped the fruits of over a decade of Jewish efforts and money. By 'dropping out' in transit sites such as Vienna or, especially, Rome, in the hope of being granted a visa to America, the drop-outs created an instant refugee camp in Italy and mocked both the Soviet Union and Israel with their blatant deceit. By the early 1980s, the Soviet authorities had had enough of supplying

America with immigrants and severely curtailed the human outflow. The drop-outs endangered the rescue of those genuinely fighting for the right to live in Israel.

It's not as if America really wanted these Jews. A quota on such immigrants was raised because of ideological anti-communism, the same philosophy that caused Jimmy Carter to accept thousands of Cuban jailbirds alongside those genuinely seeking freedom, and because some American Jews saw accepting these refugees as a humanitarian act. By the end of the decade, Israeli pressure on America to restrict Soviet Jewish immigration had its effect and most of the drop-outs were denied immediate refugee status in the US. Given a choice between staying in their transit camps or moving to Israel, most chose the good life in disused Italian warehouses or train stations. After a decade, American Jews were less than enamoured with the long-suffering Jews from the East who entered their territory. While Israel got the devoted idealists, America was getting more than its share of unscrupulous opportunists. As Soviet Jews longing to be free overcharged millions of clients in their taxis, while the FBI created a special division just to keep tabs on the 'Russian Mafia', American Jews began to wonder if the Soviets were such a worthy addition to their community.

By 1989, when the trickle of immigrants turned into a tidal wave, the gates of America were closed to all but the very privileged, and direct flights from Moscow to Tel Aviv assured that most of the Jews would arrive in Israel whether they liked it or not. But not all of them did. Over 10,000 sneaked into Germany on the pretext that they were in transit to Israel, and tried to stay, believing that with Germany's guilt, it would never throw out Jews. It was a valid try but the Germans wanted no truck with these refugees, mainly because they might set a precedent that would result in millions of other Eastern European refugees arriving in the Fatherland.

By 1990, if a Jew or a pretender left the Soviet Union, he knew it would be for Israel. But so many were desperate to escape the drudgery of Soviet life that even Israel became desirable. It was a dream come true for Israel. After 20 years of minimal immigration and a decade when emigrants from Israel outnumbered immigrants to the country, at last Jews were choosing Zionism.

At least that's how Israel painted the picture. In fact, Soviet Jews were choosing anywhere to live but in the communist bureaucratic state that repressed their lives. Little did they realise at first, that they were entering a country with a socialist bureaucracy that could outstrangle anything they had lived through in Russia. In one short

year, 1990, Israel had become such a disappointing misery for the
Soviet Jews that well over half of those planning to leave Russia
for Israel had cancelled their plans by 1991. Life in the Soviet
Union had become more attractive than what awaited them in the
Jewish homeland. By the beginning of 1992 Soviet immigration
had declined to less than 5,000 a month – not even 15% of the
two previous years.

POLITICS AS USUAL

Rabbi Yitzhak Peretz, as mentioned earlier, is Israel's Minister
of Absorption, the man ultimately responsible for the lives of
newcomers to the country. Peretz has important links with Rabbi
Shach, the man with ultimate power over the three Orthodox
religious parties and their eight seats in the Knesset. Prime
Minister Shamir would dearly love to get rid of Peretz – the two
men disagree about most matters – but has always felt unable to
sack him for fear that Shach would retaliate and switch allegiance
to Labour. In fairness to Shamir, when he appointed Peretz to his
present ministry, Immigration was a minor portfolio since less than
20,000 people a year bothered to immigrate to Israel.

As writer Sarah Honig observes, 'It is an open secret . . . that
Peretz is the wrong man in the wrong job at the very wrongest time
imaginable.'[1]

In her 1990 report, State Comptroller Miriam Ben Porat presented a stinging indictment of immigration policy and Peretz's
ministry. She noted that warnings of the impending wave of Soviet
immigration were issued for some time but only in May 1989 when
the new arrivals were already on the doorstep did the government
plan for their absorption into Israeli society. Her indignation is
couched in angry bureaucratese: 'Experts and commissions over the
years have reached the conclusion that the present administrative
structure is an impediment to absorption and a waste of funds
. . . The government ministries . . . did not prepare plans for
immigration. Their plans are only partial, undetailed and unready
for implementation.'

One government source stated that 'Peretz is doing irreparable
harm to immigration by what he says, but also by what he doesn't
do. His ministry is totally inefficient and inept, failing not only to
plan ahead but even to change basic conceptions from the days
when immigration was all but non-existent.'

Yitzhak Modai is the Finance Minister who joined the present
government after demanding and securing a $10 million bond to

be cashed upon failure to form a coalition. Of this minister, Yosef Goell writes, 'Prime Minister Shamir is saddled with a finance minister, Yitzhak Modai, who should be the central figure in the economic absorption of the new immigration. But Modai, in addition to having a notorious history of personal instability, is totally devoid of the political clout needed to force politicians and bureaucrats to pull together or to initiate new economic growth.'

Mr Modai doles out government money to various industries and is tight-fisted with political rivals. When Peretz requested $12.5 million to be used as start-up money for immigrant entrepreneurs, Modai turned down the request.[2]

Modai had a much better way to encourage employment. It was a complicated programme combining subsidies, factory expansion, encouraging investment and renewed research and development efforts. Who would pay for all this? You bet, the Americans. Right smack dab in the middle of the Gulf War, with Scuds landing on Tel Aviv, Modai flew to Washington to demand $6–10 billion worth of aid in return for Israeli military restraint. Needless to say, his nerve was not appreciated either on Capitol Hill or by the Knesset.

Of Modai's employment plans the State Comptroller writes that they are at best long-term solutions which cannot begin to increase jobs for three years. By the end of 1990 about half of all immigrants were unemployed, while the rest, 85% of whom are university graduates, had found work in the most menial of professions. Ten of Beersheva's street cleaners today have PhDs,[3] certainly the best educated dustmen on earth and sadly typical, as we shall discover, of the employment opportunities available in Israel where some 165,000 people are unemployed each month and only 30,000 jobs open up, very few of them suitable to the skills and talents of the unemployed themselves.

In terms of cruelty, one action of Modai's stands out. Immigrants are given their first six months of health insurance free of charge. That stands to reason since penniless people who have not yet started work cannot be denied health care. The six-month period assumes that after his language course is completed, the immigrant will find a job and pay for his own health plan. However, since half of all immigrants are unemployed after six months and most of the rest are working menial labour jobs, not many can afford the $50 per person monthly health charge. By the beginning of 1991 almost 70,000 immigrants had run out of health coverage and would be in debt forever if hospitalised.[4]

Ehud Olmert asked Modai to approve a $10-million addition to the Health Ministry to assure that immigrants would be covered for another six months. Modai refused partly because he apparently doesn't like Olmert, and partly because he appears not to like immigrants.

But he doesn't like Housing Minister Ariel Sharon either. Sharon needs the most money since building isn't cheap, but most of his plans clash with Modai's grandiose schemes. By withholding funds for Sharon's building programmes he hopes they will be directed towards his idea of comprehensive housing. Modai envisions 'a Silicon Valley in the Negev',[5] which would include new towns adjacent to high-tech industrial parks. A great idea if he can convince anyone to move to the blistering moonscape of the Negev Desert. This expensive but futuristic plan will not achieve fruition because Sharon is a much stronger Housing Minister than Modai is a Finance Minister. And Sharon is the director of the Immigration Cabinet, the war council of immigration planning. The position should have gone to the Absorption Minister since the post rightfully belonged to the minister responsible for immigration. However, Shamir appointed Housing Minister Sharon, as chief co-ordinator of the new immigration. If there is anyone left still asking why, the appointment was a political favour. Sharon really wanted to be Defence Minister so Shamir let him have two important posts for the price of one.

Because the government had delayed so long before doing anything about arranging accommodation for the Soviets, when they finally took action they had to find a quick way to put up a lot of housing. The obvious solution was public tender, and to keep prices really low, the Knesset welcomed international bids. A number of American companies submitted low tenders and flew to Israel to begin negotiations. Once they arrived, the naïve negotiators were given a total runaround. According to an American Embassy official, the contractors tired of the idea of building in Israel because of excessive red tape and an 'old boy network' that just wouldn't let outsiders in.[6] It seems that Israel is one big building cartel. Government monopolies control the sale of every piece of building material in the country. There is no such thing as buying a competitive bag of cement or choosing cheaper plasterboard. It's all one brand: Government of Israel or GOIS as the gentiles call it.

Two partners in an engineering consulting firm, Adek and Scott Apfelbaum, are not happy about the state of construction in Israel and they give this appraisal: 'The housing industry is very, very ill. It is inefficient, antiquated, overmanned, mismanaged and totally incapable of delivering a reasonable quality product for a reasonable sum of money.'[7]

THE WAR ROOM

Sharon, Peretz and Modai are the three principal components of the emergency Immigration Cabinet. But the picture wouldn't be complete without one more figure of repute: the Interior Minister who issues all the identity cards and citizenship papers to the immigrants, the one and only Arye Deri. Yes folks, these are the men in charge of making the massive Soviet migration a resounding success. And you can only imagine how they've handled their tasks: it took a whole year before they'd even sit down and talk civilly to each other.

In 1990, 200,000 Soviets arrived and needed housing. Incredibly, there were a thousand *fewer* housing completions that fateful year than the previous year. Of the 45,000 flats slated for construction in 1990, only 4,500 were started. This was a disaster in the making and Sharon desired action. He demanded the lifting of the tedious local licensing requirements that can hold up building for years. Interior Minister Deri refused to sacrifice this marvellous source of funds and he appealed to the regular cabinet and won.

Soon after, Sharon requested $13.5 billion over five years from Modai's budget for building costs. Without the money he predicted there would be 600,000 homeless Israelis by 1992. Even so, requesting almost a quarter of Israel's annual GNP for one ministry was a bit much and Modai fought Sharon tooth and nail over every penny, as he did Peretz.[8] Inevitably the Knesset itself had to force decisions on the warring immigration cabinet.

Finally things became so impossible that Shamir himself declared that certain ministries are deliberately obstructing each other in the task of absorption. He would have to intervene personally to put an end to the destructive fighting. By the time of the intervention Sharon had gone power-crazy, declaring that his position gave him the right to supervise the other ministries. Modai had stopped attending the immigration cabinet meetings and by the time Shamir undertook his reconciliation assignment, Peretz had boycotted the meetings for the previous three weeks and had witheld essential statistics to the government to avenge his treatment by Sharon. Shamir got all the parties to shake hands and agree to make up. And they are the team that assures Soviet immigrants a welcome they'll never forget.

CAMPING OUT

In 1990 the housing shortage became so acute that the market skyrocketed and a lot of people couldn't afford to buy or rent housing. This left thousands of Israelis homeless, and threatened the whole Soviet immigration programme.

The government decided to give each Soviet family $330 a month for rent. The wily Soviets worked out that two families living in one apartment could use the grant money left over for other purposes. But the wily landlords recognised the trick for what it was and raised their rents accordingly. In less than a year rents shot up 30% and tenants who had lived for years in their apartments were forced out by the price rises. Some landlords raised their prices but wouldn't take in Russians despite a government advertising campaign begging them to do so. An article in *Chadashot* explained why many landlords discriminated against the new immigrants. Their grants were good for only a year and after that they were likely to be stranded. In Israel it's complicated legally to throw out even non-paying tenants and not many landlords relished the thought of evicting Soviets.

But at least families had a large enough grant to pay for temporary accommodation. Single people received only $90 a month and that wouldn't pay for a gopher hole in the Negev. The government, faced with tens of thousands of homeless unmarrieds, came up with a new plan.[9] It offered to pay apartment owners some $400 monthly if they would rent spare rooms to Soviets and again they initiated a serious advertising campaign to promote the scheme. But it was a no go. In a *Chadashot* article,[10] the reason for this failure was articulated. No matter what the price or how patriotic the justification, most people would not give up their privacy to hand over a room in their homes to a hopelessly lost Russian without enough Hebrew to understand, 'Please clean the toilet after you use it'.

The rent rises combined with the lack of available apartments for sale produced an appalling housing shortage by the summer of 1990, when 2,200 Israeli families – 10,000 people – were living in semi-organised tent villages. What was the government going to do about it? According to Modai, 'Living in tents never hurt anybody', and he went on to formulate a plan for housing the Soviets in army camps. Peretz looked at the housing fiasco in the making and came to the conclusion 'that the government would soon have no other alternative but to place immigrants in tents.'

Meanwhile outside Tel Aviv, the squatters and police clashed violently when the police tried to tear down structures in one tent village. Disease spread in other camps as the weather turned colder. The local experience was proving that tent camps were no alternative to solid buildings but the government began preparing the public for the likely need to house immigrants temporarily in tents just as the last big wave of immigrants in the 1950s were accommodated.

Fortunately, Soviet immigrants wrote letters home in 1990 and warned anyone considering joining them that what awaited them was unemployment and tents. Over 200,000 expected immigrants cancelled their plans so the tents were never assembled. Other surprises awaited the newcomers, however.

HOSTELITY

Amidar is the name of the government's housing authority – it runs most public housing in Israel. After the Soviets began arriving by the jumbo-load, it was charged with finding homes for them within the public housing framework. A noble task and carried out with the usual shame that accompanies Israeli public services.

When David Levy was Housing Minister, he filled Amidar's top positions with his own appointments, people of varying degrees of incompetence. Once Sharon took over at Housing, it was his turn to return favours to his political devotees. So in the midst of an immigration wave, he fired three of Levy's appointees, including the managing director of Amidar. Needless to say, the new Amidar executives required quite some time to get the hang of their jobs. All the while thousands of apartments in the public housing sector remained empty. This spate of firings and new political appointments were hardly Amidar's introduction to corruption. No, the company has a long history of it but one incident is worth the telling.

According to *Ha'aretz*, 'For 6 years the treasurer of Amidar, Zvi Katz, dealt with company money as if it was his own, and nobody noticed. Amidar receives the rent from tenants of 60,000 apartments and transfers the money to its bank. Katz, instead, transferred the money to his own personal account and kept it there for two to three months, thereby accruing interest, before transferring it to Amidar's account.'[11] Good idea and one that made Katz a millionaire. To keep the money rolling, Katz offered car loans to dozens of Amidar employees. No one bothered to ask where this clerk, even if high-ranking, had the assets to offer hundreds of thousands of dollars' worth of car loans to fellow workers. When he finally stood trial, he was also convicted of cheque forgery. He received a lesser sentence in part for his generous car loans.

By 1990 Amidar was run by political appointees and they were determined to prove their stuff no matter how. If their duty was to get Russians shelter, then they'd find the way. Way number one was to rent shoddy hotels and convert them into temporary 'hostels'. Hostel is a euphemism for hovel. Take the complaints of 150 Soviets crowded into a Haifa hostel which once actually was a youth hostel. To get an idea of life in Amidarland, here is the agreement made on behalf of the Soviets who were living six to a room: 'Representatives of Amidar . . . and the Haifa hostel met yesterday in Tel Aviv. They agreed that the hostel's management would turn on the air-conditioners in the immigrants' rooms and provide fans in rooms without air-conditioners. An electric stove will also be put in each room . . . Amidar has access to some 7,000 hotel and hostel rooms throughout the country. Many immigrants are transferred to the rooms immediately after they arrive at Ben Gurion Airport.'[12]

Lucky immigrants. But if they don't end up in a steamy room, without a fan or stove, then there's always the possibility of a rinky-dink trailer.

Sharon purchased thousands of trailers, known in Hebrew as *caravanim*, because he was convinced they were the perfect stopgap until real buildings could be put up. In one of his wackier moments Sharon actually proposed putting trailers on the roofs of buildings and plugging them into the sewage and electrical systems thereby saving the costs of caravan-park infrastructures. How mobile homes are lifted on to roofs was never elaborated on, but mobilising a squad of Air Force helicopters might have pushed this unique scheme in penthouse-living closer to reality. However, sanity, for once, prevailed.

Sharon overstated the value of these 'mobile homes' by a third, according to the government Treasury. According to Stanford University economist, Alvin Rabushka: 'He was charging the country $20,000 for the trailers. He was buying in bulk and couldn't have paid more than $10,000 each. As far as I'm concerned, maybe half the trailer budget is unaccounted for.'

Two types of trailer finally arrived in Israel: the kingsize model, covering 45 square metres and the baby model, which was barely half that size. As for mobile-home living: 'In a joint decision between the ministry and the Holon municipality, 30 caravans are to be put in place within 72 hours, thus providing housing for 60 homeless families.'[13]

Isn't life wonderful? A long flight from Moscow followed by a restful stay in a hostel six to a room with a new fan and hotplate and then straight to Holon to share a 40-square metre home on wheels with another family.

Not surprisingly, the immigrants refused to move into the trailers and hundreds stood empty. Amidar's Sharon-appointed executives could not have his trailer plan revealed for the flop it was, so came up with a stunningly clever plan. Anyone who agreed to live in a rented trailer would be the first eligible for a public housing dwelling when available.

But not enough houses were available so Amidar decided to take action; it sent out 10,000 letters to tenants advising them to let out rooms in their homes or face eviction. The tenants let out a public scream and Amidar sent them a new letter asking them to let out rooms for patriotic reasons. But included in the appeal to love of country was a threat: 'It has come to our attention that you no longer have the right to the apartment where you are living.' Singles and couples who may have lived in the same apartment for decades were given four options: buy the apartment outright, move to a smaller Amidar apartment, take a huge rent rise or rent a room to an immigrant.

In the words of reporter Bill Hutman, 'From the outrageous to the despicable, the government's search for temporary immigrant housing appears to know no bounds.'[14]

Someone must be asking why the immigrants don't skirt Amidar and head for the rental market with their generous start-up grants. The answer is that there barely is a rental market in Israel. In the whole country, not one contractor put up a building solely for the long-term benefits of renting flats. No, in Israel, apartments are built to be bought. Those rented are the former homes of deceased parents or apartments owned by expatriates abroad who keep the properties as a last link to the land they loved and abandoned. Private-sector landlords can be very unpleasant in any case, as Naftali Greenwood, writing for the Institute of Advanced Strategic and Political Studies explains:

> Rent is largely non-negotiable, with one major exception. Some landlords who expect rent levels to rise during a year's contract insert a mid-year no explanation eviction clause ... A prospective tenant who demands receipts is deemed unethical at best and an Income Tax agent at worst ... The result is ... a distorted market typified by ... caprice, perversity, intimidation and exploitation.[15]

Another problem is that there is a lack of official protection in the private sector, and immigrants face the danger of being swindled by unscrupulous dealers. According to Moshe Herzog, a Tel Aviv attorney specialising in fraud cases, between two and three thousand Soviet immigrants have been seriously swindled by con men in the first two years of the immigration wave.[16]

One family of six rented an apartment from an agent for $250 a month and forked out a large advance. After paying the owner of the 'apartment', the agent mysteriously left the country. When the family moved in to their new home they discovered it was a one-room apartment with no toilet or kitchen. The family wanted its money back but the law backs the owner in a buyer-beware situation. The family had rented the room in a free market with no price restrictions and it was their obligation, no matter how green were their horns, to check out the purchase before putting down the money.

With the private rental market totally cut-throat, the immigrants must depend on the public rental market unless they take the only other step available short of immediate immigration to a sane country, namely purchasing an apartment.

WHY DOES THIS DUMP COST SO DAMN MUCH?

The government, through its Land Authority, owns 93% of the land in Israel. Only Albania and Cuba have a higher percentage of their land tied up in government ownership.

If someone wants to buy a plot of land in Israel, he doesn't just purchase a deed from someone else. No, he must go to the Land Authority. There he will discover which plots of land will be released for sale at a public auction or lottery. And he will be told if he is eligible to purchase land. Even if he has the cash in his wallet, he will not be permitted to buy the property for such reasons as having once owned another plot, for having no children, for not being disabled in combat or for whatever regulation is being enforced that day. If eligible for a public auction, he will pay a non-refundable fee for the right to compete against thousands of other eligibles for a few available plots of earth.

Now why, the astute reader is sure to ask, wouldn't the government want to sell land at exorbitant prices to someone willing to pay? Again and again and again, the Authority is under the influence of the agriculture (kibbutz) political lobby which finds it in their interest to keep land in escrow for future farms. In all of 1990, the Land Authority released only 250 acres of land for construction.

The contractors pay a fortune for each plot and this adds some 30% to the price of a flat. When a private land-owner offers a plot to a contractor he can demand amazing concessions, like a share in the ownership of the flats to be sold. Even with the land costs, the prices charged by the contractors are immoral. The cheapest apartment in the least desirable backwood town is $65,000, over twice the true market value. But immigrants are given only $38,000 per family in mortgage rights and single immigrants considerably less. Few immigrants had the available cash to make up the difference so contractors in 1989-90 refused to put up apartments they knew would go unsold. So, by the beginning of the new decade, Israel was heading for a housing disaster. Contractors wouldn't build, banks wouldn't lend enough for mortgages and the government wasn't releasing land to build on. No one was co-operating with anyone and someone had to do something. Enter Sharon.

Give the big man credit, it's a clever scheme to get contractors to put up buildings. Step one: offer a government promise to buy back all unsold apartments for $65,000. Now the contractor can't lose by building. But the government could lose because Israeli contractors typically took 27 months to finish an apartment (three times more than the rest of the planet). With disaster at the door the government could not afford a two-year wait for housing so Sharon came up with another incentive. Step two: give each contractor a cash grant of $10,000 for every apartment built in less than 13 months and $15,000 for a completion in less than 11 months. This money was not included in the selling price of the apartment. Instead, these lavish grants for doing work in the time considered normal everywhere else came straight from the taxpayers' wallets.

Joel Bainerman analyses the two steps: 'How much care will the contractors put into a product when they have a guarantee it will be bought? What is going to happen when they discover they can't complete the apartments in the required time to qualify for the guarantee? Will they have no choice other than to cut corners and hand over a shabby product . . . ?'[17]

If cutting corners is what is needed to make a killing in real estate, then what faster way than by buying cheap land? Sharon never wanted to settle people in the Tel Aviv area where 50.9% of all new Soviets chose to live. So he offered only a 50% guarantee to the contractors who built there. Naturally the contractors built where the guarantees were full and where the land was cheapest. By the end of 1991, the Israeli construction industry put up 95,000 units, a new yearly record, and cut their building time by more than half. But they built tiny high-rise shanties in places the immigrants didn't want to live. For instance, 28.5% of all new housing construction went up in the Negev where only 6.3% of all new immigrants had chosen to live. Another 32% was built in the depressed areas of the Galilee, while much of the rest was put up in expanding Jerusalem-area suburbs where only 9.7% of immigrants had chosen to live.

The government was repeating the biggest social disaster of the '50s, the coercion of immigrants to live in 25 'development towns'. These towns, with names like Dimona, Kiryat Shmoneh and the legendary Beersheva, were created for security reasons and to populate undesirable locations in the desert and near war-zones. They quickly became cesspools of crime and despair and remain that way to this day. There are few decent jobs available in these towns. Those factories and services that do exist were artificially created by the government and serve little profitable purpose. These are company towns and the government is their creator, employer and destroyer. Sharon's plan is resulting in the expansion of cities without hope.

The south of Israel had been depopulated over the years as unemployment and depression drove its most ambitious or desperate people to the centre of the country. Now it is destined to be repopulated by Soviets who will find no more opportunities than the natives did before. As Melvin Cohen, a member of the Chartered Institute of Building (UK) writes: '. . . to refer new immigrants to these places in spite of the exceptionally high levels of unemployment there, is a step which will aggravate an already critical social time-bomb.'[18]

Sharon's task in 1990 may have been to house immigrants but his priority was and always will be to populate the disputed lands with Jews.

The American government presented Israel with $400 million in housing guarantees with the provision that none of it be used to settle immigrants in the West Bank or Gaza. And East Jerusalem was considered disputed though the Bush administration backed down on this proviso. Immigrants were not directed to the territories as such but in a free country who was to prevent them from choosing where to live? Mobile homes were offered to new immigrants in the West Bank for as low as $40 a month rental and that meant keeping $290 in rent grants for other uses. That is certainly an incentive for moving to the Wild West Bank. By the summer of 1991, Sharon was fooling no one in Washington and the $400 million in guarantees were endangered in a showdown with Israel over settling the territories. Housing Soviets became secondary to creating housing facts near Nablus as the Israeli government refused to stop construction of new settlements, loan guarantees be damned.

It is a useless showdown. The territories are annexed and Israel should just announce it. No government in the future will ever have the power to evict 250,000 (so far) Jewish residents from their homes. Complicating matters is the issue of Jerusalem. In 1991, the Land Authority released huge areas for building near Jerusalem at half the usual leasing price. Jerusalem will be a city of a million Jews in a generation with boundaries that stretch half the width of the West Bank.

Sharon as Housing Minister has bulldozed his way to a massive budget that is too complicated to be accountable. He has succeeded in building almost 100,000 units in one year or over 90,000 more than the year before and most are sitting in slum towns, deserts and former Jordanian territory. And much of the tab may someday be picked up by American Jewry through the UJA.

Although the UJA had already guaranteed $750 million in loans to Soviet immigrants, even this wasn't generous enough. Finance Minister Modai during a New York visit declared that American Jews must carry most of the burden for housing and settling an estimated 1.2 million Soviets expected within five years. He estimated the total bill to be $50 billion.[19] Even more frightening than that figure is the thought that the UJA might try and raise that preposterous sum.

I AM A NOTED NEUROLOGIST FROM LENINGRAD. CAN I CLEAN YOUR STEPS?

Housing is not the only problem facing immigrants; employment, or the lack of it, is another major source of trouble. Admittedly, your average immigrant is prepared to work day and night at menial jobs for the sake of his family's future. But the Soviet immigration to Israel isn't typical. Tens of thousands of engineers, musicians, scientists and doctors arrived in Israel, each expecting improved opportunities in their fields. And if granted them, the whole country might prosper. Some 41% of all immigrants hold university or technical college degrees compared to 8% of Israelis.[20] The percentage of doctorates among the immigrants is six times that of the Israeli proportion, of musicians five times, of physicians nine times and of dentists five times. Israel is getting a massive injection of expensively trained manpower.

But the injection might as well have been empty, as Yosef Goell writes: '. . . on the major issues affecting absorption – economic growth, employment and adapting the economy to exploit the immigrants' wealth of professional and vocational expertise – virtually no progress has been made since the immigration began.'21

Rolando Eisen, chairman of the absorption committee of the Israel Manufacturers' Association concurs: 'The government bureaucracy where immigration is concerned is bankrupt and beyond repair . . .'

By July 1991, the once bustling reception area at Ben Gurion Airport for new Soviet immigrants was a most subdued place. From a thousand arrivals daily just weeks before, fewer than 200 were now arriving each day and the number was dwindling steadily. The great immigration of 1991 that was supposed to bring 400–500,000 Soviet Jews to Israel had ground to a halt at 87,000.

It's not as if the warnings weren't there. Back in March, the governor of the Bank of Israel warned that 400,000 Israelis would soon be jobless and 200,000 immigrants, a two-year supply at recent rates, would leave the country. He blamed the Histadrut for refusing to adopt realistic policies and he blamed Modai for scaring off potential investors in Israel. His own plan to prevent rocketing unemployment was cruel in the extreme: he suggested cutting the minimum wage, already Dickensian, and abolishing cost-of-living allowances, which would hurry the process of starving the majority of Israelis.

That same month, Michael Kleiner MK and chairman of the Knesset Immigration Committee, warned that thousands of Soviets had cancelled their exit visas because 'they did not want to venture into the fast deteriorating employment situation here.'22 Kleiner blamed the Jewish Agency for 'irresponsibly' trying to create the impression that immigration was continuing as normal despite problems with absorption here.

By April, hundreds of Soviet doctors demonstrated outside the Knesset, claiming that Health Minister Olmert had arranged matters to prevent the physicians from ever finding work. An immigrant doctor from Russia must pass a licensing exam before he can set up a practice. Until recently 90% of the applicants passed on the first try. The Health Ministry had toughened up the exam in a successful ploy to keep thousands of new doctors from competing in the open market with those already practising. Only 20% of Soviet doctors23 could pass the new test and that means 80% of the 7,000 doctors who had arrived since 1989, had to find alternative employment in very unrelated fields, like rubbish collection. Mikhail Vaksman's story illustrates this. Mikhail Vaksman is 37. He completed his medical studies at the Leningrad Medical Institute of Hygiene and Sanitation in 1976 and immediately began studies in surgery. By 1982, his talent was recognised and he began teaching surgery at the Leningrad Medical College. By 1984 he combined teaching with practical surgery at the Leningrad Municipal Hospital. In May of 1990 he arrived in Israel with his wife Victoria and their two sons. They rented one room from friends who lived near Jerusalem.

> We lived in that room because our $330 stipend couldn't rent a flat. Eventually I borrowed money from a friend and leased a two-room flat and I began to study Hebrew. I only lasted three months because our stipend wasn't enough to support a family. I had to work so I started cleaning. During this time I had to prepare for my medical licensing exam. The exam was on general medicine, only 20% of the questions had anything to do with surgery. A specialist can't pass the exam so I was denied a license to practise.
>
> In Russia neurosurgery was very prestigious and in my department I was the expert. I was number one in spinal cord injuries. I don't need to be number one here, just to earn enough to pay for living and my sons' education. But prices in Israel are out of proportion.
>
> Israel isn't a democratic country, it's an ideological country. There are so many things in common with Russian regulations and the government doesn't want to do anything, just like in Russia.
>
> I've received invitations to work in South Africa and New Zealand. I want to work in my profession and I can somewhere else. I have the alternative and the pressure here isn't worth it anymore.

A report on Israel Television in July 1991 illuminated government employment policies. One electrical engineer paid a visit to his local employment office and was offered work as a chambermaid in a hotel. As one reviewer observed: 'The employment office must take their career counseling advice from other government agencies which follow the credo that qualifications and employment opportunities are mutually exclusive concepts.'

With an additional 2,000 scientists in the country, practical solutions were suggested to employ them to everyone's benefit. Dr Herman Branover of Ben Gurion University, himself a Soviet-Israeli scientist of repute, wisely advised setting up a special college to train this brainpower in Western techniques, equipment, patent laws and marketing strategies. Science Minister Yuval Ne'eman asked Modai for $12 million, a pittance when one considers the $2.5 billion housing allocation, to set up such a training centre. Needless to say, petty bickering held up the request.

Ne'eman later softened his plans to create a scientific hothouse in Israel, presenting a programme to shift most of the scientists into teaching and at levels as low as high schools. Degrading perhaps, but better than the current fate of Soviet scientists like the 52-year-old physicist featured in a *Ma'ariv* article whose family of five was consisting daily on cabbage soup and bread.

According to MK Ora Namir and confirmed many times over by the Israeli media, nearly 1,000 Soviet women with university degrees have gone into prostitution because they are unable to find employment. In the Tel Aviv area alone some 500 work on the streets, 250 as masseuses at sex parlours and 150 for escort services.[24] At Tel Aviv University, Soviet women offered sex for lunch money. Rachel Jacoby writes: 'These women who left the Soviet Union in order to escape persecution as Jews are now suffering exploitation no less severe in the Promised Land. Until this tragic irony is recognised . . . [it] will continue to destroy the lives of Russian immigrants and undermine the ideals of immigration.'[25]

An article in the April 1991 edition of *Moment* stated that: 'Unless changes are made, these Soviet immigrants may never have a chance to build satisfying, prosperous lives in Israel.'[26]

By May 1991, figures published by the Ministry of Trade and Industry revealed that the number of jobs in industry fell by 0.8% during the past year. With over 100,000 new immigrants entering the job scene, the number of openings actually dropped, surely the last word to be uttered about the value of government intervention Israeli-style in employment.

THE IMMIGRANTS SPEAK . . . ALL YOU HAVE TO DO IS ASK THEM TO PUT DOWN THE MOP

By April 1991 the number of applicants for unemployment insurance had risen by 28% in March and over ten times the figure for the previous September. There are many human stories behind the cold statistics.

Assia is an engineer from Minsk. Everyday she rises at five to travel out of town to clean houses for $4 an hour. The rate for native-born Israelis is twice that. The pay and long hours in this honest but demeaning work for an engineer, barely covers her $400 a month rent or support for her elderly mother. 'There is no chance,' says Assia. 'No hope. I'm a realist. There are just too many immigrants.'[27]

As one Soviet Jew was quoted in an article distributed by the Jewish Telegraphic Agency, 'Some are not ashamed to say that if they had to do it over they would have stayed in the Soviet Union where most had good jobs and steady incomes and lived in relative comfort.'

Relative indeed since the Soviet Union is not known for the good life but Israel is now coming close to matching what the immigrants left behind.

Georgi Chazan is a cellist who came to Israel to master his instrument. Today he is a street busker saving his coins to escape the country. Though like most Soviets, he genuinely likes Israelis, he despises the system, which he calls, 'Just like the Soviet Union, only worse.'[28]

Luba cannot get work because the computer at the Absorption Ministry broke down and didn't register her. For two months she has been going from office to office to rectify the error. In the meantime, she isn't even eligible for Hebrew courses because she doesn't exist, nor do her two daughters need food or shelter because they disappeared from the computer with their mother.

PUTTING THEM THROUGH THE WRINGER

Early in the immigration wave, officials realised that many Soviet men had married gentiles and thus their children were not Jewish according to religious laws. Government policy was not to make a fuss lest the whole rescue of Soviet Jewry be endangered. But by 1991 even the hardened Zionists who desired immigration deeply as proof of the virtues of the ideology, were having second thoughts about many of the Soviets.

By the spring of 1991 Interior Minister Arye Deri suggested that only Russians with 'a Jewish grandfather buried in the USSR', be granted visas to Israel. Absorption Minister Peretz announced that 'we shall soon be getting twice as many non-Jewish as Jewish immigrants.' Michael Kleiner claimed that millions of gentiles were waiting to climb on the Jewish emigration bandwagon and that Israel should not pay for their resettlement.

MK Arye Eliav wanted all talk of Israel being a way-station for gentiles escaping the USSR stopped, at least such talk emanating from the government. Eliav was convinced the immigration would be hampered by 'confusion, embarrassment and apprehension lest more difficulties were added to their obstacle-strewn path to making their home here.'[29]

But the obstacles were thrown on to the path despite his worries. The Orthodox clerks of the Absorption and Interior Ministries made darn certain the doubtful Jews proved their lineage before being granted the proper papers.

First a birth certificate had to be presented. If a family's birth certificates were in Russian, which of course they all were, then they had to be translated into Hebrew. Yona Frenkel of the Soviet Jewry Zionist Forum explains the procedure. 'The Ministry offices do not have Russian-speaking clerks and the Absorption Ministry does not offer the service of translating Soviet birth certificates. The Interior Ministry further insists on notarised translations at a cost of $60 per immigrant. Imagine a family of five or six: it costs them a month's living allowance to get their identity cards.'

If there are any doubts in the mind of the registration clerk that the immigrant is Jewish, he is directed to the rabbinical court where he must bring two witnesses to verify his Jewishness. 'However,' adds Frenkel, 'even if such witnesses are available, the immigrant has to pay $35 to open a file with the rabbinical court. Why should he?'[30]

Needless to say, many immigrants, Soviet and otherwise, overcome the rabbinical court by convincing or hiring two witnesses to perjure themselves before the judges.

If the Soviets often suffer at the hands of the Absorption and Interior Ministries, they've also been given a hard time by the Finance Minister.

All immigrants to Israel are relieved of paying taxes and customs duties on most items for a few years. The Finance Ministry changed the rule for Soviet immigrants in 1990, exchanging customs exemptions for a $2,500 grant. This was highway robbery for only a few items can be purchased in Israel for that paltry amount whereas buying the goods abroad where prices are normal and bringing them into Israel is about the only way to start up a household. One Soviet Jewish official called this new grant 'a dirty trick'.[31]

This trick was followed shortly after by another. Soviet immigrants had previously received $9,000 each to get through their first year. With rent eating up $7,000 per apartment and food prices higher than anywhere in Europe, this money disappeared quickly. The Treasury cut the subsidy by $1,500 without warning or explanation.

Ida Nudel had had enough and wrote a piece called 'Letting Immigration Hopes Slip Away'. After detailing the miserable performance of the government she concludes: '. . . integrating the newcomers has been a complete failure, a catastrophe which gives world Jewry the moral right to lobby for raising the quota of Soviet Jewish immigrants going to their respective countries.'[32]

RUSSIANS, WHO NEEDS THEM?

A Russian, a Scot and an Israeli are seated on a train. The Russian takes out a jar of caviar, eats a spoonful and throws the jar out the window. The Scot and Israeli are shocked and ask him why he wasted so much. 'In Russia,' he says, 'we have too many jars of caviar.' The Scotsman takes out a bottle of Scotch, sips a small amount and throws the bottle out the window. The Israeli and Russian are shocked and ask what he was doing. 'In Scotland,' he explains, 'there are too many bottles of Scotch.' The Israeli then stands up and throws the Russian out the window.

That story is told throughout Israel and everyone gets the point. According to a recent news item: 'If Finance Minister Modai's economic plan for the absorption of Soviet immigrants is adopted at today's special cabinet session, Israelis may expect to have a lower standard of living, with an erosion of cost-of-living increments on wages and the minimum wage.'[33]

Israelis were told in 1989 that the wave of immigration on the way would raise their living standards through increases in new purchases and an infusion of ambitious entrepreneurs. They did not expect that the immigrants would cost them in bonuses to contractors, new taxes and ridiculous rent rises. Amos Glazer, chairman of the Israeli Real Estate Association, says, 'Rents have risen 50% since December [four months] solely as a result of absorption.'

Wendy Blumfield, a childbirth and infant-care specialist, sees young couples leaving Israel in droves because of the price of housing.[34] Many go abroad to earn enough for a home and stay for good. Many others who stay in Israel postpone parenthood until they can afford housing. A business consultant, Manfred Gerstenfeld, wants to cut down the Soviet immigration, a feeling not uncommon in Israel today despite the original enthusiasm for more Jews: 'It is doubtful whether Israel should try to deter other countries from accepting immigrants . . . a well-functioning country of 5.5 million in 1995 is far preferable to one of 6 million with a high rate of unemployment and emigration . . . Absorbing a million immigrants isn't an act of self-interest. It is one of generosity.'[35]

When there is bitterness, the canaries in the coalmine are the children. Thanks to the influx of immigrants, Israeli classrooms are crowded, and an average of 40 or more pupils cram each class. According to a Soviet Jewry Zionist Forum report in October 1990, 'In more socially deprived, lower-income areas, the pupils, like their parents, are often resentful of the new Soviet immigrants, fearful that their arrival may negatively affect their own upward mobility.'

The Soviet immigration is causing not only tension between native Israelis and newcomers but between some veteran Soviets, now thoroughly Israelised, who feel their hard-earned respect in society is being jeopardised by the plight and complaints of the more recent arrivals.

It used to be said that Israelis love immigration but not immigrants. This was not the case originally with the Soviets. They were welcomed by Israelis openly and sincerely. Now thanks to the bungling of their leaders, Israelis are turning sour on immigration. The country, veterans and newcomers deserve better leadership.

FULL CIRCLE

And who props up these leaders in no small part but American Jews who are underwriting much of the cost of the Ethiopian and Soviet immigration enterprises? The belief of this book is that they should stop and to the author's shock and relief, no less than the *New York Times* printed an editorial by Robert J. Loewenberg, on 24 June 1991, which supports in large part the thesis of aid perpetuating corruption:

> Israel's stagnant socialist economy dwarfs and conditions all domestic problems the country faces. The US Jewish community have long evaded this problem. But faced by the tragic failure to integrate Soviet Jews, they can no longer do so.
>
> The UJA calls for overseas Jews to guarantee $800 million in loans to Soviet immigrants . . . . Guaranteed loans to Israeli banks constitute a departure from traditional American Jewish philanthropy. US Jews send money but rarely involve themselves in the allocation of funds in Israel. If the loan guarantee is approved, American Jews would have a stake in the coalition government's maintenance of the status quo.

The Jewish Agency is madness. It has rescued Ethiopian Jews

only to have their culture torn asunder in Israel. It has transported Soviet Jews only to deliver them to poverty, unemployment and disgrace. Israelis want and need immigrants and they wish them all a good life in their new country. But the régime that runs Israel does not deserve new citizens and until it proves itself worthy of the good people who live in Israel, it does not deserve support from Jews abroad. Israelis would prefer the corruption to end and would thank world Jewry if they could contribute something worthy, like a complete cut-off of funds until the whole political and economic system of Israel is reformed inside out.

CHAPTER FOURTEEN

Oh, Those Piggy Banks

They stood in the dock on 11 July 1991, seven years after they had come close to bankrupting the country. Seated next to each other facing the judge were 17 of the nation's leading banking executives and accountants of the early 1980s, who together once controlled over 90% of Israeli banking. They were gathered together to defend themselves against the following indictment:

> Starting from the end of the 1970s . . . the accused interfered in the trading of commercial bank shares by taking steps to artificially increase the demand for these shares, thereby increasing their ability to raise capital from the public via their issues . . . By adopting these measures the bank directors caused the banks to take increasingly greater financial responsibility for the inflated rates of their shares, thereby diminishing their capital and independent sources and decreasing their ability to honour their commitments.[1]

Enough legal gobbledy-gook. Here's what happened. Way back in 1972, Yaacov Levinson, the head of Bank Hapoalim (the workers' bank run by the workers' union, the Histadrut), was tired of being in charge of the country's number two bank. He was haunted by the thought that Ernst Yaphet, his counterpart in Bank Leumi of Israel, was heading a much more profitable organisation. Levinson decided to take action. If he couldn't make as much money as Leumi on savings, then he'd make up the difference in share sales on the Tel Aviv Stock Market. He put Hapoalim shares on the open market and to make the public sit up and take notice, he directed Histadrut companies to buy up the first offering. Naturally, this increased the value of the shares for the next offering. Once the shares came on the market, the public snatched them up.

However, since the shares were inflated by artificial buying in the first place, some of the public sold their shares, lowering the value of all shares. This Hapoalim could not allow, so it directed the companies under its control to take Hapoalim money, and buy up the slack in the market plus some more. Once again the shares rose and the public bought into a rising stock. But the price of the stock really didn't reflect the assets of the bank, so some shareholders cashed in their chips, causing the stock price to fall. At that precise moment, the bank's front companies again bought the available shares plus a few more. Once again the stock value rose and the public bought in.

Over at Leumi, Ernst Yaphet was consumed with envy. Hapoalim was raking in money by illegally cheating shareholders with in-house trading. Well, he would put an end to such goings on. He'd do the same thing with his bank. So Leumi entered the same market, offering shares which were manipulated sometimes via the companies closely tied to the bank. Now the public had a choice of two frauds to buy into. But which one? They both looked so delightful. Why, the more profitable one, of course. Thus began a frenzied rivalry between the two biggest banks to pump in even more of the public's savings into grossly inflated stocks in order to earn even more of the public's savings in stock revenues.

Obviously, if the two biggest and most trusted banks could blatantly break the law, earn totally tainted funds and get away with it, the other banks would follow. Two more big banks and a few smaller subsidiary banks entered the fray and it wasn't long before the fierce competition for buyers pushed all the stocks up phenomenally. At one point each share of Bank Leumi, which had not shown a true profit in years, was worth $489, or about the cost of Chase Manhattan shares.

The bankers, however, realised that they might be riding for a fall, so, not wanting to carry a good thing too far, the directors of all the banks involved met and decided to co-operate. The manipulation would now be co-ordinated with all the banks buying each other's stocks at fortuitous and opportune moments of their own making. With stocks selling for preposterous prices, only a constant flow of new cash could keep the house of cards from collapsing. So the banks took more measures to relieve the public of eventually, one third of its savings. The banks offered credit for its customers to buy stocks and, if the carrot wouldn't work, they wielded the stick, refusing in some cases to grant credit unless stocks were bought as part of it. This was followed by powerful advertising campaigns, complete with glossy prospectuses promising a safe investment that increased in value far faster than any savings plan they were offering.

Still, not everyone wanted to buy bank shares, some people preferred to invest in mutual, provident or trust funds or in pension schemes. These were considered secure, long-term plans, suitable for the cautious citizen. Unfortunately, the cautious were caught up in the disaster with the risky because the banks took enormous sums from these funds and invested them in their own stocks. All this money was still not enough to bridge the yawning chasm between price and value, so the banks ordered their financial advisors to direct customers seeking investment or savings advice to buy the bank's stocks.

That took care of most of the Israeli public. Stocks were being purchased voluntarily because of the impressive dividends, by arm-twisting in the case of those seeking credit, by chicanery dipping into trusts and pensions, by misrepresentation in advertising, reports and brochures and by fast-talking. And still, there wasn't nearly enough liquid cash to keep the overturned stock pyramid from tipping over. So, in an incredibly risky move, the banks offered a no-risk investment to the public. If the stock fell, the bank would refund the purchase to all customers equal to the value of the stock the previous day. Now stocks not only had to keep pace, they had to rise as well, or the public would cash in, leading to a panic.

And still, there wasn't nearly enough money to cover the reality gap and sooner or later too many people were going to redeem their stocks only to find there wasn't enough money to cover the presumed value of the paper. That day arrived on 6 October 1983, when the public redeemed 30% of the banks' stocks and never saw a nickel of cash. This led to a run on the stocks by most holders, who collectively demanded over $7 billion. But the banks didn't have the money. All in all, some $7.5 billion – a third of public savings – were stolen from the Israeli public, leaving it effectively broke.

ENTER THE GOVERNMENT, FROM NOW ON YOUR FRIENDLY BANKER

The government finally had no choice but to step in. Where were they before this? They were observing the disaster in the making and letting it go on. Though laws were broken blatantly, the Finance Ministry and Bank of Israel silently nodded non-interference. Once the government got a grip on the disaster, it went straight to work sorting things out. First it closed the stock exchange to stop the run. Then, with the newly impoverished citizenry in deep shock, it promised to buy back all the shares, outstanding or not, and redeem them at full value within five years. Since the banks' debt of $7.5 billion is more than Israel's annual defence budget, the government's only hope was to sell off the banks and regain some of the cash. Or so the thinking was in 1983. Not much later the government learned that owning banks was a great way to rob the public and there were advantages to holding on to them.

Back then, the government thought it had five years to sell the banks and repay the losses to the public. But there was a snag. The government may have been the majority owner of the banks' shares but because of the crooked control set-up, the shareholders had next to no voting rights on the boards. No one would buy a bank without a majority of voting rights so the government forced the very reluctant banks to shift controlling power to the shareholders or itself.

Fine. For $7.5 billion, the government bailed out the banks. But the public was enraged and wanted answers. On the last day of 1984, the State Comptroller provided a few.[2] He concluded that the banks failed to distinguish between regulating shares and manipulating them. In choosing manipulation, the banks may have been guilty of criminal acts.

The public wanted to know if they were victims of criminality and the hue and cry was so loud that the government appointed a committee led by Justice Chaim Beiski to investigate the matter. A final conclusion reached was: 'If the banks would have adhered to the law, the manipulation would not have taken place.' Yes, the bankers were criminals.

The commission recommended that 17 bankers and consultants resign immediately. All but one (of Discount Bank) acquiesced. The Governor of the Bank of Israel was also asked to resign. Now the public wanted blood. They had been hoodwinked and a government commission confirmed it. The hoodwinkers had so far escaped trial and that had to end. The state Attorney-General, Yosef Harish, gave into public demands for a police investigation only after an unseemly long period of deliberation. This was the beginning of a series of suspicious delays by the Attorney-General.

Two years later, the police investigation recommended indictments but Harish decided not to press charges, claiming the bankers had suffered enough by being fired and the country would not benefit by their standing trial. The public disagreed as did three MKs who went to the Supreme Court and overturned Harish's decision. And it still took Harish another seven months to give in to the court and order indictments. Coincidentally, Harish had stalled just long enough for the bankers to have passed the seven-year statute of limitations of civil cases. Much of the evidence presented by the prosecutor would be disallowed and the trial of the bankers would be mostly a show.

SUFFER THE POOR BANKERS
Here are the less celebrated fates of some of the bankers put on trial for fraud: Mordechai Einhorn, Leumi's chief operations officer at the time of the collapse is today managing director of Tzmicha, a large investment firm. Giora Gazit, the former managing director of Bank Hapoalim, now earns more money in just one of his projects, consultant to the Tsur-Shamir Insurance Company, than he ever did in his banking heyday. Aharon Meir, the former managing director of Bank Mizrahi, eventually became chairman of Israel's largest private corporation, Clal. Dov Naveh, who was a senior accountant at Mizrahi, now lives in London where he is financial chief for businessman Leon Tamman.[3] All in all, they didn't suffer a bad fate for robbing two-thirds of Israeli adults of their savings, for depriving students of their college tuitions, for turning the golden years of many Israeli aged into a misery of deprivation.

BANKER, HEAL THYSELF
It had not been a good decade for Israel financially. Inflation passed 400%, the stock market collapsed, the banking system fell apart, the agricultural system imploded, the health sector went belly up, and on and on. And with each new crisis, the government came up with a bail-out of public money.

By 1984 when the government acquired controlling shares of most of the country's banks, things were so bad that the Finance Minister became 'unavailable' to foreign bankers. In 1985 Israel's foreign currency stocks were down to a few months' supply. Once used up, the country would be insolvent.

From 1973 to 1990, Israel's economy stopped growing. For 17 straight years, annual growth was less than 1% per annum, and some years recorded a loss. In 1990 there was a spurt of delusory growth caused by the addition of 200,000 immigrants who bought consumer goods on borrowed money. It is safe to say that Israel has the most badly run economy in the democratic world.

But up until 1985, the people of Israel made do even in times of galloping inflation. In 1985 the government, led by Shimon Peres, decided that inflation had to end. Hand in hand Peres and his Finance Minister, Yitzhak Modai, foisted on the public a plan to

halt inflation by impoverishing the population. First wages were
frozen and in Israel that works. An unholy cartel of government,
Histadrut and the Manufacturers Association control the salaries
of three-quarters of working Israelis. If this triumvirate wants to
stop wage rises, it will. Stage one was a success. Israelis stopped
receiving salary increases. There was no reward for hard work nor
any incentive to produce more. Salaries would be determined by
the triumvirate and not by market forces.

Stage two called for a severe reduction in available capital, which
shot interest rates to the moon. At one point the lending rate at
Israeli banks topped 200% per annum. At the same time, credit
on deposits fell to literally nothing.

Stage three called for a Cost of Living (COL) increment to be
attached to all credit and this was the killer. The COL consists of
a basket of economic indicators including the price of food items
and manufactured goods. What it does not include is the value of
capital, the worth of Israeli currency or the state of salaries. Thus
if a locust plague caused a rise in commodity prices, the COL would
rise even though Israeli wages stood still and the shekel fell in world
currency markets.

Now let us put this in practical terms. Someone takes out a $100
loan in 1991. The cost of credit was 25% at Israeli banks so each
year, of a ten-year loan, the borrower has to return $25 on the
$100. But don't forget the COL on top of the interest. Since 1985
inflation has been about 20% a year as determined by the COL. So
in the first year of his loan the borrower must pay 20% more for
the COL and the principal of his loan is linked at all times to the
COL, so he must return not 25% of $100 but 25% of $120. And the
debt is cumulative. Next year the COL will be calculated as 20% of
$120 and the interest on the loan will now be 25% of the principal,
and two years of cumulative COL adjustments. By the third year,
another COL calculation ensures that the borrower is now paying
25% interest against a loan that has doubled thanks to cumulative
COL adjustments.

This is where the treadmill begins. The borrower needed a mere
$100 to tide him through a slack period and had no choice but to
accept the murderous interest rates. He calculated that he'd be able
to return the loan based on projected profits. But no one of sanity
believed that banks of the 20th century would demand hundreds
of percent return on their risk.

To further ensure super-profits, the interest on savings was left
untied to the COL in most banks meaning a person could actually

lose their money in a savings plan. Today most Israeli banks offer an 11% gain on savings plans which means a 9% annual loss after calculating the COL. The best plan around is offered by Bank Mizrachi. It gives 1% interest after COL indexing. What is not publicised is a clause invalidating the rate if the COL is higher than 19% in any year.

The actual gap, therefore, between borrowing and savings rates in Israel, is about 30%. As Stanford economist Alvin Rabushka notes, 'They'd put you in jail in the States for that.' According to Danny Gillerman, chairman of the Israeli Trade Bureau, the interest the banks are taking is, 'worse than that of Mafia loansharks'.[4]

Obviously, the effects of such criminal credit policies would more than ripple through the economy. Throughout the world small businessmen borrow in the off-season, return the loan when goods start moving and then deposit profits to earn interest as protection against the next low season. In Israel the small businessman cannot borrow at reasonable rates nor can he save and hope to gain on the interest. So small businesses die in droves. In 1988 twice as many small businesses went bust as the year before. By 1989 almost 9,000 companies, most small, went under.[5]

The government did not step in to save any of the small businesses but when the biggest enterprises in the country became buried in debt to the banks, Clark became Superman, defender of the victimised.

In the next chapter, we will examine how the government bailed out the kibbutzim and moshavim, but for now it is enough to know that the cost to the public was over $6 billion. Another victim of the banks and its own inefficiency was the Histadrut industrial giant, Koor Industries, an umbrella organisation for over 160 companies that employ 18% of all Israeli manufacturing workers. By the late 1980s Koor was bleeding money, in one year losing almost $900 million. The government pressed the banks for the usual waiving of some debts and the usual rescheduling of loans at lowered interest rates. This bail-out, still in the pipeline, was necessitated by an American bank which called in its loans to Koor. If Israel's largest corporation failed to repay its foreign debt, then Israel's national credit rating would sink. So far, that is what's happening so the government is almost guaranteed to finance another bail-out of socialist enterprise.

Another socialist victim of the banks was the Clalit Health network. According to Yisrael Kessar, the Secretary General of the Histadrut, in one year $20 million of debt had risen to $200 million as a result of the recycling of old debts to pay off immediate commitments. Now figure it out, the Histadrut leader is claiming 1000% interest on loans.

In the last three cases – the kibbutzim, Koor and Clalit – the bank which lent most of the money was another Histadrut company, Bank Hapoalim. Since Koor is the industrial arm of the Histadrut, the kibbutzim the agricultural arm, Clalit the health arm and Hapoalim the financial arm of the same Histadrut, aren't the very same people lending to and borrowing from each other? Okay, the answer is yes. Now why would Hapoalim, the banking socialists, try to bankrupt the other socialists?

There is an answer, believe it or not. Alvin Rabushka claims, 'Hapoalim is extracting deadly interest from its own companies because socialists are too ideological to get along.' Not so simple. Everyone knows the government will eventually bail out everyone. It can't let all the farmland of the country rot, 75% of the health clinics shut down or 18% of the industrial output disappear. Actually it can and should but everyone knows it won't, so the bigger the debt, the more likely a bail-out becomes. Within this system, the Histadrut gets even more money into its coffers. Bank Hapoalim can happily bankrupt its fellow travellers and in the end it will receive the debts back in public money.

Now we must not forget that the government is the majority shareholder of Bank Hapoalim, amongst the other banks. The more Bank Hapoalim earns, the more the government earns from its ownership of the bank. So not only does the bank gain from cruel interest, so does the government. That goes a long way to explaining why the government permits the cruelty to carry on.

Right now the government claims it is trying to sell the banks and the more a bank is worth, the more it will get. So profit at all costs is the byword. Inside the banks, the current managers will have to prove their worth to the new owners, whoever they may be. So the bigger the profit, the more likely they will be to keep their jobs.

Naturally, the public and small businesses are the victims of this usury gone mad. But the banks have no reason to close small businesses if they can get a share of a hopeful firm. In return for easing credit and spreading debt, the banks have taken over thousands of little enterprises. And when a bank takes them over, the ultimate owner is the owner of the banks, the government.

So why would the government want to sell off the banks? As it is, the banks themselves are by far the most profitable businesses in Israel, recording profits that are the envy of even the diamond industry. Through debt negotiations, the banks, thus the government, own most of the health, agriculture and industrial sectors of the nation. Now add the small businesses, and the government has the ultimate control of almost all the money made in Israel. Prof. Eitan Berglas, chairman of the Board of Bank Hapoalim, admitted if the government chose to nationalise the banks instead of sell them, it would nationalise almost the whole economy.

So far, the banks have been a drain on the government. It has cost $7.5 billion to buy the worthless stocks after the crash of 1983, it has cost about $6 billion to bail out the agricultural sector after interest rates killed it and add together the price of a Koor bail-out with endless Clalit bail-outs and the government has spent over $15 billion just to keep bank victims solvent. If spent on Soviet immigration, that same $15 billion would have created 300,000 new jobs thus making a success out of the fiasco of the immigration wave of 1989-91.

As it stands now, the Israeli citizen pays taxes to finance bail-outs. But let us not forget that the public's wages have been frozen since 1985 and despite allowances added to the paycheques, earnings have not remotely kept up with the COL addition to credit. And if the interest rates, the COL additions and the frozen wages weren't enough, there is still another complication.

In 1986 the government created a new shekel which was valued at 1.5 to the dollar. To keep the currency artificially low, the government occasionally devalues it causing a run on foreign currency if news leaks too soon. In the five years from 1986, the shekel rose to 2.3 to the dollar, or about 70%.

Israelis are not allowed to hold foreign currency. They are stuck earning and saving in shekels. In five years their currency rose 70% while the COL rose 20% in each of those years, or about 200% in total. That means Israelis lost 130% of their money's value. Yet prices rose in step with the COL. Israelis then must work 1.3 days more to buy the same things they could five years before.

Joel Bainerman simplifies matters: 'Say the government let the currency float naturally. Today its true value would be close to four to the dollar. Then everything would be okay. Israelis would have four shekels in the bank for every 2.3 that they have today and they could live half normally. As it stands the government has kept inflation to 20% a year and they're proud of that. Anywhere else, 20% inflation would mean a revolution. In Israel today, buying has been curtailed, so inflation is down relatively. But the country is in a deep depression because its people are holding on to a currency so overvalued as to be worthless in foreign currency markets.'

There is a story that illustrates the sad straits the shekel has fallen into. An Israeli in Amsterdam enters a house of ill-repute and asks the madame for a lady who has seen it all because he wants to do something really dirty. She says she has just the girl for him, fearless and kinky. They are introduced and the Israeli whispers his request in the young lady's ear. Her face turns ashen, she screeches and then slaps the Israeli. 'My God,' said the madame, 'what does he want to do to you?' The tearful and shocked lady of the night replies, 'He wants to pay me in shekels.'

BANKING PRACTICES AND OTHER BREACHES OF ETHICS

Here are some of the practices legally employed by the banks, since the government is in no rush to quell sneaky tactics that send public money into its coffers.

1. *Overdraft* – If an Israeli falls behind in his payments, he may request overdraft facilities from his bank. The banks were at first reluctant, but they soon learned there was a fortune to be made by charging interest on overdrafts and began encouraging the practice. Today, the average Israeli is the proud possessor of a $250 overdraft. In 1989, 29% of the profits of Israeli banks came from overdraft interest. That adds up to almost $2 billion in revenue just from keeping Israelis in debt.[6] It's a great system.

2. *Paying Bills* – In normal countries, a utility bill is paid by mail. Not in Israel. Bills there must be paid at the bank or post office. Up until 1985 the banks were allowed to charge only a minimal commission for processing bills. As a result of the economic plan of that year, all supervision was removed and commissions were raised tens of percent even on standing orders. The banks also charge an arm and several legs to process cheques.

3. *Tax Reductions* – The government allows the banks and only the banks to present financial reports to the stock exchange which calculate the proceeds on capital after reducing the effects of inflation. Further, the banks are allowed to subtract 33% of its revenue/loss for inflation when the inflation rate hasn't been above 20% in five years.[7] The reasons for these tax breaks are to earn more for the ultimate legislators of tax laws, the government.

4. *Saving Bonds* – Let's say an Israeli wants to avoid the government and put his money into a private fund. It won't work because these funds are required by law to invest almost three-quarters of their income in government bonds. The government offers interest

on the bonds according to how much political clout the funds have. The powerful insurance companies receive bonds that gain 5.2% annually while the lowly provident funds get only 4.5% return on the bonds they must purchase. Meanwhile, the banks offer twice this unlinked interest so customers, as much as they distrust the banks, are directed towards them.[8]

5. *Interest On Interest* – According to *Ma'ariv* (April 1987), who did an excellent exposé of banking practices in 1987, Bank Mizrachi charges interest on interest already taken on credit in the same month. For instance, if a person has a 10,000 shekel debt and the interest rate is 10%, the bank should charge 1,000 shekels interest. However, Bank Mizrachi added the 1,000 shekel interest charge on to the debt, meaning the client would be paying 10% of 11,000 shekels or 100 shekels more than what he agreed to.

6. *Computer Games* – When a client does find an error, the same Bank Mizrachi claims it's because of computer error. In one case a client discovered he was being overcharged on interest he was paying. The bank owned up to the error but would not pay the difference between when the overcharging began and the value of the money at the day's rates had the correct interest been paid. The bank claimed the computer software could not be reprogrammed to make the calculation.

However, the same software was found operable when a similar error was found in favour of the bank. Another client deposited a cheque two years before which wasn't honoured. The bank discovered its own mistake and charged the client according to the rates of two years before. This time the computer worked beautifully.

7. *Damn Computer Error Again* – Bank Mizrachi and one other unnamed bank were ordered by the Bank of Israel (the country's combination of supervisor and federal reserve) to alter their software. After regular inspections it was discovered that the computers were programmed to charge higher interest than declared by bank policy, a practice thought to be common among other banks as well.

8. *Holding Bad Cheques* – Mizrachi was caught in a practice again believed to be widespread. When this bank bounces a cheque it fines the customer twice: once for the cheque and again by taking the amount of the cheque out of the account and replacing it only after a few days. The money taken from the account is placed in the bank's own account to gain interest and then replaced back into the customer's account. In the meantime he has lost his three days of

interest. A later investigation proved Banks Leumi and Discount use this trick.

9. *Holding Good Cheques* – One customer of Bank Discount has a typical story. 'I brought in a cheque for $3,000 from an American client and tried to deposit it. I was told it wouldn't be credited to my account for three weeks because that's how long it takes to send it to America and back. Five weeks and many arguments later it returned. It was endorsed after a few days and stayed in Discount's hands for weeks gaining interest before they'd release it to me.'

10. *Forgetting To Cancel Standing Orders* – One customer of a mortgage bank, Tefahot, repaid his mortgage with a standing order at Bank Hapoalim. After falling out with Hapoalim, he requested the standing order be cancelled by Tefahot. Three times he cancelled the standing order but the bank still sent out the order and charged him for the bounced cheque. For months the bank added these charges to the mortgage and nothing he did could cancel the order. One day he requested a second mortgage for home improvements. It was rejected because his standing order cheques had bounced for two years even though he had not missed a personal payment to the bank in all that time.

DISHONOUR AMONG THIEVES

Throughout Israel, people have anxiety attacks every time they step into a bank even to deposit money. Israelis despise their banks with unbridled passion, and fear them even more. Now imagine you are an Israeli who must choose a bank because life is infinitely more complicated without one. You hate them all but you will select the best of the lot as your bank. Now which one would you choose after investigating the financial market? Would it be . . .

Bank Igud – This is a subsidiary of Bank Leumi and thus the controlling interest belongs to the Jewish Agency, the keepers of most American donations to Israel. But the real owner of the bank is the government, which purchased Igud's shares from the public after the crash of '83. It was Igud who proposed not only that the government bail out the banks but also compensate them for the trouble they took in almost bankrupting the state. In the end the government actually accepted Igud's proposal, paying the banks 3% of the lost shares' value at the inflated price manipulated by the banks. Igud appointed Moshe Zanbar, Chairman of the Board of Igud's parent company, Bank Leumi, as salesman for the bank. Since Zanbar is also a director on the board of the Jewish Agency

Trust controlling Leumi, he is clearly not going to sell the bank in a hurry. The government ordered Igud to look for a buyer and it appointed the last person on earth who would gain by selling the bank, the sole selling agent for the bank – this is illegal, everywhere but Israel.

So where does this conflict of interest lead? To Drexel Burnham Lambert, an American consortium driven to bankruptcy for illegal trading. They co-operated with the Jewish Agency in order to buy the bank. A new conflict of interest. And as a condition for buying the bank, they agreed to allow Zanbar to continue as its Chairman of the Board. And another conflict of interest. Now how will Zanbar sell the bank, at an experienced interest-paying market price or to a nice company working with the benevolent Jewish Agency and promising him a chairmanship in return for a little understanding?

Corruption from on high encouraged one resourceful clerk to take matters into her own hands. She started her own swindling operation within Igud. In November 1988 many clients were horrified to learn that a clerk in the shares department of the Jerusalem branch, Ruth Amar, had cheated them of their money. She had encouraged clients of the bank to sign a power of attorney agreement, secretly giving her control of their bank accounts. She then proceeded to embezzle the accounts, actually running a bank within a bank. Over a million dollars was embezzled, leaving many customers penniless.

Another big-time Igud swindle came to light in September 1990 when the bank announced that a Tel Aviv branch manager had embezzled over $10 million.[9] The manager had executed forward transactions by opening foreign currency accounts with clients' money under fictitious names. For over a year he invested money in the dollar against European currencies but his forecasts were mostly wrong and the debts accumulated. But this was not the last nor the biggest fraud as we shall soon discover.

United Mizrachi Bank – Mizrachi is the Orthodox religious bank and, in contrast to Bank Hapoalim which is owned by the Labour Party, it is said that Mizrachi owns the National Religious Party. Until recently this bank actually gave preferential credit to members of the NRP but was stopped by a Bank of Israel directive. Still, all policy decisions are decided by a committee, 40% of whose members are ministers and party officials of the NRP.

There is a story that illustrates the dilemma of Mizrachi's greed and corruption in light of its religious ownership: A man walks up to a Mizrachi teller and tells her, 'I wanna make a goddamn deposit.' She can't believe he said that and asks him to repeat his request. 'I wanna make a goddamn deposit,' he demands again. The teller is aghast, calls the manager over and explains what's been happening.

The manager approaches the customer and says, 'We're a religious bank. We can't have you cursing in here.'

The customer insists, 'I came in here to make a goddamn $10 million deposit.'

'What!' replies the manager while pointing to the teller, 'and this bitch wouldn't help you?'

Mizrachi may be religious but it's up to its skullcap in shady dealings.

Under its chairman, Aharon Meir, Mizrachi made a number of transactions involving very large sums of money which were omitted from its financial reports. But neither Meir nor the bank faced charges for this despite the conclusions of the Beiski Report that a felony had been commited.[10] But Meir could not avoid being sued by an English citizen, Theodore Reitman, for fraud.

Reitman had held shares in the Israel Company since 1969 which, by 1981, had stopped yielding dividends. He informed the company that he wished to sell his shares and they found a buyer for him, Aharon Meir of Mizrachi Bank. Meir bought the shares, forgetting to tell Reitman that he was privy to some rather good news: the company was about to issue new shares and lots of them. Meir, the sly old fox, as well as being Chairman of the Board of Mizrachi, was also on the Executive Committee of the Israel Company. In the year between July of '81 and '82, share prices on the Israel Company rose 435% and Meir earned $900,000 from Reitman's stocks. Reitman sued Meir and won. The judge went so far as to claim that Meir had lied to the court during testimony.[11]

In this overview, we will be skipping over two of Israel's three biggest banks. Of the two, Leumi and Hapoalim, enough has been written about their dealings to give a fair idea of the state of their internal operations. Both banks initiated the shares manipulation that robbed Israelis of most of their savings. In addition Hapoalim is the bank which bankrupts kibbutzim and Histadrut organisations, eventually forcing the public to bail them out. And Leumi gave its former chairman, Yaphet, several million of its clients' dollars and sent him on a permanent vacation abroad.

That leaves Bank Discount open for examination and this bank will not disappoint the reader intensely interested in lurid displays of power.

Bank Discount – This is Israel's only family-run bank, founded in 1935 by Leon 'Jock' Recanati. Jock built his bank into a huge holding company controlling 22 industrial firms, four investment houses, six finance operations, 13 building companies, 15 marketing companies and one very big shipping company that has performed secret arms transports for the government. The bank also had subsiduaries in Switzerland and America. Recanati's son Raphael took control of Discount's board in 1981, appointing his own son, Ehud, as his assistant. The Beiski Report, following the share crash of 1983, declared that 'Raphael and his son Ehud were unfit to hold any position in the Israeli banking system'.[12] They were given three months to resign and hand over control of the bank to the government.

For some reason, Discount's board wanted to keep Raphael on, despite the fact that by 1986 the bank had accumulated a total debt of $18 million. This doesn't mean the bank had been running at a loss for 50 years but rather the losses of the 1980s outstripped all the profits of the previous half-century. Raphael had been largely responsible for the astronomical losses and it was he who led Discount into the grimy world of stock manipulation. Yet with the bank and country barely solvent in 1984, he drew a $1.4 million salary, increasing it to $1.7 million the next year.

Still hanging on to power as the only bank executive fingered by Beiski not to voluntarily step down, Raphael made a blunder. He did not block the appointment of Michael Bruno as head of the Bank of Israel. According to *Ha'aretz* finance reporter, Nechemia Stroessler, 'Before that time, the Recanatis had used influence in political circles to pull strings in order to obtain the appointment of a governor who would not clash with them.'[13]

Bruno used all his governing powers to try to get Raphael out of Bank Discount and to force the bank to come to terms with the government over its sale. Raphael used all his money and power to hold on to the bank. He was a close friend of the then Prime Minister Shimon Peres and appealed for his support against Bruno. But Peres was reportedly reluctant to defy Bruno so Raphael had such figures as Baron Edmund de Rothschild write to Peres with the message that 'harming the name of the Recanati family is as serious as harming my own name'.[14]

It now came to a cabinet vote: would the government force the Recanatis to leave their bank and hand it over to them for sale, or would Recanati's power win the day, allowing him to stay at the helm? Peres abstained from the vote thus keeping a modicum of integrity, and a very split government demanded the resignation of Raphael and immediate negotiations for the transfer of control of Discount to the government in order to be able to sell the bank.

The next day Raphael resigned, leaving behind a board filled with hand-picked Recanati loyalists.

When the time came to negotiate transfer of ownership to the government it was clear how those innocent bureaucrats had fallen into Raphael's trap. He had sold them all of Discount's holdings and the negotiators thought they had got the better of the deal. Little did they realise how hard it is to sell a bank when several dozen holdings are involved.

Not many businessmen will buy a shipping company if it means taking over a supermarket chain. Conversely, Robert Maxwell was willing to buy Discount's industrial holdings but wanted no part in purchasing the bank.[15]

Moreover, Raphael stalled on the transfer agreement until May 1990. That meant the government would be offering a tender on the bank in the summer, which is a slow period for international banking. Final bids were set for 12 September, only one week after Labour Day, when banks begin their buying season. That would not give any bank enough time to consider the proposed tender but one, Discount itself, which knew its own financial state better than anyone else.

By 12 September, Recanati had won. He used whatever means necessary to scare off all buyers. His was the sole bid for Discount and it looked to all the world that he had prevailed.

Then the decision to prosecute the bankers implicated in the shares crash came tumbling upon him. Under Israeli law, a convicted felon cannot control a bank and until the trial ended, no one could be sure if he was going to be indicted or not. This was just the pretext Bruno needed to block to sale of Discount to the Recanatis.

It had been five years since the government promised to recoup its losses by selling off the banks it acquired and not a single one had been sold.

Two banks were supposed to be sold. The government entrusted Igud with its own sale and it attempted a deal with the fallen investment house, Drexel Burnham Lambert, on condition that the Chairman of the Board keep his job and ties remain to the former owners, the Jewish Agency. Then the government tried its own hand at selling Discount only to become fumbling amateurs in the hands of the unscrupulous Recanatis.

In the summer of 1991, the Supervisor of Banks, Amnon Goldschmidt, came up with a solution. The Supervisor is entrusted with keeping the banks honest and the public protected from shady practices. Goldschmidt had represented mortgage banks to the government finance committee and convinced them to raise fines on people who had the temerity to pay off their mortgages early. He proposed selling the banks on the stock exchange. (Wasn't that where all the trouble began in the first place?) His reasoning was deceptively logical. By splitting Discount holdings and selling them separately, the bank could be sold, and by selling all the other banks, money could be immediately raised to finance Soviet immigration.[16]

How thoughtful and humane. What he forgot to mention was that the Recanatis, with their estimated $400 million in assets would buy back controlling shares in Discount 30 seconds after trading began, followed by the Histadrut who would purchase Hapoalim back in twice the time.

If there is a hero in all this, it might be Bruno. But one cannot forget that Bruno was acutely aware how badly the public is being treated by the banks and had taken only a few steps towards a national rescue operation. According to government thinking, the banks must be incredibly profitable in order for them to be sold at the highest possible price. Bruno had forced the Recanatis out on one hand, but had turned a blind eye to the endless exploitation of Israel's people on the other. There are no heroes in a government which controls 90% of Israeli banking, just vested interests masquerading as public servants.

Agriculture Bank – This is a government-run bank whose main clients are the Jewish Agency and farmers. One of these clients is Doron Gruper, son of Pesach Gruper, head of the Farmers Association. This organisation is affiliated with the Liberal Party faction of the Likud headed by Finance Minister Yitzhak Modai. Pesach Gruper is a member of the Knesset belonging to Modai's faction. He sits on the Knesset Finance Committee which approves government allocations.

In 1990 Doron Gruper received about $220,000 to cover his farming debts from the Knesset Finance Committee, on which his father sat. When Agriculture Minister Raful Eitan discovered the transfer of funds, he termed it 'corrupt'.

Not satisfied with mere nepotism for monetary gain, in 1990 Doron also made a concerted effort to become chairman of the Agriculture Bank. Since his father is an associate of the Finance Minister, such a candidacy would be patently illegal in any normal country, but in the diseased democracy of Israel, he has an excellent chance of seeing his fondest wish come true.

In the spring of 1991, the Agriculture Bank succeeded in securing $32 million from the Treasury to tide it over until bankruptcy. Since this bank was already insolvent, there was no real point in the public supporting its continued existence. The executives of the bank knew they had no real case for receiving government help so they tried to deceive the Knesset Finance Committee. First they convinced the Finance Minister and comrade of Pesach Gruper to approve their request for funding. Next it was off to the Finance Committee for approval. Normally junior executives present such requests to the committee yet for this meeting the bank sent the Director-General of the Treasury, Shalom Zinger, as well as its budget director and the chairman of the Government Companies Authority to present its case. The appearance of such a high-level trio of lobbyists backfired. The Committee became suspicious of the loan. MK Avraham Shohat, a Committee member, told the triumvirate, 'When I see you three here, I know there's something going on.'[17]

Indeed something was going on, for the Chairman of the Finance Committee, Moshe Zeev Feldman, declared the meeting 'confidential', and barred witnesses from discussing anything they heard with journalists. Feldman justified his declaration by claiming the public might be shied off from using the bank if its financial status was revealed. This explanation did not fool other Committee members who were well aware that the 'customers' of this bank were primarily the Jewish Agency and the Farmers Association. What the public might be disgruntled about was the fact that $32 million was going to a bank about to be headed by Committee member Gruper's son. By the end of the meeting, the Committee turned down the bank's request for money.

Enter Bank Supervisor Amnon Goldschmidt once again. He convinced the committee to approve the request of the Agriculture Bank for $32 million. His reasoning was was simple: if the bank didn't get the cash, it would not have sufficient capital to balance its outstanding loans. How this argument swayed the Committee is anyone's guess but one Committee member, MK Chaim Kaufman, refused to participate in the vote saying the money transferred to the bank was pointless since the bank was already insolvent.

But it's solvent enough to someday approve Doron Gruper as its director. And if that day comes, one will better understand why the Knesset Finance Committee, whose Minister is Yitzhak Modai, whose fellow party member is Pesach Gruper, handed over the money to the Agriculture Bank.

North American Bank – This bank began operations in 1978 with $30 million of start-up funds given by several investors including Nissim Gaon. To refresh the reader overwhelmed with Hebrew names, Gaon was the Swiss millionaire who backed the avocado plant in Mexico where Amiram Nir last operated before his untimely death.

There was something about Latin America that attracted this bank to do business there. According to *Ma'ariv*, by June 1985 the losses of the bank were out of this world. Over $12 million were lost on the shares crash, $7.2 million disappeared as a result of fraud, and $2.25 million granted to companies in Panama were at risk because of the country's insecurity. Now what was this Israeli bank doing in Panama with customers' money? Readers of this book shall never know but are asked to remember that in Panama, companies do not have to register the names of their owners.

Like most of the other banks, North American Bank (whose acronym is the fitting NAB), lost its shirt in the shares crash. But unlike other banks, it did not sell out to the government, preferring to bail itself out. It helped that most of its shareholders were 'interested parties' within the bank, who did not demand instant repayment, and not the outraged public.

Ever incorrigible even after the crash, NAB continued manipulating its shares on the market. In October 1984, the bank granted credit of $4 million to seven clients in order to buy its shares. The atmosphere of corruption at the bank led to a massive and complicated case of theft that made Igud's $10 million embezzlement seem like loose change. While customers were being embezzled in Jerusalem's Igud branch, three blocks away at NAB, patrons of the establishment were being robbed blind by branch manager Moshe Stern. He simply stole about $30 million from his mostly North American Orthodox clientèle.

Stern skipped the country but when later tracked down in Paris, most of the money was gone. This led investigators to suspect that the money was given to haredi institutions and yeshivas. The investigation did prove that Stern was not alone in NAB theft. The Director General of NAB, Hadassah Munsa, was also charged with stealing from the bank accounts and while Stern got seven years in jail, Munsa received five.

And onward did the investigators reveal the conspiracy. Soon after the first two convictions, the chairman of NAB management, Yehoshua Halperin, was charged with theft. He was joined by Shmuel Barzel, NAB's well placed legal advisor and Director of the Board of the bank, who was charged with defrauding numerous customers.

Now try to follow closely because here's where the politicians come into the picture. Jerusalem city councillor, Morris Rejwan, discovered that he had $1.3 million stolen from his account by Halperin. Did he go to the police like any honest politician would be obliged to do? No, he demanded his money back or he'd squeal to the cops.

However, when Yehoshua Halperin outlined his plan for unofficially granting customers loans at extremely high interest rates, Rejwan was more than keen to get a piece of the action. When he was finally caught, he had already seen a $6 million profit. He kept out of prison by giving evidence against Halperin, who was convicted of theft, false entries in a bank ledger and fraud.

The investigation of NAB led to a most unexpected trail that stopped on the doorstep of Health Minister Ehud Olmert. While Halperin was under investigation, his good friend Olmert called a senior police investigator, Yoram Gonen, and inquired if Halperin could leave the country. Olmert was called to testify at Halperin's trial by the prosecution which was interested in Olmert's interference or inquiry, depending on what his real motives for the call were. Certainly Olmert and Halperin shared some profitable times together. Olmert received a loan of $50,000 from NAB to purchase a home. The terms were most favourable, nothing had to be returned. Five years after taking the loan, Olmert had not made even one payment on it. When this disclosure went public, was Olmert fired from the government? Come on, this is Israel!

Once again the reader will ask, isn't there some body like the Securities Exchange Commission watching over bank activity on behalf of the Israeli public? Well there is, we keep telling you: the Bank of Israel. Way back in 1984 the BOI discovered that $24.5 million of credit granted by NAB was at high risk. This was three times more than the liquid capital of the bank and far more than was permissible. Clearly, the clients of NAB were at great risk, but needless to say nothing was done to protect the public.

First International Bank – FIB is a privately owned bank that was founded by the government. Back in 1972, Finance Minister Pinchas Sapir decided that Israel needed another bank. He arranged the merger of two existing banks, the Foreign Trade Bank and the Export Bank (if anyone can figure out the difference, send a note to the publisher and you'll win a choice of Israeli party favours) to form the First International Bank. Now there must have been a purpose to founding this bank. Daniel Doron, an expert on the Israeli economy, says, 'Sapir didn't do anything by accident. He ran the treasury like his own personal kingdom. And he certainly contributed to the general public perception that Labour was corrupt.'

Of Sapir, *Ha'aretz*'s financial expert Nechemia Stroessler writes, 'Until 1977 the Histadrut had a big daddy in the Treasury, Pinchas Sapir. He was their patron. Everyone in the Histadrut understood that for survival, one had to pray in his direction every day.'

Sapir's use of patronage, to put it mildly, made the news constantly. In one case, a man named Allison requested help from Sapir to expand his foreign sales. Sapir turned his request down. But Allison was a fast learner. He donated $250,000 to the coffers of the Labour Party. Unsurprisingly Sapir had a sudden change of heart and granted Allison a million dollars in export subsidies.

Now knowing a little about the man, one would expect that the bank he founded would run a parallel function to Hapoalim, that is, supporting the Labour Party, Histadrut, the kibbutzim and other like-minded organisations. But that is not what happened. Sapir, or whoever in the government told him to make a bank, had other ideas.

Sapir invited a Pennsylvania bank to buy 42% of FIB leaving the government 26% to play with (the remainder stayed in common stock). After this agreement, the Pennsylvania bank dropped out of the picture when an American businessman named John D. Marsh bought its FIB shares.

Interested parties went looking for John D. Marsh and he was nowhere to be found and no one had ever heard of him either. Strange too, was the government's decision to sell a majority position in an Israeli bank to an American bank. No other Israeli bank is controlled from abroad, because Israel's enemies could buy control and wreak total havoc on the bank and its clients.

After John D. Marsh was found to be a phoney, rumours floated through the Israeli financial world that the bank had been taken

over by Arabs. In large part to quell the gossip, the bank revealed
that John D. Marsh was really Shaul Eisenberg, the richest Israeli
in the Far East and probably the Middle East as well. His money
largely comes from ventures in the Orient as a writer for *Asia Today*,
and *Readers Digest* Asian editions explains, 'Eisenberg's fingerprints
are found in Taiwan, South Korea, Singapore, everywhere along
the Pacific Rim. He worked with Marcos closely. But somehow
he covers all his tracks. Nonetheless, he is literally Israel's trade
attaché to the whole Far East.'

Joel Bainerman simplifies matters: 'He is Israel's biggest arms
dealer. If a régime needs Israeli expertise without letting anyone
know, they call Eisenberg.'

According to Andrew and Leslie Cockburn in their book, *Dangerous Liaison*, 'To understand Israel, it is necessary to know Eisenberg.
There are many rich Israelis but by common assent, he is the
richest of them all. He represents the ultimate confluence of arms,
intelligence and political power.'

One thing Eisenberg did not appear to need was a bank but he
became quite obsessed for a while with FIB and in 1978 he bought
all non-government shares from the remaining shareholders. That
left just Eisenberg and the government as owners and it made no
real sense for either of them to have been involved in this most
fledgling of operations. Unless, the bank was a handy funnel for
secreting foreign (read Asian) currency into Israel.

The logic behind such an argument fades quickly when Eisenberg
sold his shares in FIB and they were taken over by a failing financial
corporation called Danot. Danot was totally mismanaged and on
the brink of bankruptcy. To stave off the inevitable disaster, it sold
a 28% ownership of FIB to Bank Discount but even this infusion of
cash could not prevent Danot's landing up in receivership.

Once again FIB went up for sale and although Israeli businessmen
bid strongly on the bank, it was eventually sold to an American
tycoon by the name of Jack Nasser. But there was something
about Jack Nasser that was eerily similar to Shaul Eisenberg.
Nasser had made his fortune manufacturing textiles in Marcos's
Philippines and had extensive ties and interests throughout the Far
East. Something there was about this bank that attracted Asiaphiles
to its ownership.

But although Nasser was the official owner of FIB, it was still
another John D. Marsh pretence. Nasser was neutralised from the
outset. He didn't attend board meetings and was even denied an
office at the main branch. This was certainly rude treatment for

someone who supposedly controlled 32.6% of FIB's capital and 51% of its voting power. If he wanted to he could have voted himself a whole office building. Clearly someone else was seated behind the throne.

In a mere 14 years the bank changed hands four times. The first sale to the Pennsylvania bank seems to have been an obsfuscation intended to leave a paper trail behind the intended owner, Eisenberg. The announced sale to John D. Marsh was clearly intended to mask Eisenberg's acquisition of the bank. Why was Eisenberg so determined to hide the fact of his ownership of FIB? And what strangely bashful owner was Jack Nasser fronting for? *Ha'aretz*, on 9 September 1990 did a little investigative reporting on the bank and discovered hints of connivance between the Israeli government and one of the world's richest bankers, Edmond Safra.

First, Safra loaned Nasser the money to buy FIB shares without collateral. This should have been hint enough that Safra was the real owner of the bank. But *Ha'aretz* discovered correspondence between Safra and the Finance Minister of the time, Moshe Nissim, which hinted at more than a little collusion between Safra and the government over this bank. After Director General Bino Zadik* left FIB in 1987 for a better offer at Bank Leumi, Safra complained to Nissim about the move, claiming that 'he was only involved in the First International Bank as a result of Zadik's presence.' Clearly Safra entered the local banking scene at the behest of some Israelis. And although the public was kept in the dark about Safra's ownership, the government was acutely aware of it.

Nissim convinced Safra that Leumi, still reeling from the Yaphet scandal, needed Zadik. Shalom Zinger succeeded Zadik at FIB but not for long. By 1990 he was appointed Director General of the government Treasury. As Pinchas Landau observes, 'This is the first time that a banking executive went directly to the head of the Treasury. It's usually the other way around.'

The implication is that Zinger was a government man appointed to head FIB. At the very least his was a private appointment rewarded soon after with a lavish government position. Either way one must ask why the government was so interested in this supposedly privately owned bank. And for that matter, what was Safra's interest?

* According to a report in *Yediot Achronot* by Benny Barak and later confirmed by Barak to the author, Zadik was asked by the government to shore up the shekel by taking a suitcase full of FIB dollars and dumping them on the black market for shekels.

Safra is a Lebanese Jew who owns the Republican National Bank in New York. He once owned the Trade Development Bank but chose to become a millionaire several hundred times over by selling it to American Express. He does not need FIB in his portfolio.

Being a Lebanese Jew, Safra has enough understanding of the Middle East to have extensive ties throughout the Arab world and Asia. His position as a Jew in a hostile continent would seemingly be compromised if his ownership of FIB got around, or at least that's what Pinchas Landau believes was the reasoning behind Safra's reluctance to reveal his part in FIB until the game of hide and seek ended two months after the *Ha'aretz* article appeared in 1990. Bainerman disagrees. 'All his Asian clients knew he was a Jew and they wouldn't have ended profitable business with him because he owned one itsy, third-rate Israeli bank.'

Of government interest in the bank, a case can be made for the transfer of the North American Bank (NAB), to FIB's portfolio. After the NAB thefts, the government transferred the full ownership of NAB to FIB. There was no public tender as in the case of all the other banks, FIB was simply rewarded with a gift.

The government justified the transfer by claiming FIB's experience dealing with religious clients was the best as a result of its subsidiary ownership of a rather odd little establishment called the Poalai Agudat Yisrael Bank, which services elderly haredi clients mostly. Still the critics said if NAB wasn't profitable, FIB wouldn't have taken it. If it was profitable then it should have been sold by the government by open tender.

However deep the government involvement in this bank, one fact stands out: the bank has changed hands four times since being established less than 20 years before. It is difficult to fathom how a bank can maintain any consistent policies on credit and long-term aims if it changes hands every four or five years. And FIB's owners are not your run-of-the-mill businessmen, they are amongst the wealthiest Jewish magnates in the world. What attracted the likes of Nasser, Eisenberg and Safra to it in the first place is beyond immediate comprehension but a legitimate guess is involvement in international arms trading.

The day-to-day working of FIB is like any other Israeli bank only much greedier. Most competitors admit that FIB is unique in its ways of extracting money from its clients' accounts through unwarranted interest. According to a *Ma'ariv* investigation in 1987, money at FIB takes a much longer route before it finally arrives in a client's account. Thus when a client sells shares

or cashes in a savings account, he loses a few days of interest.

Clients who put up their shares or savings as collateral against
credit provided by the bank, found that when they asked to sell
their shares, the money was delayed before entering their accounts.
A short investigation proved that after the sell order, the clients'
money took a ride through FIB's system. When a client opens a
share portfolio at FIB, he unknowingly opens a parallel portfolio.
The client's account has a prefix of 105 while the parallel account
has a prefix of 131. The 131 account is where money is deposited on
the day shares are sold, and only a day or two later does this money
arrive at the 105 account, the only account the client is aware exists.
Thus a likely situation exists, where the client's personal account
is in debit and paying the bank for it, while the 131 account is in
the black with the bank earning the interest. In inflation-plagued
Israel, such a delay taking place thousands of times a week, adds
up to real money.

Moreover, FIB actually charges the client for each transaction:
depositing the money in the 131 account without the client's
knowledge, transferring the money from the 131 to the 105 account
and then depositing the money into the 105 account. Clients, in
essence, had their money 'stolen' by FIB for a day or two and then
paid three times for the theft.

As you will recall, in Israeli banks, bad cheques are fined after a
similar amount is removed from the client's account for the bank's
own use. All other banks charge a management fee at the end of
each quarter for processing bad checks. FIB charges the account
management fee several times a month or quarter. Thus when
FIB charges interest, it is constantly on bank charges instead of
quarterly.

The First International Bank of Israel (its official acronym is
FIBI but the author finds FIB more appropriate and lyrical) runs its
clients through the same treadmill of interest on principal plus COL
on interest plus principal as do all the other banks. But it is unique
in the viciousness with which it pursues its creditors. A well known
Tel Aviv attorney calls it, 'the bastard bank. None of the other Israeli
banks, even the big ones are as prepared to terrorise creditors like
FIBI.' Yaacov Buzaglo, head of the Banking Victims Organisation
concurs: 'First International is the last bank anyone should cosign
a loan for. If things go wrong with them, your life is ruined.'

Your life might not be ruined if you have political connections.
On 31 January 1992 Kol Hair reported that MK Ariel Weinstein,

the Likud Deputy Head of the Knesset Finance Committee, cut a deal with FIB's Director General to forgive a $40,000 debt incurred by some well-placed guarantors. According to legal expert Moshe Negbi, both Weinstein and FIB broke numerous parliamentary and civil laws in this blatant display of favouritism.

Israeli banks have branches throughout the world. Bank Leumi has over 25 branches in New York alone as well as branches in such far flung localities as Frankfurt, Melbourne, Milan and Mexico City. Bank Hapaolim issues notes internationally floated by its subsidiary in the Antilles Islands. Anyone abroad who patronises an Israeli bank branch or purchases issues from an Israeli bank is supporting a corrupt banking system which results in the misery of hundreds of thousands of ordinary Israelis. As is the case with charitable donations to the Jewish Agency, anyone who supports an Israeli bank is contributing to human suffering and is thus partaking in an act of immorality.

CHAPTER FIFTEEN

Bankrupt Cows, Meadows, Sheep and Corn

The kibbutzim not along ago considered themselves the harbingers of a new equal society. And if equality means the whole country sharing their debts, then they've achieved their aim. The kibbutzim were always underachievers and covered their failures with government bail-outs. Let's summarise how this system of communal villages went $4 billion into debt in the 1980s.

In the early part of the decade, when the money supply was abundant and credit was easy, the kibbutzim borrowed to expand. There was no problem getting money – all a kibbutz needed to do was ask at any bank and the manager would hand it out without any more security than knowing the government would never allow the bulk of Israeli agriculture to go under.

Oded, a member of a modest-living and solvent religious kibbutz (the religious kibbutzim and a few dozen secular kibbutzim are the exceptions to the vast majority who ran up the debt) puts matters more precisely: 'They took out loans and bought swimming pools, villas, cars, fancy dining halls, state-of-the-art gymnasiums and trips around the world. They frittered the loans away.'

Of the money spent on new factories, former kibbutznik and now private economic consultant, Daniel Brod, suggests reasons why the investments mostly failed.

> When the system works it is based on the willingness of an individual to behave altruistically – to sacrifice personal gain or comfort for the good of the community. Studies suggest that individual identification with the kibbutz has deteriorated over the years, and this process no doubt contributed to the debt crisis; the irreconcilable rising expectations of individuals drove the kibbutzim to violate their budget constraints.
>
> Within industry, attention wasn't paid to the importance of marketing . . . Bad investments were also the result of the desire to achieve an idyllic, closed society . . . ventures with outside partners weren't given the weight that they should have. The kibbutz factory

225

was also seen as part of the kibbutz and unjustified efforts to save failing factories were influenced by undue emotional attachment and feelings of identification.[1]

This translates into a uniquely kibbutz-style method of blowing money intended for burgeoning industry. Each kibbutz viewed itself as a self-reliant entity, capable of earning its keep without inviting expert advice from the outside. If a kibbutz didn't have a marketing expert, then it would appoint a member as marketer. If it didn't have a resident economic expert, then some member would be asked to learn economics on the job. If a factory suffered production difficulties, then a member would be asked to master specific technology. All this to prevent partnerships with successful outsiders.

Bringing in outsiders meant paying them the appropriate salaries for an engineer, economist or marketer. This would upset the apple-cart since on a kibbutz there is ideally no salary difference between a doctor and chicken-feeder. Either the outside expert accepted a chicken-feeder's salary or stayed where he was overpaid.

Yet despite the ideology, the individual kibbutznik had become downright materialistic and demanded his yearly trip to London. Chicken-feeder and doctor alike were affected by the new influx of borrowed cash and demanded their piece of the treasure.

However, if the factory was losing money, it could not be closed because that would symbolise a failure of the kibbutz. And one of the primary reasons for factory failure was a kibbutz philosophy that insisted factory managers be constantly rotated, so no one would get big-headed and everyone would have an equal opportunity to botch things up.

Another weakness in the kibbutz system was the philosophy that all kibbutzim were part and parcel of the same federation and if one kibbutz suffered bad times, the others would pitch in to help out with a friendly loan. Thus, as Brod concludes, 'the kibbutzim perceived that no serious damage in terms of standard of living could befall them as a consequence of bad economic decisions.'[2]

A very bad perception, indeed, when most of the kibbutzim went into deep debt at the same time. Here's how it happened . . .

The kibbutzim pooled their money at their federation head-quarters where decisions were made how best to use it. When a kibbutz made a good profit, on say, the export of a crop, it wasn't worthwhile depositing it in an Israeli bank because there was little if any interest on savings. It was far smarter to loan the money out to companies refused bank credit at higher rates than the banks charged to acceptable creditors.

Mediators between the kibbutzim and the borrowers were hired and one after another robbed the financially innocent farmers blind. Just one mediator, a shark named David Balas, was given massive amounts of cash which he used to play the stock market instead of lend. He defrauded the kibbutzim of over $100 million.[3]

In 1988 the collective debt of the communes was over $4 billion. By then the annual output of the kibbutzim was $600 million annually. Debt repayment amounted to $530 million a year on interest alone, leaving just $70 million to pay back the principal, provided all human activity ceased. Even without life-sustaining expenses, it would have taken 60 years to repay a debt accumulated in just five years.[4]

While most Israelis are also in debt, few have friends as good as Shimon Peres. He arranged for the banks to waive $1 billion with the rest of the debt to be repaid at reduced interest over 20 years. Thus the banks and government, which are one and the same, rescheduled $40,000 worth of loans for every kibbutz member and waived $11,000 per kibbutznik. This cost the rest of Israel $1,200 per family.[5]

The kibbutzim cost more than just the price of bailing out their debts. The government also subsidises their inefficient farming practices. In 1988 the cost of protecting the farmers from cheap imports was $253 million. For instance 35.8% of each sip of milk an Israeli took, came out of his tax money.

The kibbutzim are pampered and protected. They have to be or 90% of them would be broke. Leftists worldwide point to the kibbutz as a socialist system that works. In fact, economically it doesn't work and never in Israel's history has it. As Daniel Brod notes: '. . . failed kibbutzim will continue to be a burden on the government budget and the economy . . . The kibbutzim will find it more difficult with each passing year to justify the present system under which they function.'[6]

The kibbutzim are deeply demoralised today. As *Yediot Achronot* notes, during the 1980s, over 50% of kibbutz offspring left the kibbutzim. In percentage terms, kibbutz offspring are more inclined than anyone else to emigrate.

According to Abraham Rabinovich:

A poll taken at 19 kibbutzim earlier this year [1991] showed that 28% favoured the idea of individual members earning money for

themselves from over-time work – a notion that contradicts the basic
kibbutz principle that no one earns more than anyone else, be he/she
a highly qualified engineer or a seamstress . . . One delegate noted
that the 28% probably represented a much higher percentage of the
younger kibbutz members and was thus a cause for real concern
about the future direction of the kibbutz movement.[7]

To accommodate these feelings, kibbutzim today are allowing
members to live in the kibbutz but work in the cities. That is a
significant concession and an admission that the communal work
ethic is not fulfilling to everyone.

Far, far more worrying are trends that signal trouble in the
social opportunities of kibbutz life. The kibbutzim have always
prided themselves on the lack of crime among their young. But
publicised cases of rape in recent days, including a gang rape of
one kibbutz teenage girl by eight kibbutz youths over four days,
is changing the perception of well adjusted kibbutz adolescents in
Israel. Something is very wrong with the kibbutzim and its youth is
beginning to rebel. If debt doesn't wipe out this hapless experiment
in communal settlement, then social discord just might.

JUST AS BROKE MOSHAVIM

Even though they survived on state subsidies and government
bail-outs and hogged an undeservedly large proportion of prime
land denied to private citizens, the kibbutz still acted as the
landed aristocracy of Israeli society. When hundreds of thousands
of Sephardic Jews arrived in the 1950s, they were sent to moshavim
because the kibbutzim were unwilling to accept them, partly
because the Sephardim weren't very often socialist and partly
because the kibbutzim were too often snobs.

The general situation of bankrupt moshavim under the care of the
Jewish Agency was reviewed. What follows is an addendum of gory
details. Let us permit Ezra Sohar to provide some background:

> The concept of the moshav was originally based on four principles:
> family farming, settler labour, mutual assistance and co-operative
> marketing. The first moshav was established in 1921. Today there
> are 450 moshavim, of which about 280 belong to the Histadrut
> moshav movement. The political establishment twisted it beyond
> recognition in its eagerness to control the moshavim, thus spawning
> a social, economic and demographic monster that cannot exist with-
> out a ceaseless flow of money. Today the moshavim are in economic
> and social distress, and many are on the threshold of collapse.[8]

Although moshavniks have, for the most part, purchased their own land and homes, the real owner is the government which licenses the farmers, and controls their destiny through the moshav committees and their purchasing organisations. Again we turn to Ezra Sohar:

> The committee is only the first layer of the mighty establishment that smothers the farmer. Above it is the purchase and credit association . . . They were established in order to centralize and economize on commodity purchase prices and to improve marketing profits. These organizations gained strength as time passed and rather than serving the moshavim, they came to dominate them. They decide what will be bought and through whom to market . . . They establish bureaucratic empires including company cars, entertainment in hotels and meals in luxury restaurants. They establish enterprises (many inept) including a plethora of packing houses, many unnecessary and doomed to fail. As all these decisions are made, the farmers are never consulted, only billed, whenever an enterprise collapses.[9]

It was the credit and purchase organisations which took the moshav farmers' money and ran up a debt of $2 billion in five years. They fell into the same trap as the kibbutzim, playing the stock and grey markets and the pattern of collapse was also the same.

The moshavim borrowed when interest was low in the early 1980s. In the second half of the decade, the interest rate rose to 200% and even at the best of times the gap between lending and borrowing was never lower than 40%. Since farming relies heavily on credit, selling all the produce didn't cover the interest. So new loans were taken and the cycle began again.

Yet no matter how deep the debt became the purchasing organisations continued squandering money on luxury villas, the mandatory tennis courts and gymnasiums and of course, high salaries for officials of the organisations. Drive through almost any moshav and one will see the handsomest homes in Israel and totally bankrupt families within them.

Now why did the moshavim buy homes beyond their means? Easy. They assumed, correctly, that the government would eventually bail them out. By 1988 the Knesset Finance Committee approved an agreement between the government and the banks that wiped out some of the debt and spread the rest of it over many years at 6.3% interest.[10] As generous as this agreement was, the one concluded by the kibbutzim after was even better, so by 1991,

the moshavim were pressing for even easier terms and as sure as
Shamir means dill in Hebrew, they'll get their way.

Farmers who try to be efficient find themselves defeated not just
by the government's banks but by the total control the government
has in the production and marketing of their produce.

IT'S KAFKA TIME ON THE OLD FARMSTEAD

The government totally controls the farmers through production
and marketing boards. Let's say a farmer wants to raise chickens.
He must register with the Poultry Marketing Board. They will
order him by law to produce a certain number of chickens and
no more. This board is obliged to keep in business weak moshavim
who can't raise chickens to save their lives. So, no matter how
cheaply one farm raises chickens compared to another, the public
must pay the average price between the most expensive producer
and the cheapest. There is no such thing in Israel as a brand-name
chicken or different brands of eggs. Almost all producers are under
the auspices of one production board and marketing company, a
Histadrut monopoly called Tnuva.

Sam Dubiner, Israel's grand old man of market reform, expounds
on the price of chicken in Israel:

> My research reveals economic waste created by the Poultry Board's
> marketing monopoly to be more than $2 billion annually . . . For
> the past three years I have been comparing prices of poultry in
> Florida and Israel . . . Average prices for fresh chicken in south
> Florida work out to $0.90 a kilo. The same fresh first-quality fryer
> in Israel is $6.50 a kilo, more than six times the price in south
> Florida.
>
> The most meaningful comparison . . . shows that it requires 90
> minutes on average to earn the cost of a kilo of chicken in Israel
> compared with five and a half minutes in south Florida. This makes
> chicken more than 15 times costlier in Israel.[11]

In order to provide work for inefficient farms that happen to be
considered vital for security, quotas are placed on the well run farms
for every item of produce imaginable, from avocados to citrus fruit
to dairy products to beef to flowers. And every farmer is obliged
by law to obey the quotas imposed on him by the boards.

And this isn't the end of the harassment. Farmers must market
most of their produce through Tnuva within the country and
through Agrexco, a government-Histadrut monopoly abroad.

The boards are inefficient and overbloated. According to Sam

Dubiner, Florida processing plants paid farmers $235 per ton of oranges in 1988 while Israeli farmers received only $90 a ton. For every $300 worth of fruit, Israeli farmers receive some $60 from the Citrus Board. The effects on Israeli citrus growers have been nothing short of devastating. Think of this. Only a decade ago weren't Jaffa oranges the most popular brand in Europe? When's the last time you've seen a Jaffa orange on the fruitstand? In just ten years Israeli citrus exports have fallen from over a million tons annually to less than 350,000. The industry, once the pride of Israel, is dying from government strangulation.

There may be hope on the horizon, however. Two brothers named Aharoni raised 20 tons of kumquats a year but the Citrus Marketing Board would only sell 5 tons.[12] The brothers sued the board and the High Court of Justice ruled in their favour. The way may soon be open to independent citrus marketing in Israel.

The bureaucracy breaks people and sends them abroad. And not only farmers. In fact, all Israelis are victims and perhaps 150,000 have escaped permanently to Los Angeles. In the next chapter, we dissect the heartless taskmaster, the deservedly despised Israeli bureaucracy.

CHAPTER SIXTEEN

Will Someone Get Those Bureaucrats Out of My Soup?

Politicians and bureaucrats are everywhere. No Israeli can escape them, no matter how hard he tries. They stick their noses into everything, especially into affairs that are none of their business. This includes Israel's sports – politicians meddle with both clubs and players – as well as its radio and television.

The country has only two TV channels, both of which are state-owned (there is no access to independent or satellite TV) and for which the public must pay an extortionate licence fee. Equipment used by Israeli Television (ITV) is antiquated and very expensive to maintain. Every year viewers must suffer the same poor quality of programmes, shoddy service and striking workers. According to one editorial, '(ITV) is a haven for featherbedders, a bureaucratic monstrosity and . . . a nationally owned institution whose employees care little for the national interest.'[1]

With an annual programming budget of less than $6 million, one can only imagine the poor quality of programming available to the Israeli public. Still, it is better than no programming at all, a scenario which seemed likely in March 1992. All television broadcasts were threatened with cancellation because of funding difficulties. The government's communications minister, the one person who could really make a difference, doesn't even own a TV set.

Sport and broadcasting are not the only sectors touched by the interfering hand of bureaucracy. Red tape, permits, licences and form-filling permeate every area of the citizen's life. Israelis must have their ID papers in proper order and on their person at all times. If a citizen needs his passport renewed, if an immigrant needs to apply for ID papers, if a tourist requires a visa extended, all must visit their local Interior Ministry office. If someone expects to find friendly, helpful staff gently guiding the client through the paperwork, then he is going to be sorely disappointed. Service is slow, surly and inefficient, and any good intentions a clerk may have will be thwarted by interminable queues, unnecessary paperwork and staff shortages. Nothing is simple in the Israeli system. A man wishing to go abroad on holiday must first receive permission to leave the country from his army unit. This will entail a journey in person to his unit's headquarters, even if they are located 200 miles away. Once the tourist-to-be has the necessary passport, ticket and army slip, he must pay a $125 bribe to the government in the form of a travel tax, in order to leave Israeli soil.

It goes without saying that the clerks do little to speed up or facilitate the process. Discussing the 1991 government Ombudsman's report which investigates complaints against the civil service, one editorial observes, 'The report provides numerous examples in which public sector employees . . . have, through ignorance, or in the worst instances, maliciousness, exercised their authority without considering that they are paid not to make the citizen's life miserable but to ensure the smooth running of society's business'.[2]

So why are so many Israeli bureaucrats determined to complicate the lives of fellow Israelis? One reason is the thwarting of the ambitions of large numbers of creative, bright Jews. Had these same bureaucrats lived in a free society, they would have found professional outlets for their energies. Many, no doubt, would love to run their own businesses but they, better than anyone else, know how the system drives independent workers insane with taxes, regulations, court appearances and daily harassment. Frightened away from self-fulfilment they devote their imaginations to terrorising those with the courage to try and survive outside the system that eats the souls of the bureaucrats themselves.

Israel's bureaucracy was invented by socialists and it developed along the same lines of those of the Soviet Union and Eastern Europe. But unlike Poland or Czechoslovakia, the powers-that-be in Israel are not prepared to break up the bureaucracy and with it all the hidden joys of socialism. As Stanford economist, Alvin Rabushka notes, 'Israelis are one of the few peoples who know why Yeltsin will never create a free society. The bureaucrats will never willingly give up their empire.'

YOU CAN'T GROW TEACHERS ON A CHERRY TREE

The bureaucrats demand control of all Israelis starting from the age they're weaned from their mothers' breasts. Pre-school children with working mothers need day-care and the government, through the Women's Employment and Status Division (WESD) of the Ministry of Labour and Welfare, makes sure it is provided haphazardly and inconsistently.

One of the two stated objectives of WESD is 'To encourage mothers of small children to participate in the labour force, especially in full-time and preferred occupations, with those holding jobs in industry at the head of the list.'

Now how can the government ministry in charge of day-care direct women to menial factory jobs and why should it? The latter question is best understood in light of the Israeli government's strategy of controlling the nation through a centralised economy. The ministry charged with providing day-care also pitches in to provide the economy with underpaid female workers.

Now how does WESD go about shifting mothers into industry? It charges a fortune for day-care, then offers subsidies for lowly paid mothers. The cost of government day-care for infants up to three years old is about $250 a month per child. If a woman earns less than $200 a month she pays only $70 for day care. The scale of parental contribution rises with income. A mother earning a paltry $400 receives no subsidy whatsoever and day-care eats up most of her salary. If she has two children in day-care, it costs more to keep them than she earns.

So, why work hard and get a promotion when the pay raise will possibly not cover the cost of looking after the children? The reader abroad no doubt cannot believe that day-care could have the power to affect employment so significantly. That is because day-care in normal countries is in the hands of private people who charge affordable rates.

If a child survives this system, he or she will go on to the kindergarten network. Once again, it's the government and teachers' union that have the children in the palms of their hands. Three weeks before the end of the 1991 kindergarten year, and giving just three days' notice, the Education Ministry announced that kindergartens would close half an hour earlier, at 12.30 p.m. instead of 1 p.m. Thousands of working mothers were asked to reschedule their jobs immediately or possibly even quit them. One government official feebly tried to explain the shortened classes as a favour to the children: 'It really is difficult for young children to stay in kindergarten for so many hours.'[3]

After the blissful years in kindergartens, the Israeli child must enter the real thing: elementary school. According to the 1991 State Comptroller's report, elementary school principals do not require an academic degree. All they need to do is undertake a three-year training course, which may be completed on the job. Sadly, only 27% of all principals had finished or were taking the course.[4]

And if the academic standards for principals are low, the teachers below them are wallowing in under-achievement. Israeli elementary school teachers are not required to have an academic degree and in fact, only 16% ever graduated from university. Yet as underqualified by world standards as these teachers are, according to the report, 'the educators themselves are not under the proper supervision needed to ensure that a high level of teaching is maintained'.

After suffering through the elementary school years with teachers who are barely better educated than their students, it's on to high school. Education is supposed to be compulsory and free but because the government has cut back its share of the teaching budget to 75% of the total, it is the parents who must make up the difference at a cost of about $300 per student. And because the government cut back classroom building despite the immigration wave, the teacher-student ratio soared past 40:1. Few teachers can maintain discipline. In the same way, because the government controls the textbook selection, classes are standardised, unimaginative and totally unspontaneous. As Shai Lachman, head of the Jerusalem Parents' Association says, 'Education is no longer a top priority in Israel.'[5] It was his association that forced high schools to grade all their teachers in a nationwide achievement test. The results couldn't have been very encouraging because the Histadrut teachers' union refused to allow them to be made public.

One of the tragic failures of Israeli education is the poor academic results of Sephardic children. With over half the Jewish population Sephardic, they constitute only 16% of the university population. However, they do dominate the drop-out rate overwhelmingly. Liberal educators have tried redressing the imbalance by integrating schools. The main result has been a fall in the standards of Ashkenazi high schools and terrific tension in the classrooms. According to a 1991 Tel Aviv municipal study, over 60% of the city's pupils had reported violent incidents at school.

The entire education system is a shambles. Hundreds of students needing special education have nowhere to go because the government isn't implementing programmes on their behalf. At university level, students suffer because the yeshivas have been bleeding the education budget. According to MK Avraham Shohat, the government invests $32,000 in the average yeshiva student versus $9,000 per university student. The effects on higher education have been tragic for Israel's academic standing worldwide.[6]

Parents who can afford it, send their children to private tutorials or pricey group lessons. Students whose parents cannot afford private lessons suffer deeply. The gap between the less well-off Sephardic and the richer Ashkenazic students is widening, leading to future inequalities and a division of Israeli society. One hopes that cool heads prevail when today's generation of Israeli students enter the workplace and find very different opportunities awaiting them.

The bureaucracy gets hold of infants in their cribs and doesn't let go no matter how hard the child struggles. It saps the child's intellectual curiosity, formalises his perceptions, disregards his worth and divides him from his people. But perhaps this is the most suitable education an Israeli student could need if he is to survive other bureaucratic garroting that will make a mockery of any hope for a normal adult existence.

ALWAYS A COP AROUND WHEN YOU DON'T NEED ONE

Israelis are arrested and jailed ridiculously often but according to Amnon Rubinstein (a genuine rarity, a reformist MK with integrity), only about 7% (based on 1983 statistics) of those arrested are eventually indicted. Thus some 93% of Israelis dragged to police stations for investigation have no business being there. But even if eventually exonerated, as Rubinstein says, 'An arrest is half an indictment, half a conviction. The suffering involved is indescribable.'

By far the greatest number of arrests involve debts presumed owed to the banks and the tax offices, both staffed by the most amoral of all bureaucrats. Commenting on two recent cases where a total of seven well-known Israelis were arrested and then found totally innocent in court, Rubinstein notes, 'The nightmare could happen to any Israeli . . . We've become used to the fact that the police, tax authorities, the production councils – I don't know how many bodies – have the right to arrest since the Knesset bestows this authority on every clerk. What difference does it make to an income tax official or police officer to send someone to jail? It means nothing to them.'[7]

According to Israeli law, it is illegal to detain someone merely suspected of a crime. The evidence must be airtight before an arrest is made. Nonetheless the most common reason given by police for arrests is, 'the requirements of investigation'. What that means is putting a suspect into jail until he breaks down and confesses.

Naturally, many suspects are given such treatment that confessions come easy but not always sincerely. There are a number of prisoners convicted on the basis of confessions made early in the investigation and occasionally justice triumphs much too late. In one sensational incident, Amos Baranes spent well over a decade in prison based on a false confession wrung out of him by the police.

Professor Kenneth Mann, an expert on Israeli criminal law, cites a number of reasons why the police get away with so many arrest abuses. First the courts are so backlogged that judges cannot properly evaluate warrant requests. Secondly, the court often doesn't inform the suspect of his rights to an attorney, nor is there a system of court-appointed lawyers for suspects unable to pay for their own defence. Half of the accused in Tel Aviv Magistrates Court trials are not represented by attorneys.

According to Mann, there are two ways to convict a suspect: get him to confess or collect evidence against him. 'In societies which respect human rights, the second method is, to use an understatement, preferable. However, it is also costly . . . For a financially strapped country like Israel, the direct approach is obviously more attractive.'[8]

Once in police custody, the suspects can be subjected to bodily persuasion. In 1980, 47.5% of all complaints against the police involved brutality. By 1987 the figure had risen dramatically to 77.1%.[9] The 1990 State Comptroller's report discovered that it takes up to two years for the police to investigate complaints of excessive force used by fellow cops, curiously close to the three-year statute of limitations for disciplinary offences. It was also found that 'Even if the complaint officer found the complaint justified, that by no means guaranteed that the police officer involved would be punished. Ninety of 149 officers who were found to be objects of a justified complaint were ultimately acquitted . . .'[10]

For proven brutality only eight out of 149 guilty policemen actually were sentenced in court. The Israeli Police protect their own before the public and subtracting the fear of retribution can turn a cautious cop into a bully. The attitude of Israeli police officers is very different from what one finds in Europe or the saner parts of America. They don't so much talk to the inquiring public politely as bark at them. They are trained to bellow as a means of winning respect and fear and often just can't break the habit even when it's inappropriate to intimidate someone. The police are the strong arm of the bureaucracy, enforcing the haphazard decrees of incompetent clerks throughout the civil service. They are mere actors for the big directors in the Knesset but they play their role with far too much relish and independence. And there is one hint of the coming end of all pretence of democracy in Israel: the decent, honest and law-abiding people of Israel fear their police force far more than they would like to admit.

THE YELLOW ROSE OF TAXES

No country taxes its citizens like Israel. And no taxpayer is as heavily burdened as the self-employed worker. If he earns half the average American wage he will be forced to pay a 48% income tax, an 18% VAT and over 15% towards social security, the excess of which goes straight to the government. Add it up, 81% of a self-employed worker's income is lost to direct taxes. And with only 19% of his income on hand, the end of taxation is not in sight. Israelis also pay property tax, land betterment tax (on the sale of real estate), excise duty, stamp tax, car licence tax and municipal tax, among others.

Until recently all VCRs coming into the country were charged a fixed tax of $440. In 1990 the tax was cut by 50% and much to the shock of VAT director Mordechai Baraket, smuggling was halved and customs duties quadrupled. The astonished bureaucrat observed, 'The more we lower the tax rate, the higher our revenues will be.'

The result of the gargantuan tax load is summarised by Jack Menes in a paper on tax reform published by the Institute for Advanced Strategic and Political Studies: '[The system collects taxes] in a way which creates inequities, stifles initiative and growth, turns most of its "clients" – the taxpayers – into petty cheats and fosters alienation and bitterness among the people towards the government . . .'[11]

As if the taxes themselves weren't enough of a burden, the income tax is collected from the self-employed in such a way as to add an additional tax on the original one. Income tax isn't collected at the end of the fiscal year like in normal countries, but is instead collected before the year begins and is assessed on the previous year's turnover and tax paid. Thus, without knowing how the forthcoming year will turn out, or even if in full knowledge of an off-year, the businessperson must pay last year's taxes for the coming year thus incurring a debt which may require a bank loan even before the first receipt comes in.[12]

At the end of the year, the tax people return money if the businessman had a poor year but without the additional interest incurred by the taxpayer as a result of the original tax payment. On the other hand, if the tax department underestimated the year's turnover, it will demand and receive the difference with interest calculated as well. But the tax people are hardly enthusiastic about returning money. And when an overestimation of income is made but the income tax authorities are slow to offer the promised rebate, the results, needless to say, can often be devasting.

All independent workers must pay the VAT collectors 18% of income every month, necessitating daily accounting on top of the yearly calculations demanded by the income tax and social security departments. An independent worker includes anyone unsalaried. So every piano teacher, plumber and newspaper vendor must add 18% to his bill and return the money monthly to the VAT authorities. In essence, all unsalaried workers are state tax collectors.

In 1990 the police arrested two senior income tax officials and nine private detectives along with two of their secretaries. The tax employees were selling confidential information to detectives, who in turn used the info against their clients' enemies, business rivals or spouses in divorce cases. Eventually a total of 13 private detectives were rounded up for paying off the two tax employees. According to two Tel Aviv detectives, 'For the right price you can get any information you want from any government office.' As one editorial commented, 'Once the corrupting of government employees becomes an accepted mode of behaviour, nothing can stay immune to abuse, even when it may endanger the very life of the country.'[13]

Wire-tapping and sending out confusing letters are among the many ways used to gather missing facts or just check up on people randomly. Thousands of Israelis each year receive ridiculous demands for tax payments because the law allows the taxers to make assessments based on pure guesswork. Tax terrorism is a fact for self-employed Israelis or the employers of salaried workers. Salaried workers are left alone since presumably not much can be squeezed out of them.

However, new sources of tax income are always sought out. In all normal countries, there are tax-exempt charities. Not so in Israel where even the most benevolent charities are assessed on non-profit activities and on the salaries of their workers. The effects of the Israeli tax system is ably described by Ezra Sohar:

'Although income tax brings in no more than 25% of the state's revenue, it severely damages the economy and public morale. It interferes with citizens' lives and makes labour so expensive that even though Israeli electronics engineers take home less than half an American engineer's salary, they cost their employers more. Israel's income tax hounds small businesses and the self-employed.

It brought into existence a huge industry of consultants and accountants. It spawned an underground economy. It set prices on an
unrealistically high level. It makes Israeli products non-competitive
on world markets unless subsidized. It stifles labour productivity
and throttles investment . . . Because they must show results, the
clerks hit well-known taxpayers with huge assessments and send
them scrambling to prove their innocence . . . Israel's tax collection
apparatus has thousands of employees, and is typified by an absence
of professionals, numerous errors, unchecked harassment, damage
to the public . . .'[14]

And the bureaucracy continues its damage to the public in still
more insidious ways.

According to criminologist, Dr Kenneth Mann, the tax authorities chase and harass small businessmen because the big players
hire accountants whose talents far exceed those of government salaried clerks and they get outclassed by the sophisticated accounting
techniques. The store-owner is much easier to nail.[15]

And the tax offices are far from the worst offenders in the Israeli
war on small businesspeople. The municipal bureaucracies wage
clever battles against the independent merchants of commerce. A
Tel Aviv municipality pamphlet intended to help the businessman
set up shop, is quite comic for bureaucratic literature. To obtain
a business licence, one must first apply to the city's Business
Licensing Department. After that simple task, the applicant is
as good as running the store once he obtains approval of the
Planning and Building department, the Fire Department, the
Ecology Department, the Veterinary Service, the Public Health
Department, the Police, the Ministry of Labour, the Ministry of
Health and Other Agencies as warranted.

The reader will undoubtedly notice some repetitions of approvals
but that should not bother the businessman provided he can get the
approvals in a week or two. Unfortunately, each department has its
own team of bureaucrats, ready to find unnecessary tasks for the
applicant to do before he gets his approval. Multiply that by a dozen
offices and it's five months before the licence is granted, if ever.

If the small businessman wishes to increase his profits, in many
fields he would be wise to further dive into the bureaucracy to obtain
a Government Approved Enterprise certificate. The winner of this seal
of approval gets to an exemption from company income tax, a further
exemption of dividends from personal income tax as well as investment
grants. Without this deal, certain businesses cannot compete in Israel.

More tales of lunacy coming up.

DRIVEN TO DISTRACTION

A sure sign of a collapsing nation is its crumbling transportation network. If someone decides to build or widen a road, he will have to seek approval from 19 local authorities, the Transport Ministry, the Housing Ministry's Department of Public Works, the Interior Ministry's Building and Planning Authority, the Ayalon Highway Authority, the Israeli Police, the Ports and Railways Authorities and so on. Since co-ordination between these offices is almost non-existent, it can take up to 20 years to have a road plan approved.[16]

Back in 1984, the government located 222 kilometres of 'red road', where the death toll was the highest, and planned for its repair. Five years later less than 100 kilometres was repaired – and those only shoddily by applying one layer of asphalt instead of the two needed to prevent quick deterioration.

Money was collected in a strange way, as expected. Israelis pay three times the American price for fuel because of high taxes but only 1.5% of the tax money goes to road repair and 42% of a driver's licence fee goes to municipalities who are under no obligation to repair roads. Not surprisingly, Israel's road maintenance investment is as low as it takes to keep up dirt tracks. Israel spends $13 per vehicle on the upkeep of roads compared to $103 in Switzerland or the $173 spent by Austrians. By 1990, according to the State Comptroller, 'No less than 46% of the inter-urban road network is in need of complete overhaul, compared to only 2% 15 years ago.'[17]

Tales of bureaucratic horror in the running of vehicle licensing abound and no visit to the registration centre is complete without witnessing one fistfight in the queue. Vehicle registration clerks are unique in their seating behind shatterproof glass.

The traffic police are understaffed and prone to gathering in fines by way of ambushes. They use the most modern photographing equipment but 70% of the time the machines don't work, while their radar equipment is boggled by two or more cars so can only be used catching speeders on empty stretches of road where no accident is likely to occur.

The courts for traffic offences have judges who are, as MK Uriel Lynn notes, 'generally on the lower rungs of the judicial ladder'.[18] Lynn was reacting to a judgment handed down to a 19-year-old who drove on a sidewalk and killed two children. The judge was not pleased by the great media attention given to the trial nor by the bereaved parents' outbursts of emotion and to teach everyone a lesson for disrupting his courtroom, he gave the sidewalk murderer a six-month public-service sentence.

Once a year a car owner must pay $375 on average, to have his car tested by a government-approved mechanic for safety defects. Adding licence and registration fees, insurance and testing, it costs the average Israeli some $3,000 just in paper before he can drive. But the bureaucratic torture isn't over. If he accumulates two tickets over any length of driving time, he must pay for twelve hours of preventative driving classes. At the end of the course, he must pass a test before his licence will be renewed.

In the past ten years, Israelis have been getting parking fines in numbers beyond comprehension. In Jerusalem cars are fitted with steel locks or wheel clamps around their tyres whether they are parked in an obstructive manner or just overparked by a few minutes. The municipality discovered that locking tyres is a great way of generating cash, as one employee relates: 'We lock tyres wherever we find them because we get paid for bringing in city revenue. I hate the job and the people we lock hate me. If someone finds me a job abroad I'd quit in a second and leave, that's how much I hate what I'm doing. I'm actually causing deliberate harassment on behalf of the city. How'd you like to wake up in the morning and do my work?'

No thanks, I'd much rather be a Tel Aviv parking inspector. In the spring of 1991, a man named Avraham Ezra was stopped by the police who, when they searched his car, found a large bundle of parking tickets. Now, not many people collect other people's parking tickets so the police's suspicions were raised. They discovered that Ezra, a Tel Aviv meter man, was ticketing people and punching the tickets into his modem which registered the tickets at city hall. The inspectors were paid a 15% bonus for handing out over 350 fines a month and Ezra devised a time-saving method to get the extra pay. He would sit at a café or at home, take down the registration number of passing cars and ticket them. Ezra alleged that all the local inspectors were doing the same thing and the police subsequently discovered 'a gang of supervisors which forges parking tickets'.[19]

As one Tel Aviv writer noted, 'The outrage is ten times greater when you realise that what you had attributed to your paranoid imagination is actually true: many or most or all of your tickets were fake.'[20]

Now surely, in the thousands of tickets forged, someone must have noticed that they weren't parked at either the place or time marked on the ticket. So why wasn't there even one complaint raised? The same Tel Aviv writer explains, 'To avoid interminable hassles, most people pay the fine without a murmur.'[21]

Let's say an Israeli is tired of the bureaucratic morass involved with car driving and chooses to utilise public transportation. Surely, his life will improve? Sorry, but there is no escape in a collapsing country in the firm grip of political interests. The government-run trains are obsolete, so much so that the Jerusalem-Tel Aviv run takes about three times as long as by car. According to the 1988 State Comptroller's report, 24 of the 34 main lines ran at a deficit.

And no wonder, if another criticism of the report is part of a pattern. Of $120,000 budgeted for safety projects, only half was spent. Whatever the other half was used for, it had nothing to do with making train travel more secure. By October of 1987, railway workers were inspecting less than half the country's crossings for safety defects.[22]

Intercity buses are the exclusive domain of one Histadrut co-operative, the Egged Bus Line, while another monopoly called Dan has a good chunk of the Tel Aviv concession. Moshe Glazman sums up bus-riding in Israel today:

'. . . the transport co-operatives – sluggish, cumbersome and swollen beyond their natural dimensions – could not provide the passenger public with service worthy of the name . . .

This situation could create a convenient culture for the development of corruption, entanglement in dubious economic deals and misuse of budgets and authority – to name only a few of the phenomena plaguing the co-operatives at present . . .

The co-operatives operate under conditions of tremendous budget deficit. According to early 1989 figures, Egged's earnings from passenger fares do not even cover wage costs. Thus the co-operatives need massive government support in the form of a public transport subsidy . . . Furthermore, the co-operatives are noted for a rude and inconsiderate attitude toward passengers.[23]

If you want to escape from Israel by air, and it's comfort and friendly service you seek, the choice of airline had better not be El Al, an acronym for Every Landing Always Late. During the 1970s, El Al's dozen unions plagued the airline with strikes, work-to-rule orders and sanctions. The unions had sunk the airline's reputation worldwide but in June 1982 the unions destroyed the airline's good name even within Israel. A week into the Lebanon War, while young Israelis were dying amongst the cedars, El Al went on strike and disrupted all flights. The government made a decision to close down the national airline and placed the company in receivership. Eventually the politicians ran the airline with their usual care.

In 1991, the Zagat Airline Survey rated El Al the world's third-worst airline. Only Greece's Olympic Airways and the ever-dependable Aeroflot of the Soviet Union were rated lower. Some customer complaints included 'rude staff', 'packed cabins', 'not a very pleasant atmosphere', 'second only to Aeroflot for brutal service', and 'all travellers were treated like enemies'.

And this is the airline that is supposed to lure tourists to Israel.

WELCOME TO ISRAEL, THIS IS A STICK-UP!
The government even sticks its tentacles into the body of tourism. Imagine the American government appointing a Secretary of Tourism whose duty it is to regulate the tourism industry. Absurd, impossible, a total waste of public money? All of the above and more in Israel where there is a Ministry of Tourism whose minister sits in the cabinet and votes on sensitive military issues.

Now since the public is paying for a Tourism Ministry what does the public get for its cash? The answer is a lot of interference and a lot of hotels. Believe it or not, in the fantasy world of Israel, the government gives hotel owners 40% of their construction costs and then asks nothing in return.

The 1988 State Comptroller's report documents several cases of the Tourism Ministry throwing away public money on useless hotels. In one instance the hotel owner couldn't afford to complete his building so the government gave over $1 million to help him out. In another case, without the Tourism Ministry even requesting a full financial report or other relevant documentation, the incompetent Shiff hotel chain received millions of dollars though its losses were well-known to the public.[24]

It's not as though the country is short of hotels: in the summer of 1991 during the peak tourism season, Israeli hotels had an occupancy rate of only 40% – and two-fifths of these were native Israelis taking advantage of cut-price deals.

HELLO, CAN YOU HEAR ME? I'M CALLING FROM TEL AVIV
Until 1984, the government directly operated the phone company in the inimitable government style which meant a five-year wait for a line to be installed unless you were a third cousin of the Communications Minister's wife's hairdresser and you were willing to bribe a technician. In one candid camera sting operation, Israel

Television's consumer watchdog programme filmed a technician demanding a $2,000 bribe to install a phone.

In 1984, the government relinquished direct ministerial control of the phone company, and formed a government company called Bezek to run most of the country's communications facilities. The government claimed the move was undertaken to improve phone services but in fact the new company was the result of a conspiracy between the Histadrut and the government to bypass government salary restrictions and allow phone company workers to earn a pirate's trove in wages. What this means is that the workers created the company and the workers run it (into the ground). Bezek is blessed with not one but two workers' committees and when one strikes, the other follows. Unfortunately, Bezek also operates Israel's radio and TV transmitters, so when the phone company is on strike, the TV screens go blank.

In 1989, Bezek issued stocks on the Tel Aviv exchange and the workers demanded that telephone services be raised so the dividends on the stock would be increased. Of course, higher dividends meant increased wages, so the motivation for enriching capitalist stockholders was entirely justifiable to everyone but the Israeli public. A telephone call to Haifa at noon from Jerusalem costs approximately the same as a call to New York at midnight.

Two years after Bezek was formed, Aharon Dolav of *Ma'ariv* summed up its achievements: 'As Bezek's second year of operations draws to a close, telephone distress has reached new heights. Israelis have run out of patience and despairing calls for civil disobedience have been sounded.'[25]

Instead of civil disobedience, two private anti-Bezek organisations were formed whose findings led to an official body handling complaints against the phone company. The findings of the three bodies and the cases they handle would be mind-boggling if this wasn't Israel.

Bezek overcharges and no one is certain if this is policy. Because less than 40% of Israeli phones are digital, bills cannot be itemised. Instead, the phone bill is based on mechanical meters. (Digital phone bills are not itemised either. The customer must pay for an itemisation in cases of suspicious bills.)

One caller to a Bezek watchdog group received two enormous bills in a row. He spent days trying to persuade various Bezek personnel and committees that the bills were way off but because the meter read what it read, he got the brush-off time after time. The watchdog group did a little investigating and discovered that an electric short in the meter was accelerating costs.[26]

In cases of a busy phone, Bezek often estimates the bill and very subtly announces the fact with a single Hebrew letter beside the amount. According to an article in *Yediot Achronot* in April 1989, a Petach Tikveh businessman received two bills in a row of about $1,500 and based on these, he calculated his phone usage. His third bill shot up to about $4,000 though his actual usage had not changed. What happened was the first two estimates were way off and the difference was attached to the third bill. This is hardly conducive to accurate business planning.[27]

In 1989 the Israeli Consumer Council published the results of a survey conducted on public attitudes towards Bezek. It found that 30% felt they were cheated on their bills and of these people, 60% complained to Bezek. In only 15% of these cases did Bezek persuade the complainers that they were in the wrong, thus forcing the phone company to investigate. And wouldn't you know it, after a little detective work, Bezek found that a majority of the complaints were justified or worthy of further consideration.

But a simple complaint does not mean filing a claim with a helpful clerk. As is always the case with the Israeli bureaucracy, the consumer is guilty until proven not so or worn down until he acquiesces.

It is the attitude of the bureaucracy that leads to hyper-tension and migraines. Israelis are afraid to challenge it for fear of getting into deeper trouble. Zelda Harris, a leading Israeli reformist cites two examples. In the first case residents refused to report a known neighbourhood criminal because his cousin was on the police force. In the second case a dentist's office was barged into by the VAT hounds while the dentist was in the middle of performing delicate work on a patient. The agents started harassing the dentist, loudly accusing her of withholding taxes while her hand was literally in the patient's mouth. But instead of complaining or suing, the dentist let the incident pass for fear of greater harassment. If she had been taken to court herself over this matter, she, like every other Israeli, would not be guaranteed a fair hearing or even a remotely competent judge.

FAST SERVICE IN THE BACK COURT

The Israeli judicial system is politically appointed so once again and as usual, hacks are given jobs as a reward for loyalty. And, as is always the case, the system is crumbling through inefficiency, lack of manpower and the wrong kind of manpower.

As for inefficiency, *Ma'ariv* on 18 January 1987 provides a somewhat humorous example. A Tel Aviv judge, in the middle of hearing important evidence, left the courtroom to answer a phone. It seems the caller was very persistent and would not stop ringing and there was no one else in the courtroom permitted to answer the call. So, while the defendant's fate was held in the balance, the judge interrupted proceedings for a chat on the phone.

The lack of modernisation is better illustrated by the fact that the Israeli court system is still not computerised. That means before a judge can render a decision, he must tramp off to the law library and look up relevant precedents by himself or with the help of a speedy librarian.

Dr Kenneth Mann of the Law Faculty of Tel Aviv University did a little research and found that on average, the time between the first hearing and the presentation of evidence in an Israeli courtroom is 171 days. It then takes a further 75 days to hear the evidence and by the time a verdict has been reached, 315 days have passed.[28] Some courtroom waits in Israel are legendary.

One example is the suit by the residents of a Tel Aviv building against the government housing company. The residents claimed their building was unfit for human habitation and demanded extensive repairs and reconstruction. But one does not sue the government with all its resources of public money without expecting a great deal of heartache. It took ten years before a final verdict was reached – the residents lived in squalour for a decade while justice was being decided.

Nor does one simply sue doctors for malpractice since all but two hospitals in the country are government or Histadrut controlled. No matter how obvious the malpractice, the patient has little recourse to seek fair compensation.

In December 1986, a doctor named Ben Dor was sued by the family of a soldier who was rather summarily examined and declared fit for army duty. He died soon after of a cardiac arrest. The court began hearing testimony in February 1986 and the final summations were not concluded until December 1987. When asked what took so long, the judge explained that he had 72 pages of protocol to consider as well as two medical books to peruse. Even if he had never taken a speed-reading course, the task required perhaps a week to complete. But Israeli judges far too often fail to take into consideration the pain of a bereaved or suffering family seeking justice. In this case, the long delay did nothing to relieve the suffering of the mourners. The doctor was cleared of all charges.[29]

There are apparently ways to get around the log-jam in court. One simply must bribe the court secretaries who arrange the schedules of judges. In 1988, six secretaries from courts throughout the country were charged with offences ranging from sexual blackmail, fraud, theft, forgery to obstructing justice. Throughout the nation, wherever justice was meted out, it seems there was one clerk willing to schedule a quick trial with an 'easy' softie of a judge in return for some nookie or cash on the table.

And perhaps this unique method of raising cash for ill-paid court clerks is preferable to the present system, which isn't working at all. By 1990 Israelis were presented with a rather unique and enticing possibility: the entire court system was bankrupt and might be forced to close down. To victims of injustice everywhere, the thought of no lawyer's fees because there were no courtrooms was truly exciting. But the government thought different and $18.5 million was pumped from the Treasury to the judicial system on condition it be made more efficient. Without going into the drab details of the Treasury's efficiency programme, let it be said that it wasn't adhered to in the strictest sense, which in Israel means it wasn't adhered to at all.

What becomes of a people beset by bureaucratic injustice but with no faith in their judicial system? To say the least, Israelis have become extremely tolerant of cheating the system and bribing to get around it. A study conducted in 1991 at Bar Ilan University revealed some rather discouraging facts. Amongst them were the following: 75.3% of Israelis put their children in private after-hours classes to supplement the pathetic school system; 34.4% have subscribed to illegal cable stations to escape the monotony of government television; 15.3% have paid bribes to doctors to jump the queue waiting for operations (43.6% support such bribery in the case of a serious operation); 75% of Israelis feel it is not immoral to trade currency illegally while 60% think there is nothing wrong with cheating on VAT. Furthermore, 45.1% of Israelis believe that most of their countrymen cheat the tax authorities by over half the amount due.[30]

These are the signs of a people who have lost all respect for the system that governs them, a system that has turned a majority into cheats of one kind or another. And the cheating is seen as justified, especially in light of an economic system that picks the public's pockets as a matter of twisted principle.

CHAPTER SEVENTEEN

The Decline and Decline of the Israeli Economy

As an introduction to this chapter, it has been decided (following the advice of Stanford economist, Alvin Rabushka) to take a quick look at simplified Israeli economics, in order that the reader, on being presented with the gruesome statistics below, might be better prepared for the description of the causes of the mess which follow.

So here goes.

In America, the government spends about 30% of the nation's GNP. In Israel, Bainerman and Rabushka claim the Israeli government spends 80% of the GNP, while Sohar insists that government-spending actually exceeds the annual GNP. In other words, after the government is finished paying for running itself, there is no money left in the hands of the people according to one source, and about 20 cents to the dollar according to two others. To further facilitate comprehension of what this means, imagine that the American government triples its budget and the citizens are forced to pay for the expense through taxes. Now put this scenario into perspective: the average Israeli salary is one-third that of Americans, prices for everything are higher and yet, the public must pay three times more to support the government.

The government itself is waste incarnate. Because it insists on maintaining control of the economy, thus strangling private enterprise, it must prevent the collapse of inefficient businesses through subsidies. It subsidises loss-making industries, loss-making farms, loss-making hospitals, loss-making bus companies, in fact a whole loss-making economy. The subsidies even outstrip the defence budget and add up to over 10% of the whole GNP.

To further protect its loss-making industries, the government puts up trade barriers in violation of its free-trade agreements with the EEC and the US. If it lowers the barriers, local factories long protected from realistic pricing, threaten the government. In 1990 the government dropped the import duty on Asian thread, so the textile industry, backed by the Histadrut, threatened sanctions and strikes. By protecting shoddy local products, Israelis are coerced into purchasing them, although most Israelis would prefer to buy quality goods even if that means paying double for imported brands. The Tel Aviv Chamber of Commerce estimates that Israelis lose $2.5 billion a year on trade restrictions.

To make this fact digestible – 4.8 million Israelis annually shell out $2.5 billion extra for foreign products overpriced by duty. This occurs in the name of keeping local dross on the market and employing the workers who manufacture it. If all duty was dropped, there would be $2.5 billion more in the pockets of Israeli consumers, which means most Israelis would be better off. As it is, the government pockets the money and distributes it to enterprises which have no business existing in the real world.

Prof. Rabushka agrees with David Magen, Israel's Minister of Economic Planning (whatever that means), that 11 ministries in the government are useless, including his own, and should be eliminated.[1] One quarter of the Israeli government's non-defence spending is directed at thoroughly unnecessary ministries and programmes adding up to another $3 billion.

According to a study conducted by the Jerusalem Institute for Israel Studies, the percentage of Israelis employed in businesses with fewer than 100 employees fell from 43.2% in the early 1970s to 36.2% in the late 1980s. All the plots against small businessmen are working to order. The share of sales from the surviving small businesses fell during the same period from 40.6% to 28.9%.[2] This bucks a worldwide trend exemplified by the situation in America where, between 1980 and 1986, small businesses added 574,000 jobs while big industries lost 1.2 million. In the meantime, Israelis have to find work where it's available, so in one year – from 1989 to 1990 – the number of public service employees rose by 18,000, this despite the fact that a quarter of such state-paid workers are estimated to be redundant.

According to figures presented to the government by the Manufacturers Association at the beginning of 1991, unemployment would reach 14% by the end of the year. The government predicted a rate of merely 10.1% at the same time. By the end of the summer of 1991, the rate of unemployed approached the 12% mark. An unemployed Israeli with a family receives only $400 a month in dole money and that means by 1992, hundreds of thousands of people will not be able to survive. Tens of thousands, understandably, will leave the country.

To support an unsupportable economy, Israelis pay a tax rate estimated variously at between 45% and 56%. About $3 billion is lost annually because of criminal or desperate tax evasion. In comparison, only 13% of Syria's economy, as bad as it is, is paid for by taxing its citizens. Thus Syrian soldiers may someday meet far more demoralised Israelis on the battlefield, the consequences of which may be tragic.

The government budget deficit in 1990 reached 5.5% of the GNP and it keeps growing.[3] By 1991, 76% of all foreign aid reaching the country went to servicing government debt and not, as many donors and Congressmen think, to the immediate needs of Israelis.

Price rises between 1986 and 1990 are beyond comprehension. The cost of an Egged bus ride rose 180%, a haircut 275%, a falafel 150%, a pizza 166%, a cup of coffee 300%, and a phone token 500%.[4] During this period, the Consumer Price Index outpaced the shekel-dollar rate by 40%, meaning every tourist arriving with dollars pays 40% more for everything. To illustrate true inflation, what cost one shekel in 1948, would cost almost seven million shekels today. Mark Feldman, a level-headed and successful tour agent, insists it is cheaper for an Israeli to spend a week in Turkey than in a local resort even with the cost of airfare and taxes included.

With Israeli salaries lagging behind the official Consumer Price Index, bare existence is threatened. With salaries lagging behind the true cost of living by hundreds of percent, a disaster of immense proportions is imminent.

How did things come to this state? It's easy when one considers the extent of government control of the economy: 40% of all Israelis are employed in the public sector and 18% work for Histadrut, or Labour Party, industries. That makes 58% of the working population dependent on politicians for their wages. Ezra Sohar includes Jewish Agency workers and kibbutzniks in his calculations and comes up with a figure of 66% of Israelis working directly for political interests. Since the small private sector controls only 30% of the entire economy, Sohar's figure may be accurate.

With over half of the country's workers employed by politicians, they are dependent on the whims of government for their paycheques. And with all public servants represented by one union, the Histadrut, they rely on their leaders to defy the government to get (largely undeserved) pay-rises. The tension between the government and the Histadrut is probably the most important reason why the Israeli economy has been brain dead since 1973.

STRIKE THREE, LABOUR'S OUT

Economic policy is determined by a sinister triumvirate of government, industry (represented by the Manufacturers Association) and labour (in the shape of the Histadrut). At one time the Manufacturers Association was the odd man out since the Labour Party and Histadrut conspired to create a workers' paradise. Thirty years of this socialist attitude led to bankruptcy in the public, agricultural and health sectors, as well as a good chunk of the industrial sector. It is the present government's task to stave off utter ruin by pinching pennies, cutting corners and introducing free-market reforms. It can accomplish none of this without the co-operation of the Histadrut which represents so many of the country's workers.

The reader is asked to imagine that all American workers are represented by only one union, say the Teamsters. If one sub-union, say the auto-workers, calls a strike, every other sub-union might be obliged to join in out of worker solidarity. The Histadrut saves its totally paralysing national strikes for special occasions but when one is called, the following services close up: the phone company, the post offices, most health services, TV and radio, banks, most schools, public transportation (except taxis) and all government-owned industries. The private sector is badly disrupted as workers can't travel to their jobs and mothers must stay at home with their children.

If the Histadrut was remotely responsible, the strike threat might be a legitimate weapon in the armoury of labour protection. But the Histadrut is a loose cannon on the brink of defeat by the forces of the free market. To stave off the inevitable end, the Histadrut disrupts all government attempts at economic reform. What follows is a partial recounting of the 1989–90 season:

– July, October and November '89, saw shutdowns by immigration employees. Soviet immigrants needing vital documents were greeted with closed doors.

– In March '89 employees at the Tel Aviv Stock Exchange went on strike, demanding pay-rises equal to those received by the banking and insurance sectors.

– In the same month, the Histadrut threatened a national strike over linkage of salaries to the COL. Meanwhile over at Zim Shipping, the administrative staff began sanctions in order to receive increased clothing and car allowances.

– The Histadrut, in order to protect its pathetic construction industry, in March 1990 denounced government importation of prefab homes for immigrants. Dock workers were ordered to prevent offloading of the cheaper and more threatening housing for immigrants.

– In large part to prevent the increased liberalisation of imports, the Histadrut called a national strike in June. For two days, 800,000 workers stayed away from their jobs, turning the whole country into bedlam. It cost the economy an estimated $100 million in lost production before the government gave in to union demands.

– In the same month, Bezek, the helpful phone company, suffered a strike of half its workers whose demands included air-conditioning in repair trucks.

– On 3 July 1990, 12,000 Histadrut doctors were on strike in protest at the cancellation of a second working shift.

– Shortly after, representatives of 90,000 workers, including El Al and municipal employees, threatened to strike if the government lessened the tax burden on those earning $1,500 a month or more.

– And shortly after this threat, workers at the Employment Service went on strike for real, delaying the cheques of everyone collecting unemployment benefit, not an unconsiderable hardship since 10% of the population wasn't working.

– In September, workers at the national water company, Mekorot, planned a strike, jeopardising the entire country's water supply.

– And if this wasn't bad enough, in October the agricultural marketers went on strike, preventing the delivery of fresh food to stores.

– In mid-October, the Histadrut threatened another national strike. This time the primary reason was a government plan to tax pension funds. In preparation for this strike, the head of Histadrut's Trade Union Department, Chaim Haberfeld, declared, 'If Modai thinks that we are talking about a one- or two-day strike, he is simply mistaken. We are preparing our forces for a struggle that will continue until a positive agreement is reached. The battle against the economic programme will be waged on land, sea and in the air. We shall fight to the end and paralyse the state of Israel.'[5]

Of these patriotic sentiments, S. Zalman Abramov, former deputy speaker of the Knesset writes: 'A general strike is a resort to force, for it is not directed against an employer but against a nation and its elected parliament . . . What is at stake is not just a grave economic setback but a challenge to the democratic order.'[6]

Miraculously, this general strike was averted, though some people chose not to obey. For four days, starting on 30 October, the unions of engineers, technicians and liberal arts academics struck.

– The strike that was averted in October took place in early
December when 500,000 Histadrut members shut down the country
for two days. The strike ended when Modai agreed to withdraw
proposed legislation and agreed not to tax employee pension
benefits up to a ceiling of twice the average wage.

– But the strike season wasn't yet over. On 13 December, 8,000
government hospital doctors took strike action for three days,
demanding higher wages. One can only recoil at the thought of
a train crash or terrorist attack occurring at such a time.

Altogether 1990 was not a bad strike season. Twice the doctors
stopped working and twice the nation was paralysed by general
walk-outs. There are certain to be better strike vintages coming up.
Of the Histadrut's 1990 season Alvin Rabushka writes:

> Histadrut clings to a discredited, troglodyte economic policy . . .
> it is worth reciting against whom Histadrut trade union members
> have struggled: Histadrut's own industrial empire, state-owned
> enterprises, government-subsidised firms, government-sanctioned
> monopolies and cartels, government-owned banks, the Government
> itself . . . Histadrut, in short has struggled against itself and
> its political allies. Rhetoric has replaced reason and reality at
> Histadrut.[7]

BROTHERS IN HARMS

Yes, incredibly, the Histadrut, Israel's labour union, has been
known to strike against itself. MK Ariel Weinstein describes the
union as a Dr Jekyll and Mr Hyde. It exploits labour as an
employer while defending them as a union. The organisation is
ruled by the Labour Party and Labour's political supporters are
paid off with jobs to the detriment of managerial efficiency.

The imbeciles appointed to ruin Histadrut factories run them into
the ground forcing staff lay-offs. When the firings start, so do the
strikes. A few are outstanding. Strikers at a Histadrut tyre factory
actually held management hostage, while at an electronics firm, the
executive boardroom was taken over. Further insanity took place in
September 1990, when management ended a six-week strike at the
Soltam munitions factory by setting 40 attack dogs on the strikers
and further ejecting those unmoved by canine capers with clubs
wielded by the human employees of a private security firm. It was
later claimed that Histadrut officials were behind the decision to
use dogs on the workers.[8]

Histadrut's apparatchiks ran their companies with an almost total disregard for productivity and profit but in other cases besides Soltam, without regard for the physical well-being of the workers. Tadiran, Koor's electronics arm, has been accused of exposing workers to dangerous fumes for years with management well aware of the health risks.

But Koor was much too busy going bankrupt to keep tabs on the health of a few hundred workers. As Alvin Rabushka recounts: 'The Saga of Koor Industries Ltd, which lost $300 million in 1989, was $1.2 billion in debt and should have been declared bankrupt, reads like a tragi-comedy. Asking Histadrut to manage Koor profitably is akin to empowering the Communist Party to direct the transition from socialism to free markets in Eastern Europe and the Soviet Union.'9

Koor's holding company is called Hevrat Haovdim or the Workers Company. It employs 20,000 workers (down from 31,000 in 1987) in dozens of companies and is the industrial arm of the Histadrut. If it went bankrupt like it should, 20,000 unemployed workers would vent their anger in ways the government doesn't wish to discover. The general manager of Koor, David Levitan, claims, 'It's still less expensive to keep Koor afloat than it is to pay unemployment for 20,000 workers.'

The calculation is a hidden threat. It is cheaper to fire 20,000 unproductive workers in the long-run even with the cost of unemployment insurance. But it is not wise for the government to defy the Histadrut and its power to call national strikes. So the government has agreed to another bail-out, this one to the tune of some $600 million of public cash. So far $100 million has been forwarded to the company, much of it in debt waivers from the government-owned banks. The cost, as in all other bail-outs, was passed on to the Israeli consumer in the form of even higher interest rates on borrowing and even greater personal debt.

One of the banks agreeing to the debt waiving was Bank Leumi, which the reader will recall is owned by the Jewish Agency. Leumi is Koor's largest creditor and by waiving huge parcels of debt, foreign donors to charities administered by the Jewish Agency inadvertently bailed out a labour union and its incompetent industrial corporation.

There was no need for all this manipulation. In 1990, the American entrepreneur who made $2 billion from Disney acquisitions, Stanley Gold, offered to buy Koor. His deal was tempting. He would take over all of Koor's debt and pay $100 million, plenty of cash to pay off old management for leaving.[10] But Koor turned the offer down, convinced it could get a better deal from the Israeli government. It was a bad decision because not all of Koor's debts are to Israeli banks. Several foreign banks, including Bankers Trust of New York, own huge chunks of Koor and they threatened to declare their shares worthless in court unless they saw some return on their investments.

This put the government in a more realistic position. If the foreign banks declared Koor a write-off, Israel's credit-rating worldwide would sink, this at a time when large bank loans were being sought to finance Soviet immigration. The day of reckoning had to be put off and the only way was to prove that Koor could be made solvent.

With a total government bail-out now out of the question, Koor began selling off companies. So far only $12.5 million has been raised by selling assets but the pattern has been set. The Histadrut empire is slowly crumbling.

But not slowly enough. To this day, at Histadrut gatherings, the *Internationale* is sung to red flags. In 1991, for the first time ever, Histadrut workers did not take the day off on 1 May, the communist workers' holiday, supposedly to make up for work lost to Scud attacks. As one editorial notes, 'Israel can hardly afford a labour federation which still believes that the good of "the workers" can be had at the expense of the welfare of the whole nation.'[11] But that's exactly what Israel is stuck with. In the name of labour rights, the Histadrut is blocking every effort at economic reform. And with three-quarters of the country's citizens belonging to the union (mostly because of health-care plan membership), it has the muscle to grind the nation to a halt. One economic reporter (who begged not to be identified) called the Histadrut, 'the greatest enemy of the Jewish people. It does more harm than the PLO.'

Former Knesset deputy-speaker, S. Zalman Abramov, concludes: 'It would seem the last Mohicans of World Socialism are in Israel, located in the Histadrut establishment. There, the clock of history stopped ticking in 1920 and ideological creativity remained in deep-freeze.'[12]

THE MANASS HOLE
Next in the troika of vested interests that choke the Israeli economy is the Manufacturers Association. This group represents the owners of all private companies employing over six workers. In total some 245,000 workers are controlled by this group, about a quarter

of Histradrut's number. So why does it get equal billing with the government and Histadrut in the formation of economic legislation? Haifa University economics professor, Steve Plaut, has kindly consented to sort out the complications inherent in this section:

> To begin with, every ministry is an empire headed by a minister wanting to consolidate power along with bureaucrats carving niches for themselves. There are three ministries alone co-ordinating economic policy; the Finance Ministry, the Ministry of Economic Planning and the Ministry of Trade and Industry. All the ministries compete for patronage instead of co-ordinating national policy.
>
> So let's say one minister hands over government money to set up a factory in Bet Shean ... The people of the town will remember who improved the unemployment situation and therefore his constituency will expand as will his power base within his party.
>
> So the politicians find the Manufacturers Association a useful vehicle for consolidating power and the manufacturers find the politicians more than willing to supply them with favours.

To further simplify the role of the Manufacturers Association (from now on abbreviated to 'Manass'), let us examine and analyse a brief press clipping from 1991:

> Dov Lautman, the president of the Manufacturers Association has urged Finance Minister Yitzhak Modai to permit industrial monopolies to readjust the prices of their products in conformity with agreed supervised prices.
>
> He said Modai should not delay such permission because of the increase in the price-index basket of commodities, and the higher prices he is recommending had already been approved by the Ministry of Trade and Industry.
>
> Manufacturing monopolies have been restricted in their prices under an arrangement outlined and agreed with the Treasury, the Ministry of Industry and the Manufacturers Association. The agreement provides for updating prices when a 3.5% index increase has occurred, or after six months since the last adjustment, whichever comes first.[13]

If the language seems foreign to the reader, it's all too plain to the astute Israeli. As explained previously, the value of savings, the currency, and wages to a lesser extent, are tied to the Consumer Price Index. This is a basket of goods whose prices are recorded and the total rise in prices determines the Cost Of Living. About one quarter of the items are subsidised by the government and others are imported, so this guide is artificial and very faulty.

Prices of most goods are also determined by the government and apparently Manass wasn't permitted to raise prices because of a bad deal cut with the government. So Manass first went to the Ministry of Trade and Industry and persuaded its minister to approve new prices for Manass's products. We shall not learn from this item what goodies Manass promised the minister in return for approving its higher prices but we do know that they are playing one ministry off the other. If the Treasury wants to keep pace with the patronage, it had better fall in line.

The first two words of the third paragraph say it all: 'Manufacturing monopolies'. In return for generous favours, the government protects certain industries from competition, turning them into monopolies. The list of private companies without real competition in Israel is long but it includes products as diverse as wood, aluminium and formica. The method utilised is tariffs. A minister can unilaterally slap a tariff on any imported product, making it uncompetitive in the local marketplace – Steve Plaut explains: 'When a minister wants to reward a businessman, he simply orders the customs office to slap high duty on foreign competition. The law allows ministers to increase duty without Knesset approval. And it protects them after by denying any legal redress of the duty. An importer cannot approach a court to challenge the legality of the duty. The court will not address the claim. Everything is set up in a way that legitimises favouritism.'

The effects of the tariffs are expanded on by economics writer Evelyn Gordon:

> The consumer suffers twice: the appliance he wants to buy is made artificially expensive, while Israeli manufacturers are not producing appliances that answer his needs.
>
> High customs duties have given Israeli manufacturers a captive domestic market which permits them to ignore consumer preferences. This fact contains the key to Israel's enormous trade deficit . . .
>
> If Israeli products had to compete with imports on an even basis, they would be forced to adapt their products to prevailing tastes or be out of business . . .
>
> It seems the government has decided that the comfort and convenience of the average Israeli should be sacrificed in the interest of filling the public coffers one way or another.[14]

But let's give the government their due. In the face of mounting public criticism of the tariffs, in 1990 the powers that be took the rather bizarre step of lifting import restrictions on steel, castor oil and shoes with leather uppers. This step will no doubt improve the lives of Israelis substantially while at the same time protecting the interests of unrelated Manass products.

Getting back to our newspaper item, the poor monopolies have been restricted in their price rises by an agreement forcing them to freeze prices until there is a 3.5% rise in the COL or six months after the last adjustment.

Six months? Who is kidding who? In July 1991 alone, the COL rose 3% and with the rise came a threat of 40% inflation. Either someone was very optimistic or deluded to the point of institutionalisation because not once in recent memory has the six-month COL rise been remotely close to 3.5%. Since Manass got taken, it was hopping mad. Thus the demand for new price rises and the inter-ministerial politicking.

Tariffs cost the Israeli taxpayer some $2.5 billion each year but subsidies outstrip even that figure, surpassing the $3 billion mark. The government uses subsidies to further reward compliant businessmen. The way the money is passed on is a bit complicated but basically companies receive grants for opening factories in backwoods and impoverished towns, through cheap credit at banks, tax concessions on equipment purchases and free money for Research and Development.

The manufacturers have devised clever ways of duping the government. Some have accepted grants for opening out-of-the-way factories. In fact, 'the factories' are often mere workshops employing a small staff while the main operations site remains in the more sensible coastal area. But technically a factory was opened in a development area so the grant is secured. Another trick is to receive concessions for equipment purchases, buy very used equipment abroad for a pittance, charge the government for new purchases and pocket the change.

According to Ezra Sohar:

A short time after Eli Hurvitz resigned as chairman of the Manu-facturers Association, he said that aid to industry amounted to $1.5 billion a year . . . Mr Hurvitz apparently flinched from describing the state of affairs in its full gravity because his figures do not include the voluminous loans given to 'approved enterprises', direct support at times of crisis, fuel and water subsidies and more.[15]

Paul Rivlin conducted a study called 'Industrial Subsidies In Israel' for the Institute for Advanced Strategic and Political Studies. Among his discoveries is the fact that:

> The Law accords government officials and ministers wide discretion in handing out grants to those industries which they favour. They can also designate towns or regions as development areas. The State Comptroller's report testifies that grants are misallocated, that the Investment Authority at the Ministry of Industry does not always operate inside the Law and that ministers intervene.[16]

Of the politicking of Manass and the sly transfer of public money to preferred companies, Joel Bainerman has a good question: 'Why not just put the taxpayers' money directly into their pockets? . . . Then the exporters won't have to waste time lobbying the government for their bonus every few months.'[17]

The final method by which Manass milks the government to be examined here is by free government cash awarded for R and D (Research and Development). In 1990 the amount totalled $110 million. The effect of these hand-outs was studied by a team of economists at the Technion College in 1986.

The Technion Report claimed that money was handed out based on the 'administrator's intuition', and the 'applicant's persuasiveness'. Money was allocated without marketing reports or proper economic justification. The report concluded that the government's control of R and D funding was especially devious since it locked experienced venture capitalists out of the field.

Much of the R and D capital is funnelled through the Office of the Chief Scientist. One Canadian worked as the Jerusalem manager of an American technology import company. He describes some of his experiences with government subsidised projects:

> A lot of projects we examined were out and out frauds. One Soviet inventor claimed he had developed a cheaper method of producing pectin for jam. We did a patent search and found out he was pawning off stolen Soviet technology as his own. And he wasn't the only Soviet guilty of that trick but the Israelis weren't so straight either. One showed us a terrific new imaging system. After another search we discovered he had stripped down a new German machine and tried selling it as his invention. A real embarrassment took place when we investigated the possibility of putting an aquaculture company on the New York Stock Exchange. The boss conveniently forgot to tell us that he had already placed his company on the Denver

exchange as a penny stock. After a year of this constant deceit, the company shut down its Israeli operations.

In the early '80s, it seemed that private industry was about to boom in Israel. Companies like Scitex, Optrotech, Laser Industries, Elscint were all making bundles of cash abroad. But by 1990, most of the hope had faded. Of all the high-tech companies, only 20% planned any expansion. Even the biggest private holding company, Clal, the private sector's version of Koor, was rocked by charges of corruption in a series of articles in *Ma'ariv*. In the end, the reporter was fired for endangering the paper's Clal advertising and the chairman of Clal stepped down after the Attorney-General began investigations of his misconduct though he claims the two incidents are unrelated.[18]

The Israeli government backs Manass, because it manufactures durable goods. Yet the rest of the First World has shifted its economy away from manufacturing into the realms of services. Hundreds of millions of dollars yearly are shifted into the pockets of manufacturers and researchers with little to show but diminishing returns or none at all. Of the $100 million pumped into R and D, only a quarter of the projects ever break even.

Dani Gellerman, president of the Israeli Chambers of Commerce is most perturbed by the cash grants and subsidies to manufacturers to the exclusion of the service industries, which are not represented by the politically active Manass:

> Israeli policy in the service area is a type of Marxist pornography which states that only somebody who carries a 5 kg hammer is economically productive. The rest of the advanced world discarded such anachronistic ideas long ago yet Israel continues to discriminate between manufacturing and services by offering subsidies and cheap credit only to the former.[19]

Of course, in the rest of the world there aren't any Manasses dictating economic policy to the government. Of this combination of Big Government, Big Union and Big Industry, controlling the economic fortunes of the hapless Israeli, Steve Plaut concludes:

> When Coke and Pepsi fight publicly, it's for the good of the consumer. Quality goes up and prices come down, that's the way of business. But when the Histadrut and Manufacturers Association bicker, it's not for the ears of the consumer. Their only audience of interest is the government. Each are vying for political favours, the public

means little to them. Economic decisions in Israel are political and
every time government sticks its nose in the marketplace everything
goes wrong.

A truism proved by the government's own debilitated companies.

PUBLICLY RUINED MONOPOLIES

To give the reader an idea of how pervasive monopolised industries are in Israel, the following products are 100% controlled
by one local company: tyres, cement, canned food, beer, metal
pipes, starch, cigarettes, asbestos and lightbulbs. Over 90% of the
following products are controlled by one monopoly: paint, paper,
chocolate, margarine, instant coffee and pasta.[20]

Obviously with monopolies controlling such a wide range of
goods, the Israeli shopper is not exactly overwhelmed by variety.
A very common comment by Israelis returning from abroad is
that after shopping at a Marks & Spencer Food Emporium or
even a lowly Safeway, they realised how drab their choices were
in Israel.

As we have seen, most of the monopolies are government-
protected sweetheart deals in which the company rewards a
minister in manifold ways. Now we enter the twilight zone of
government-owned monopolies, industries forbidden competition
by the government itself.

According to the 1985 Report of the Board of Government
companies issued by the Treasury, there are 209 government
monopolies of which 100 have commercial purposes. The scope
of government business interests is quite astounding and one must
wonder why the public is asked to own a wedding hall in Tel
Aviv, three large hotels, the Israel Wine Institute, a restaurant in
Jerusalem or the Habimah Theatre.

Some of the monopolies are best categorised as cartels. There are
three energy companies and six oil-drilling companies (which have
offices but don't drill for oil) all owned by the government and each
sanctioned by different ministers.

As journalist Gabi Kessler explained in *Ma'ariv*:

> The government companies serve *inter alia* as a highly powerful
> political tool for those who hold the reins of power . . . The election
> of public figures to boards of the government companies has long
> since become one of the ministers' prerogatives and a tool that they
> use to hand out goodies and honoraria for their party cronies.[21]

Some 65,000 people are employed in these monopolies and the value of the companies the government owns outright or has shares in is estimated at $15 billion. That figure is equal to five years of American government aid to Israel and if the companies were sold, and if the economy were reformed, Israel would have no need for outside charity.

But there is a more pressing reason for the government to sell its companies: Israel has a total of $64 billion in external and internal debt, a government deficit over 5% of the GNP and a widening trade gap that increased 49.6% in 1990 to $3.5 billion. The country is in fit state to apply for a Chapter 11 bankruptcy.

To stave off the world debt-collectors and save its people from starvation, the government for years has declared its intention of selling off its assets. But because approval of such sales from the various government ministers was a prerequisite, nothing got done. No minister was willing to give up his fiefdom, his appointments, his favours, his patronage or his guarantee of a happy retirement in an executive industrial position to a bunch of strangers crazy enough to buy a bankrupt company under his tutelage.

By the summer of 1991 no less a personage than Shamir himself stepped in to streamline the selling process. He forced the cabinet to restrict the ultimate say in selling to just three ministers, including himself, thus locking out the other two dozen ministers. But even like this, it has been business as usual with one sale or another blocked, stalled or cancelled. What follows are some examples of Israeli government salesmanship.

The government announced that Weizman Science Press was up for sale. The owners of a Jerusalem firm called Laser Pages attempted to bid for the company but the government selling authority would not meet with them or comment on their proposal, nor would they okay a meeting with Weizman Press officials. They were but one of several bidders who complained the government never replied to their proposals and discouraged all attempts to obtain information about the sale. Further, the government added a very dampening caveat giving it the right to change its mind about selling or alter the sale conditions. These are hardly the acts of someone sincere about selling his property.

Then there was the case of a Histadrut company called Rami Refractors which offered an open tender to buy. There was only one taker, the Provident Group headed by a Canadian, Marc Belzberg. After Belzberg agreed to buy the company for a million dollars more than it was worth, Rami announced that negotiations had broken down. This was a shock to Belzberg who thought things were going well. Shortly after, the Minister of Industry and Trade, Moshe Nissim, submitted a bid by a government company in his fiefdom, Israel Chemicals, to buy Rami. Belzberg reacted rather heatedly to the shenanigans saying Nissim was 'sending a message to the world that there is no room for the private sector in Israel'.[22]

Now if the government is trying to sell its assets, what is it doing buying another one from the Histadrut? What it's doing is extending its hold on the economy while cynically claiming the opposite. Time after time companies intended for sale to foreigners have been blocked for supposed security reasons while alternative attempts at selling shares of companies on the stock exchange have been halted because of a supposed fear that the Israeli public doesn't have the funds at hand to pay a proper price for the stocks.

Daniel Doron explains the likely reason why many leaders in the present government are opposed to sales of public companies: 'As long as such companies are in the hands of limited investment groups, what is termed "sweetheart deals" can easily be accomplished behind the scenes with a few phone calls. There is also the danger of interlocking directorships in which former government officials become company executives and vice versa helping each other out.'[23]

This very same Israel Chemicals is one of the companies the government is supposedly going to sell and MK Yair Levi of Shas has an idea of what should be done with the profits. According to Ha'aretz: 'When the Finance Committee discussed the sale of Israel Chemicals, Levi expressed the opinion that, "The company should be sold and the proceeds transferred immediately to the religious school system".'[24]

Besides the losses the public must swallow on operating expenses, the government shells out another $1.2 billion a year on very helpful subsidies. That is $100 million more than what America transfers yearly to Israel in the form of economic aid. The companies have to go, if Israel is ever to stop begging for foreign hand-outs, but the blockages never stop.

Israel Chemicals, Israeli Aircraft Industries and Agridev, an agricultural consulting company, are all meant to be put up for sale but because of supposed strategic considerations, no foreign group will be given controlling interest, hardly a conducive condition for an overseas purchase.

And it's not like overseas investors are rushing to Israel. In all of 1990, only a pathetic $100 million of foreign capital was invested in Israeli companies.[25] Word is out, Israel is a bad place to do business in.

Morton Mandel, an American industrialist, invests in Israel despite its awful reputation. But he has some words of caution for others contemplating the same thing: 'Government rules and regulations range from hostile to oppressive to stupid. They do not encourage a free market, nor do they give sufficient encouragement to export industries. And as far as privatisation goes, this has been handled poorly. All in all, it's harder to do business in Israel than it should be. If I wasn't Jewish I wouldn't bother.'[26]

Yet there are about 150 American corporations in Israel and some, such as Motorola, IBM and Digital, report success. Other stories aren't quite as happy. The government handed Intel over $50 million just to open up shop in Israel.[27] This was a dead loss as Intel sent most of its profits and results back to its head office with Israel gaining only in lower unemployment figures.

Sometimes Israel does not see eye to eye with its foreign guests. The Ministry of Labour and its deputy minister, Porush, actually sued American computer giant National Semiconductor in August 1991 for keeping workers on the job during the sabbath. An official at National Semiconductor was not overly thrilled at the prospect of having to pay a $2,000 fine for every employee violating Israel's arcane sabbath laws and subtly hinted that this insult could mean the end of the company in Israel. He vowed the company would stay, 'unless they make life too miserable for us'.[28]

With the threat of closure and the resultant loss of 500 jobs in one town of 15,000, a ministry official was asked if he would back off the suit. 'No,' he indignantly replied. 'What's important to us is the sabbath.'[29]

There is no choice. Israel must convince foreigners to buy its companies, partly because Israelis don't have the capital and in greater part, because America is demanding it. In October of '91, the American government ordered Shamir to sell off politically owned companies lest he endanger Israel's request for $10 billion in loan guarantees. Shamir reponded by heading an inter-ministerial committee on privatisation, which was nothing but a bluff. The Prime Minister has no interest in free market economics and the committee reflected his apathy.

SHOCKWAVES AGAIN

The Water Company (Mekorot) and the Israel Electric Company (IEC) are both government monopolies but to increase cost-efficiency, they have separate company structures. Throughout 1990 the electric company cut off power to the water company for unpaid bills. And without electricity, the water company cannot run its pumps and the consumer has empty pipes.

The water company owed the electric company $10 million at the beginning of 1990 but could not pay the bill because it was already $45 million in debt. So the electric company stopped sending power to pumping stations that were behind in their bills. The Knesset Economics Committee transferred an emergency $5 million to the electric company so the power went back on.

But by 28 November the IEC cut off power to four pumping stations because of an outstanding bill of $20 million. So the Ministry of Finance transferred another $2.5 million to the water company and the power was restored. By 20 December the electric company sent the water company a bill for $7.5 million more bringing the total debt to $25 million. And the electric company badly wanted that bill paid because it was in the red itself to the tune of $75 million. The water company was very careful to pay the power bills at its administrative centres, so its executives never had to read in the dark. It let the pumping stations run up bills, so the public wouldn't be able to wash and would shortly after place demands on the government to fix the intolerable situation.

Without delving into the core of matters, the water company belongs to the Ministry of Agriculture, while IEC is subject to the authority of the Energy Ministry. They don't always get along and it is up to the Finance Ministry to settle the differences. And all this trouble when the bills paid come from the same source, the government Treasury.

If the picture of water being cut off because the government's water company didn't pay the government's electric company seems bizarre, may we also point out that this same electric company gave itself illegal raises and allows its workers unlimited electricity. Daniel Doron justifies their behaviour:

> . . . those electrical worker monopolists who bind us to the electric chair with their hand on the switch, were not the inventors of our distorted, dishonest and sometimes violent economic system . . .
>
> Under this atrocious system, Israeli workers, who possess a human potential second to none, have to make do with a shameful wage of $1,000 a month. For this reason they must seek any avenue, legal or not, to 'finish the month'. Only thus can they provide their families with a decent level of housing, health and education . . .
>
> Those who fashioned such an iniquitous and corrupting system, those who maintain it by all kinds of 'arrangements', adjustments

and subterfuges, have no right to complain when others resort to similar tactics.[30]

There is a problem with Doron's logic: there are too many people justifying their own illegal cartels by comparing them to government practice. Examples abound but two will have to suffice.

A Scottish Israeli, David Wolfe, looked into opening a small business importing Scotch. He was threatened by his local liquor monopoly with violence if he pursued his enterprise. He wisely backed off.

A garbage collection contractor in the Galilee was not persuaded to refuse his winning municipal tender by hired representatives of the rubbish cartel, and was stabbed and had his car torched as a reward. Government monopolies have inspired private monopolists with such tactics.[31] It all conspires against the businessman trying to turn an honest buck.

If the government causes endless pain to the public when providing monopoly services, sometimes it gets a little back.

DA OILY BOID GETS DA WOIM

The government owned one of the big three networks of petrol stations called Paz. In the name of privatisation it sold the company to an Australian named Jack Lieberman for far less than it was worth. Lieberman later sold the company at a steep profit to two Poles.

In the meantime, though it lost its marketing branch, the government still maintained strict control on the cartel by owning the country's oil refineries. The refineries were criticised by the State Comptroller in 1990 for everything from poor maintenance and improper record-keeping of equipment to financial irregularities.

Privatisation of petrol marketing was a farce since the refineries charged the same price for fuel to all three marketing companies, regulated the price at the pump and determined the commission charged by agents of the companies. Though it sold its petrol stations, the government did not relinquish power over the monopoly.

But finally, the government got a taste of its own chicanery. The two Poles who bought Paz from Lieberman were involved in a huge fraud scheme that bilked the Polish government of up to $300 million. The fraud was Poland's Watergate and it led to the dismissal of the head of the central bank and criminal charges against seven top bankers.

Israel found itself in a real mess by the middle of August 1991. One of the Poles had taken Israeli citizenship and the Polish government wanted him extradited. A nice thought but Israel has no extradition treaty with Poland. Both he and his partner were put on Interpol's most wanted list. And here they were, the new owners of a former Israeli government company.[32]

By selling Paz on the cheap to businessmen totally uninterested and inexperienced in the petrol field, the government was asking for trouble. So why, oh why, we ask again, did they do it?

We don't know exactly but we do know more certainly that when the government is actually serious about selling a company, it sometimes makes the deal without open tender behind closed doors. That's how the American company Bear Stearns acquired the Jerusalem Economic Corporation for a fraction of its value and that's how Jack Lieberman got Paz. And that's how Paz was picked up by two chancers (and an Israeli partner) who just about broke the back of the fragile Polish banking system.

AN ACQUIRED TASE

Despite an economy built around socialist principles, Israel does have a stock market, a very peculiar one called the Tel Aviv Stock Exchange (Tase). Its practices are often unknown or unused in similar exchanges throughout the world.

The Tase is the only exchange open on a Sunday and the only one which prohibits simultaneous bidding. Stocks are offered one at a time and their daily prices are determined by one sale a day. So, if an oil stock is bought at 9 a.m. and civil war breaks out in Saudi Arabia at 9.30 a.m., there is no selling the stock until the next day when half of the kingdom's oil fields are ablaze. Because of this one-at-a-time selling approach, there is no official closing time at Tase. On a slow day, the traders can enjoy a peaceful early supper, on a busy day they may miss their evening viewing of *Dynasty*.

But what really separates Tase from other exchanges are unique regulations – or a great lack of them. Stocks may be and are sold with no or minimum voting rights, depriving stockholders of any say over how the company they partly own is run.

A far more serious deviation from normal stock trading practices is explained by former Tase managing director, Yossi Nitzani: 'In Israel, the board of directors of one financial institution can act as a company's banker, broker, mutual fund manager and underwriter.'[33]

What this means is that a board member of a bank may also be a board member of an insurance company. There is no Securities Exchange Commission to prevent such a blatant conflict of interest. If the bank issues shares, the board member can prevail upon the insurance company to purchase some of the stocks. Essentially, the little guy is locked out of the Tase by legalised manipulation of the companies issuing stocks. And as the reader will recall, in 1983, the banks exploited the flimsy regulations and lost the Israeli public a third of its savings.

The consequences of sanctified conflicts of interest are predictable enough: high volatility, instability and cheating. In 1990, 13 charges were filed for insider trading. The crimes need not be recounted. Let the example of Paz Oil Exploration suffice. Geologists discovered signs of oil and before Paz went public with the news, it informed an investment house which bought a large number of Paz shares just before they shot up.

Tase is government-run, hardly a surprising revelation in light of all that has been written. And as such, it is run incestuously. Yossi Nitzani, the previous Director-General, left his job for a better one as head of the government body in charge of selling public companies. Now since some of these companies have or will be sold on the Tase, Nitzani's appointment is a conflict of interest that would never be tolerated in any government professing honesty. Yet such is the way of the Israeli civil service where lateral career movement is compulsory and pensions start at age 40.

SHARING THE SYSTEM WITH OUR ARAB FRIENDS

Lucky Arabs of the disputed territories. They get to participate in the Israeli economy whether they want to or not.

It all started so hopefully back in 1967. Within a decade of Israeli rule, the Arabs saw their average incomes double, health services improve and school networks expand. But then again, Israel inherited a very poor populace to begin with. Once a level of prosperity bordering the decent was achieved, the Arabs stagnated with the rest of Israel.

Unfortunately for them they are subject to Israel's tariffs and import laws. Their economic fate is decided by the Civil Administration running the territories and the CA uses its privileges on Israel's behalf. The CA can interfere with the arranging of letters of credit, rewarding obedience with money transfers and punishing unco-operative behaviour with a denial of cash. It restricts the amount of Jordanian dinars brought into the territories to 70 a month per person, a genuine hardship since most of the population

save at Jordanian banks. The reasoning here is based on past
experience when the PLO transferred funds from Jordan to be
used for terrorist activities.

Other restrictions are less benign. Many well protected Israeli
business concerns are terrified by the prospect of Arab competition.
Labour in the territories is far cheaper than Jewish workers and
many Israelis are absolutely paranoid about being undercut. In
order to prevent the 'unfair' competition, they prevail on the CA
to deny permits to prospective businesses.

Nesher Cement has successfully prevented the building of a
cement factory in Hebron, while the kibbutzim have blocked a
chicken hatchery in Ramallah. It took 12 years of kibbutz objections
before a citrus processing plant was approved in the Gaza Strip
despite it being a joint venture with the Italian government and
the United Nations.

With opportunities denied them at home, the Arabs had to seek
work in the undisputed territories or what is known in some circles
as Israel proper. Before the 1987 uprising, 100,000 Arabs a day
crossed the Green Line to work. Instead of a trade in goods, there
was a one-way trade in cheap labour. The territories, especially
Gaza, became dependent on Israeli wages for their economic
viability.

But with the uprising came strikes and sabotage. Arab workers
became undependable and industries that relied on them, such as
orchards and construction, suffered significantly. Housing prices
rose as did the price of tomatoes in the winter of 1989, when
there weren't enough labourers to pick them and tons rotted in
the fields.

The Arab workers had to be replaced and with unemployment
hovering around the 10% mark, there should have been no problem
with that, right? Wrong. Israelis had become spoiled after 22 years
of cheap Arab labour and not enough would lower themselves to
take on this essential but menial labour.

So impoverished Israel imported 3,000 foreign workers, many
from Portugal, to make up the loss of Arab labourers. These 3,000
arrived on government visas, while undetermined thousands of
others entered the country on tourist visas and went straight to
work. Such are the opportunities for honest labour in a country
with over 10% of its workforce unhappily idle.

There are economists who claim the *intifada* was ignited and
fuelled by the Israeli stranglehold on the territorial economies.
As one economic observer notes, 'Difficult economic times make

for a very unrestful and resentful population.' As do endless taxes, tariffs, permits, licences, documents and bureaucrats.

SPEAK FRANKLY, EXPERTS

In August 1991, the government released figures asserting that the average Israeli family must spend just over $1,800 a month to live. However, the average Israeli family earns just under $1,125 a month. How do families make up the difference? They go into deeper debt, that's how.

Those figures alone sum up the tragic situation of the Israeli economy. But to drive home the point, here are the views of some experts. According to a *Jerusalem Post* editorial:

> Israel's main strength is in its creative, ingenious and enterprising human material. Its main impediment is that its collective genius is shackled by a malstructured, suffocating system . . . A country which could develop the fastest computer chip in the world . . . should be one of the world's most thriving economies, not an economic basket case.[34]

Indeed, basket case is not far off the mark. Israel's GNP is a trifling $42 billion a year compared to that of another small country, Denmark, which is over three times as large. What has barren Denmark got that we ain't? Alvin Rabushka lists some of the delights Denmark lacks:

> Israel's economy is ridden with money-losing state-owned enterprises, Histadrut's own debt-ridden industrial conglomerate, a huge government bureaucracy, massive public spending consuming three-fifths of the national income, dozens of official monopolies and cartels, massive taxpayer subsidies to manufacturers, price controls applied to a quarter of all consumer goods, tariff and non-tariff barriers to free trade, foreign exchange controls, government domination of the capital markets, government ownership of 93% of Israel's land, oppressive levels and rates of taxation and bureaucratic hurdles to entrepreneurship.[35]

See? Israel's got it all and more. Daniel Doron describes the fruits of such a fine tree:

> It is getting late. Our statist system has already managed to punish a most talented people with a failing economy . . . Large parts of our productive sector are collapsing. Our famous agriculture is facing

bankruptcy; our banking system and pension funds are threatened
with insolvency; the health system is failing; education is in decline,
water has become scarce and poisoned and the air is polluted.
Our system of political patronage radicalises competition between
ethnic and national groups and between secular and religious. By
weakening us materially and morally, the system jeopardises our
very security, robbing us of true independence.[36]

Robert J. Loewenberg, president of the Institute for Advanced
Strategic and Political Studies expands on Doron's last essential
point and the author will take the liberty of expanding on it still
further:

Israel's present system of political economy was created by the
Labour Party. Fed by the institutions created by Labour, the Likud
Party continues the old system. Both parties promote their fortunes
by means of economic policies which are essentially gambits to
assure themselves the means to sustain the present system. These
would-be economic policies are disguised as foreign policies. It is for
this reason that Israel has no economy and no foreign policy.[37]

Economics are politics in Israel and politics, economics. By
binding the hapless people to the economic system, the government
glues it to the wretched political system.

But the ploy is backfiring miserably. A broke Israel is a paralysed
Israel and a paralysed Israel can make no imaginative foreign
policies. Instead it is driven by the whims of an uncaring world.

We try to imagine a prosperous, confident Israel. It makes daring
moves first, it sets the tone and tenor of its own diplomacy, it
stands tall and true. It views the hopeless situation of holding
on to the Gaza Strip objectively. It realises that Egypt is in good
part responsible for the miserable condition of its people. From
1948 to 1967 it kept Gazans imprisoned in squalour, refusing to
invest in their future, rejecting students from its universities and
preventing the construction of universities within Gaza. It wiped
out the aspirations of a generation of Arab Gazans.

With 750,000 people crowded into a strip 36 miles long and eight
miles wide, Israel cannot afford to offer any sort of statehood for its
people. Any nation would be inherently unstable and unviable and
would pose a threat worse than fractured Lebanon only 40 km from
downtown Tel Aviv.

But next door to Gaza is the huge Sinai Peninsula, three times
the area of Israel but with only 50,000 inhabitants. If the Gaza Strip

were extended another 50 miles into the empty Sinai, there is the possibility of creating a workable state. If the desert was irrigated by Nile water, a country could more likely stand on its own feet.

Daring, independent Israel offers the world an option. It will release its hold on Gaza and permit a Palestinian state on condition that Egypt donate an equal area of land in the Sinai for such a state. Yet Egypt would never give up an inch of its holy soil nor allow a country of over a million radicalised Palestinians near its border. But the ball will be in her court for a change and Israel can lie back on its hammock and watch world pressure mount on Egypt.

The independent and proud economic miracle of Israel looks at the West Bank and takes action. It has promised autonomy to the Arab residents and grants it. All troops are withdrawn from Arab cities and towns. They will stay withdrawn provided the residents get on with their own lives without resort to violence against Jews. And if the autonomy holds, Israel will initiate the final stage – full autonomy. The land will be shared under a system called dual sovereignty. Jews living in Judea and Samaria will hold Israeli passports, while Arabs will travel under Palestinian passports. Civil law will be the concern of a united parliament, while land is sold at public auction.

If the Arabs abuse the autonomy and use the unpoliced cities as terrorist bases, Israeli troops will return and with the general understanding of the sane nations of the world. By invoking the autonomy promises of the Camp David Accords unilaterally, Israel created a bold new diplomacy, one the world respected for its attempt at fairness. And if the plan was not universally admired, there was a secret admiration for the Israeli government for its independence and courage in implementing it.

What a wonderful world it would be. But the real Israel 'don't know much about history' and does not instigate policy because it has no confidence in itself. And why should it? The place is broke, corrupt and pathetic. So it allows itself to be pushed around and outmanoeuvred by an American administration substantially hostile towards it. It permits itself to fall into diplomatic traps in order to get aid and loan guarantees to prop it up another year.

And soon, the paralysis is going to be very costly. Since the Gulf War, America has sidled up to the violent and unscrupulous Syrian régime. In return for joining in the alliance against Iraq, if not for actually fighting against Iraqis, Syria has been rewarded with promises by America to twist Israel's arm and secure for it the Golan Heights. No other prospect would lure Syria into talks with Israel. And since only 11% of Israelis are willing to give up the Heights for any agreement, Israel is about to be diplomatically isolated, an object of world derision and poorer, much poorer by the day.

It may be too late but Israel must reform its economic system completely and immediately. Once the government loosens its hold on the country's money, political reform will inevitably follow. But no economic reform is possible until American non-military aid is cut off and for good.

REMOVE THAT AID, YOU SCOUNDREL, AND BE DONE WITH IT
The sensitive reader will rightfully ask, if the government is hoodwinking the people out of its scarce funds in order to strengthen its grip on their lives, why don't the people of Israel in one voice demand change?

The answer lies in what the author coins, the '*Baruch Hashem* syndrome'. This concept tries to explain the defeatism of almost all Israelis.

Baruch Hashem, literally means, Blessed is His name. In our context it means, thank God for that. At the founding of the state, Israel had little industry, meagre housing, an expensive military responsibility, and as many new immigrants as oldtimers. Most of the newcomers had barely escaped death at the hands of anti-semites and were grateful to be alive at all. No matter how poor they were in Israel, their fates were infinitely better than what they had escaped. Even if they lived in unheated, leaky shacks in winter and lacked proper clothing, there was enough to eat. A new immigrant in 1952 would trudge to his grocer, buy a cheap subsidised loaf of bread and remark, 'At least there's enough to eat in Israel', to which the grocer would reply, '*Baruch Hashem*'. Thank God for that.

Forty years later one economic observer notes, 'Israelis are still grateful when they buy an egg. They think someone has blessed them.'

Israelis will not protest against the thoroughly corrupt statism and the politicians can continue riding roughshod on them at will. No power within the state can deflate or defeat the appalling theft of the people's money by the powers that govern, be they cabinet ministers, bankers, union representatives, manufacturers or executives of the Jewish Agency. The only hope available that can possibly put an end to the economic crimes that characterise the Israeli status quo comes from outside. Foreigners, mostly American, pump over $6 billion in aid every year into Israel and by doing so, they finance a dying system and prop it up for another long season. If the aid stopped, Israel would have to become efficient, equitable and fair to its people.

Most of the aid arrives in four ways: German reparations payments, charity, through the sale of State of Israel Bonds and via American government assistance. There are many objections to the continued purchase of State of Israel Bonds. The Bonds were first issued in 1950 and monies raised by their sale went into building the infrastructure of the state. Four decades and many billions of dollars later, the bond sales go not directly to construction projects but straight into the Treasury where they cover the government's debts.

During the 1980s, over a billion dollars of bonds were sold to construct a hydroelectric project called the Med-Dead Canal. This futuristic scheme described in many a glossy brochure was a terrific sales inducement. Unfortunately, the canal was never built and it is not known if any bonds purchaser received his investment back.

Bonds purchasers make a sacrifice; the return on Israel Bonds is considerably less than is offered by almost all other bonds on the market. Even with the added tax deduction that comes with the purchase of the bonds, a gift from Uncle Sam, they are still a pretty dreary investment. Yet they are among the most successful bond issues in the world, raising about a billion dollars annually. Since Shamir promised that 1990's bonds would build homes for immigrants, we will assume that a decent amount of the money was received by the Housing Minister, Ariel Sharon. If so, as previously described, it eventually landed in the pockets of overpriced and unscrupulous government-connected contractors. Bonds purchasers, in essence, contributed to the well-being of Israel's uniquely tainted Housing Ministry instead of to honest private builders who would have been called on to construct homes in the absence of a government budget large enough to handle the task immorally.

As long as well-meaning friends of Israel buy billions in bonds, they are helping to finance the deficits of the ethically bankrupt Israeli government and are delaying the emergency reform measures needed if the country is ever to survive. By giving money to Israel Bonds, buyers are helping to kill the state.

The situation is similar but more complicated when discussing American government aid. A little background is needed before diving into these contentious waters.

Up to the Yom Kippur War in 1973, Israel received very

little American aid, about $50 million a year (discounting the aftermath of the Six Day War in 1967 when aid topped $650 million). Without aid, the Israeli economy grew at about 8% a year despite the economic system. In 1973, Israel received over $2 billion in American aid and since has received an additional sum of some $45 billion.[38]

It is not a coincidence that in the very year, 1973, that Israel accepted its first huge infusion of American aid, the economy ground to a halt. Since that year Israel's yearly economic growth has fallen from 8% to zero or, in some years, less.

Long-term aid is bad for every country. One thinks of nations such as South Korea or Taiwan which weaned themselves from American aid and compares these vigorous economies with the miserable state of such ongoing aid recipients as Mexico, Egypt and the Philippines. Aid tends to stay in the hands of those in power and once there, the hands become very dirty. It is rare when the intended recipients of the aid, the peoples of the countries, benefit from the largesse.

The government-run economy has so sapped the Israeli worker of desire that productivity is only $27,000 a year per labourer, or half that of well-run nations. And every penny of American economic aid coming into Israel, is one penny less, not more, in the hands of the Israeli worker.

As Joel Bainerman writes in the *Wall Street Journal:*

> The loss of US aid would be a blessing for Israel's economy ... Israel is dependent on US aid only because of its foolish economic choices. The moment that the US ceases to pick up the yearly overdraft, Israel will be forced to change its ways ... the economic shock of an aid cut-off could well precipitate political reform – particularly a stronger executive and the abandonment of the decrepit political system that gives tiny extremist parties veto over national policy.[39]

Had Israel used the massive aid received in the 1970s and 1980s properly, it might have been helpful. However, instead of funnelling the money into investment, the government, beginning with Rabin and continuing rampantly with Begin, directed it towards personal consumption. The philosophy was that voters with additional money will support the government at the next elections. This strategy worked wonders for the Likud in 1981 when tariffs were lowered and a buying spree erupted just before the election. However, this aid-inspired prosperity led directly and quickly to 450% inflation and the near collapse of the economy.

Aid became an addiction as the economy went into a tailspin and only more aid could bail it out. By 1991, foreign aid totalled 7% of the entire GNP and junkie Israel needed a yearly injection lest it suffer through a very painful withdrawal cold turkey. The time had come for Israel to recognise its disease for what it was and take the necessary measures to get unhooked. A piece appearing in *Newsday* in July 1991, explains why nothing was done to cure the patient: 'Israeli politicians would rather stand in line for charity than diminish their stranglehold over the economy. Why? Because control over the economy translates into political domination. This ugly fact of Israeli life is the key to understanding what makes Israel tick . . .'

American aid is divided into two: $1.8 billion is for military purchases, while $1.1 billion is targeted for civilian economic aid. Most of the aid is in the form of easy credit and must be returned. The debt on these credits now totals about $10 billion.

The military aid mostly stays within the American economy since it is used to purchase American equipment. As long as the US supplies the Arabs with massive amounts of sophisticated weaponry ($20 billion to Saudi Arabia in 1991), it has a moral obligation to assure that Israel is not annihilated by these weapons. But instead of forcing Israel to beg for its annual military assistance, life would be much simpler if Israel was included as part of the permanent US defence budget in the same way that NATO or South Korea are. But such a logical move would decrease presidential leverage on Israel so will not be taken.

It is the civilian aid which is so futile. Every year Israel must repay $1.2 billion on its $10 billion aid debt and that is almost precisely what it receives in civilian aid. Israel's highest-ranking government ministers must trek to Washington annually to beg for money that stays in the US anyway. It would be so much simpler to cancel the $10 billion debt in return for an end to future civilian aid.

The *Journal of Commerce* on 9 January 1990 contemplated the effects of debt forgiveness for aid cancellation: 'If Israel and the United States came to a new arrangement, Congress wouldn't have to pass an aid package every year and Israel would no longer be the No. 1 recipient of US foreign aid. The State Department would no longer be able to manipulate Israel by warning, "Do what we say or we'll cancel this gift we give you."'

The issue of aid for US diplomatic blackmail is doing possibly irreparable harm to relations between Israel and the US. It is an unhealthy way for two sovereign nations to be allied. Since the unexpected arrival of the wave of Soviet immigrants and the government botch-up of their absorption, Israel has become terrified of losing its US aid connection. And Israelis must witness the sad spectacle of their leaders touring the White House on their knees.

Soviet immigrants worried Bush/Baker because inevitably many would be drawn to the territories – not because of government directing. Lower housing prices, due in part to government incentives, had the potential of attracting many thousands of indigent immigrants eastward. Bush/Baker decided that such incentives must be stopped in order to put a real freeze on 'settlements'.

Their chance to put their policy into action came in 1991. Right in the middle of the Gulf War when American lives by the thousands were at risk, Finance Minister Modai demanded $10 billion in aid as payment for Israel's restraint. The demand was crude, insensitive, led to the wrath of Congress and the deep shame of Israelis.

That ploy having failed, the Israeli government lowered its expectations and later requested $10 billion in loan guarantees to absorb immigrants. Bush/Baker saw their opening and pressed ahead with their 'settlement' freeze and even threw in talks with Syria over the future withdrawal from the Golan Heights as a condition of the guarantees. Israel's addiction to American aid was becoming very, very expensive.

Arye Stav, editor of the Israeli publication, *Nativ*, comments on the turn of events:

> . . . all the advantages together are as nothing compared to the urgent need to be freed of our status as the rather stepped-on doormat of the opulent Americans. The unbearably heavy price of this self-abasement . . . is paid by us daily, starting with the amazingly nasty remarks of the Secretary of State, who would not dare direct them to the least of the banana republics and ending with the brutal pressing of Israel to embrace the explosive booby-trap of a Palestinian state . . . Israel must detach herself from this dependence, which embodies losing political independence, which in the Israeli situation means endangering its very existence.[40]

Accepting aid is deeply humiliating for Israelis no matter how many psychotic justifications they come up with for the handouts.

In order to be eligible for charity, a person or a country must be in a pitiful state. If Israel wasn't pitiful, then it would not deserve pity in the form of aid. Businessmen are not interested in investing in a pitiful nation and tourists don't flock to visit one. As long as Israel chooses to portray itself as pathetic in order to secure American aid, it will be treated with scorn by the very people who could contribute to its prosperity.

Israel has the admiration of most Americans for its guts in standing up to its enemies, but much of this goodwill is thrown away when it begs for aid. No issue causes such bad feelings between Israel and the American people as the aid hand-out. Millions of Americans resent throwing their money into a black hole from which it will never return.

America has its own debt to take care of and that must come before Israel's. And the American lower and middle classes are losing financial ground. The tougher their economic situation, the more they will turn against Israel for taking their tax money. And who can blame them? In a world where hundreds of millions starve, well-fed Israelis are hardly the most deserving of American foreign aid. America shouldn't be giving it and Israel shouldn't be taking it.

The Israeli people are far prouder than their leaders. Most work hard and pay their own way. But few are independent because their government has made them dependent on it for economic survival. Now these same oligarchs, rascals and scoundrels that have demeaned their productive lives have made their country dependent on America to cover its debts.

American aid must be cut off for the sake of the Israeli people and the nation's pride. Any American Jewish leader or pro-Israel congressman who pushes for continued aid, no matter how decent his intentions, deserves the wrath of all Israelis longing for freedom and prosperity.

The author has but one plea in his book and it is to all pro-Israel American politicians:

PLEASE CUT ALL AID
IT IS CONTRIBUTING TO THE FALL OF ISRAEL

CHAPTER EIGHTEEN

Back to the Creepy Knesset

The cycle of this study is complete. It began with a look at the politicians, continued with an examination of a system abused by the politicians and will now end where it began, at the Knesset.

Months have passed since this study began and since then either new events or new discoveries by the author prove that things are becoming far worse. Over and over, the author was warned that if he didn't balance criticism with positive developments he would be labelled a crank with a bone to pick. Certainly, the Israeli system has produced some glory in the past: major breakthroughs in solar energy, the invention of arid-land farming techniques including drip irrigation, legendary military feats. But the weight of evidence that supports internal collapse is so overwhelming, and the danger that all the accomplishments will be crushed by the rubble of a fallen nation so great, the author has chosen the muddy route taken. If the reader needs any more facts to support the thesis that Israel could fall under the weight of its own governmental corruption, here are a few: former MK Shmuel Flatto Sharon was sued by one Paul David for defrauding him of $9 million in a phoney African jewel deal; the speaker of the Knesset presented a list of cabinet ministers who had refused to reply to questions put to them in one session of parliament. Not surprisingly, Ariel Sharon of housing misallocations notoriety led the pack, refusing replies to 33 queries. Second on the list was Yitzhak Peretz, the minister responsible for botching immigration. He was followed by our old friend, Arye Deri. No action was taken against those ministers who refused to explain their policies and actions before their fellow MKs; 17 MKs failed to provide income statements to the Knesset by the legal deadline, a procedure intended to quash conflicts of interest. Among these shirkers were Aharon Abuhatzeira, previously indicted for embezzlement of public money, Pesach Gruper, who shifted government funds to his son's farm and bank, Michael Kleiner, the advocate of immigrant rights, Yair Levy, the Shas MK everyone thought had run away to avoid a police investigation, Shimon Peres, the man who destroyed the only party strong enough to oppose Likud incompetence, Chaim Kauffman, the importer of Lego toys and Barbie Dolls who makes sure high tariffs are slapped on the competition, and Yisrael Kessar, head of the Histadrut – need more be said?[1]

High-level Israeli politics is sinking to new depths. A review of recent events in the three main power blocs more than adequately describes the state of putrefaction.

ORTHODOX BEHAVIOUR

Amost half a year after this study began, Arye Deri is still Minister of the Interior. This is despite the fact of a report in August 1991 by the State Comptroller which traced $40.5 million misused by Deri and the subsequent fining of his party for misallocations of funds.

On 26 July, Eli Landau, the Likud mayor of Herzlia made a powerful accusation in print. He claimed that back in 1987, he approached PM Shamir and informed him that Deri was shifting government money illegally to his cronies. 'Shamir said, "I see," but nothing happened.'[2] If his accusation is true, then the Prime Minister of Israel allowed embezzlement to carry on for over four years in his government. This would make him no less an accomplice to a crime than Beilin or Peres who have been accused of keeping track of the graft and later exploiting their knowledge to bring down the government.

Landau offered one alternative for Shamir. He 'should demonstrate a respectful sense of responsibility and resign.' The author believes there is another possibility. He, along with Peres and Beilin, should be put on trial as willing accomplices in the massive misuse of Israeli public money.

Landau, paraphrased, sums up the present ruling system. 'It all comes down to a rotten government that was built on the basis of a few shady deals that effectively ridiculed the intelligence of the country's citizens.'[3]

One Orthodox politico who was put on trial was the secretary-general and treasurer of the Degel HaTorah Party, Menachem Carmel. He was indicted on charges of filing false statements in order to defraud. During the last national election campaign, Carmel, a man of God, falsely submitted a report to the government claiming $410,000 of donations were actually loans, in order to make his party eligible for higher government election recompensation.

In another scam, TV reporter Moshe Shlonsky obtained documents strongly suggesting that some Orthodox men were defrauding the social security office by claiming army compensation without actually doing army service. The Deputy Minister of Religious Affairs, Moshe Gaphny of Degel HaTorah, had Shlonsky arrested in an attempt to both intimidate him and find out who gave him the sensitive evidence of religious fraud.

LOVE, LABOUR'S LOST

Over at the Labour Party, it was business as usual, which means Peres was trying to find new ways to stay in power and further his party's demise. As noted previously, a 1990 poll by Rafi and Hanoch Smith revealed that only 21% of the electorate supported Labour.[4]

On 14 July 1991, the same Smith brothers unveiled the results of another poll. They asked the public who they would prefer as the leader of Labour and only 17% of Israelis chose Peres. To give an example of the lack of choices plaguing the country, twice as many people preferred Rabin, and the next year he did take over the party leadership. But with only 21% of the population supporting Labour, Rabin took over what was Peres's corpse.

To revive the cadaver some younger Labourites have been demanding change. Even Yossi Beilin, 'Peres's poodle', as Rabin calls him, demanded the end of Labour's symbols, the red flag, the singing of the *Internationale* and May Day celebrations. Any rational person could see that the hundreds of thousands of Soviet Jews who will vote in upcoming elections, will not support a party that reminds them of the politics they left behind. But Peres and the party's old guard rejected the changes, Soviet voters be damned.

In a further attempt to resuscitate the corpse, Labour initiated a membership drive in 1991. The results were pitiful and most humiliating. So the party turned to the Histadrut which set up membership booths on the premises of its factories and other interests. Suddenly membership in the party soared, much to the joy of its leaders. Such happiness was not long-lasting, however, when the press reported that the new membership had been coerced into joining the party if they wanted to stay in the good graces of their Histadrut bosses (or, more likely, if they wanted to keep on working). Six months later, Peres came to regret his party's decision to use the Histadrut to up its membership. Histadrut chairman Israel Kessar had gathered enough political support to challenge Peres for the Labour Party's leadership. He attracted 19% of the central committee's vote, just enough of a shift to allow Rabin to take the prize from Peres.

There seemed to be no end to the shame and finally the remaining rationalists of the party decided to take action. A movement was started that will surely lead to future leaders being chosen through primaries instead of by the central committee. In a democratic system, Peres wouldn't have stood a chance of staying party leader. However, when primaries were instituted, they did not determine party leadership, only the pecking order of rank and file. The leadership was still determined by a vote of the central committee. Nonetheless, to thwart the primaries before they had a chance of being instituted, the astute old leader of the Opposition called for early elections, much to the chagrin of the rest of his party. Reports suggested that he and Shamir, who also has reasons for preferring an early election, would soon be colluding to that end. It would be just like Peres to have led his party into an election which it would have lost miserably, just to keep his leadership. And it would have been just like his party to fall into the trap. And indeed the party did fall into the trap but Peres fell into one of his own. Shortly after the announcement of early elections, his party replaced him with Rabin as leader.

YOUR HONOUR, MEMBERS OF THE JURY, THE LIKUD . . .
After funding national, municipal and Histadrut elections since 1988, the Likud is broke. Very broke. It owes almost $40 million in bank loans and at one point didn't even have enough cash on hand to send letters to its members.

Legal funding of parties is restricted to party memberships, individual donations up to $10,000 and most important of all, a Knesset allocation of about $16,000 per MK per year and double that in an election year. Corporations are not permitted to donate to parties and soon we'll see how the Likud skirted that section of the funding law, but first a look at the Knesset allocations.

In late 1990, the Likud and Labour were both broke and in a rare show of unity, passed a bill in the Knesset raising their public allocations by 36%. After the parties grabbed the loot, the High Court declared the bill illegal and demanded that the parties return the extra cash. Only two parties, Eitan's Tzomet and Rubinstein's Shinui, began returning the money. Likud and Labour held on to their share of the bonanza and were so reluctant to give it up, that in defiance of the highest court of the land, they passed a bill in the Knesset retroactively legalising the allocations. On this strange technicality the Knesset voted itself $9 million in public money, against the will of Israelis and their judicial system. On this issue alone, the Knesset proved it has little respect for the laws other Israelis are forced to obey.

The Likud was smart enough to know that flouting the funding law too openly would cause a backlash so it created some straw companies and a slush fund so that corporations could bypass the legal system and donate to the party. In both 1988 and 1989, the State Comptroller charged that the Likud did not audit its income properly and in both years fined the party a million dollars, significantly adding to its debt.

The people in charge of Likud Party finances were an accountant, Mordechai Yahel, and his two superiors, Menachem Atzmon and Health Minister Ehud Olmert. Of Olmert, much has been written. His greed is nationally renowned and one joke is that his law firm charges $10,000 a meal for clients to eat at the Knesset cafeteria. The implication of the joke is that he sells influence, for there is no other reason for paying $10,000 to eat the bland fare offered in this government setting.

In June 1991 the press reported that a deputy minister, Sharir, and two ministers, Patt and Olmert, were investigated by the police for misuse of public funds. All had taken vacations abroad with party money, and Olmert even took his family with him on his 'fund-raising trip'.

For those counting, that makes three more ministers (or deputies) of the present government who underwent a police investigation. (Two, if you delete Olmert on grounds that he had already been investigated for shady dealing with the North American Bank.) Never in Israel's history have almost a dozen government MKs been put through police investigations.

The above-mentioned trips abroad were discovered when the police perused the files of a fictitious company set up by the Likud. In the national election year of 1988, Yahel set up two straw companies. One was foolishly called B.M.Y. Shachar. The foolhardy, carefree and blithe accountant used the initial of his wife Bruria, added his own, 'M' for Mordechai, 'Y' for Yahel and completed the clever word-play with his son's name, Shachar. It wasn't difficult for the police to establish a connection between Yahel and the phoney company he set up for the Likud. However, no connection was established between Yahel and his boss, Olmert. The literate accountant took the whole rap for the scheme and he was charged with tax evasion.

Meanwhile, the 'funding' scam worked like this: corporations otherwise banned from making political contributions instead charged one of the phoney companies for some consulting service and the fictitious company returned a receipt. The money then went straight into Likud party coffers. The corporations thus donated to the party in clear violation of the law but their transactions were on the books as consultancy fees.

Over 60 companies donated to the Likud via this back door and two are worth noting. The Israel Diamond Exchange, reportedly the biggest single enterprise in the country, donated $90,000 – who knows what concessions they expected to extract – and a car importer intimately connected to Bank Discount chipped in another $45,000.[5] There may not be a connection but it is worth mentioning that Shamir later supported the Recanati family's claim on the disgraced and corrupt bank despite the large role Discount played during the shares crash of '83.

During the later municipal elections, the Likud came up with a simpler plan for evading the law. They hired a number of PR firms which agreed to record direct cash transfers for the campaign as company business. After recording the donations as company income, the PR firms returned receipts to the corporations. In July 1989 Haolam Hazeh reported that among the companies which agreed to support the Likud through this back door was a large importer of Japanese cars, Elite Chocolates and Coca Cola. One wonders if the folks in Atlanta know their Israeli subsidiary partakes of illegal political funding.

As clever as these tricks were, still the Likud found itself in desperate financial straits. So it pulled yet another rabbit out of its hat. Israeli law prohibits individual donations over $10,000 and not many Israelis have the kind of cash Likud needed. The answer to its financial woes could be found in sympathetic foreigners, if a way around the individual donation restriction could be worked out.

And yes, the devious minds of the Likud fund-raising team came up with a beauty. It involved getting foreign multi-millionaires to guarantee bank loans for the party. Now, let's say the Likud couldn't repay the loans . . . well then the guarantors would just have to pick up the tab. The reader has to admit, it's a neat way of getting someone to donate indirectly. And whilst the whole scheme might be legal, it undoubtedly flaunts the spirit in which the law was enacted.

And who better to put the scheme in action than, you guessed it, Olmert? In March 1991, smack dab in the middle of another threatened doctors' strike, Health Minister Olmert flew to Zurich and London on 'ministry business'. The people he met symbolise all the shady and rancid connections between the Israeli government and money.

In London, Olmert met with Robert Maxwell and an American magnate named Alan E. Kasaden. Maxwell had been seriously investing in Israel since the Likud took power but had not then been accused of suspicious dealings with Israel. In the aftermath of his death, the story of Maxwell's involvement in Eastern European arms purchases funnelled by Israel to the Contras began to come to the surface. And Kasaden was involved in a most disreputable chapter of recent Israeli history.

The reader will remember, if all the corruption hasn't turned him comatose, that Yitzhak Modai refused to join the current coalition unless the Likud guaranteed him $10 million in case it did not form the government. Well, the Likud buckled and turned to Kasaden to guarantee half of Modai's demand.

While in Zurich, Olmert met with Edmond Safra. The author realises it's getting late so to remind the reader, Safra is the inexplicable owner of that most peculiar institution supposedly unconnected to the government, the First International Bank of Israel or FIB for short.

The meeting must have been an unconditional success, for Olmert and FIB apparently reached an understanding. According to *Haolam Hazeh* on 29 May 1991, Likud spokesman Gil Samsonov confirmed that loan negotiations had begun and with, who else but Bank Discount of recent under-the-table donations notoriety and FIB, that infamous independent bank without government connections?

Revelations of Olmert's secret life appeared again in *Haolam Hazeh* on 24 June 1991 and this episode epitomises all the dubious dealings American Jews innocently support when they donate to the UJA. The Jewish Agency sold a losing real estate company, Hachsharat Hayishuv, to the Nimrodi family in March of 1988. The head of this family is the very same gentleman who was one of the original Israeli go-betweens in Iran-Contra and who was later investigated by the police on suspicion of having something to do with $2 million missing in the whole messy affair.

Nimrodi purchased the company shares from Bank Leumi, which is owned by the Jewish Agency, and which funnels most American charitable donations to Israel. According to *Haolam Hazeh*, by the mid-1980s the late chairman of the Agency, Arye Dulzin, had tacit understanding with Leumi chairman, Ernst Yaphet. Yaphet agreed to let Dulzin do what he wanted with Hachsharat Hayishuv, if Dulzin gave Yaphet a free hand at Leumi. That hand eventually took $7.5 million of customer money and ran to America after its owner was implicated in the great bank robbery of 1983.

Now every great deal needs a great lawyer. And who negotiated this very profitable transaction? You uncannily guessed it again. And give Olmert credit, he was very useful to Nimrodi. He arranged the sale thanks to his close political ties to Irwin Levy, Chairman of the Board of Governors of the Jewish Agency's Companies Department. A little later Nimrodi sold 50% of the company at a great profit to the Bernard Moss Group of Australia. Now how did the Nimrodi, a humble provocateur in Irangate, find such a willing buyer? You guessed it again, Olmert did a little matchmaking.

For arranging the two deals, Olmert demanded a fee of $1 million from Nimrodi. Nimrodi refused to pay such an outlandish amount so the dispute was settled by a mediator, namely Yosef Chechover, chairman of Bank Discount, the same institution that 'donated' funds to the Likud, through the phoney company set up by the accountant working for Olmert. Chechover apparently decided that Olmert deserved $400,000 for his difficult work. Now since he was about to be a minister in the 1988 government, Olmert couldn't just accept a cheque like that and, almost as soon as it was issued, he resigned from his law firm. We assume his associates found a way to get the money to him somehow.[6]

It's all so ugly. And it's not just Olmert. The Israeli political system is diseased and the public's trust is violated daily. So why, oh why, isn't the cry for change ringing throughout the land? The truth is, it is but it's a cry muffled by a government of mediocrities conniving to hold on to all the advantages that come with power.

IF YOU DON'T REFORM THE SYSTEM I'M GONNA HOLD MY
BREATH 'TIL I TURN BLUE
Of the failure to handle the recent wave of immigration, Yosef Goell writes:

> The single and deadliest [reason for the failure] must be attributed to the endemic incapability of any Israeli government to govern, owing to the pernicious combination of a paralysis-inducing system of government and the most feckless bunch of political leaders in Israel's history . . .
>
> The question confronting our political leaders at this time is how much nearer the brink of catastrophe the country will have to be brought before they are ready to buckle down to the task of altering the manner in which we govern ourselves?[7]

One thing is certain, it will not be Shamir who leads the country to reform. Of Shamir, Goell notes succinctly that he 'seems indifferent to the values of good government, the rule of law and the need for clean-fingered politicians'.[8] His point was proven in the summer of 1991 when the public and a few decent politicians demanded that the Knesset vote on a new law that would lead to the direct election of the Prime Minister and a Knesset half selected by the public in representative elections.

In brief, four different MKs proposed electoral changes and one of the MKs was Uriel Lynn of the Likud. He was appointed to head the Knesset law committee which would meld the best features of the four proposals into one bill. With him at the head of the committee, it seemed like reform was a sure thing.

The public wanted change, that was clear to even the densest of politicians. In 1990 hundreds of thousands had gathered outside Tel Aviv's City Hall in Israel's largest-ever demonstration, demanding electoral reform. By 1991, according to a poll conducted by the Teleskar Institute, 76.9% of Israelis wanted the electoral system changed while a mere 9.9% preferred to keep things as they were. And to keep these 9.9% satisfied, and retain the status quo, Shamir decided to prevent passage of the reform bill. He could not openly oppose reform without a huge public backlash, so he put immense pressure on Uriel Lynn, a reformist MK and previously a man of great integrity, to delay introduction of the bill when it was up before the committee Lynn headed. Shortly before, David Wolfson, the director of a reform organisation had asked, 'Will Mr Lynn risk his party seat for this bill, or will he too be part of the erosion?'[9] He suspected long before anyone else what Shamir undoubtedly did – i.e. threaten Lynn with the loss of his job. Lynn reacted to Shamir's pressure by employing a variety of stalling tactics, meaning that by the end of the Knesset session, the reform bill remained in limbo, unvoted upon and unpassed. As a result the next election will be conducted like all the others.

Israel is not the first nation stuck with a system based on internal party selection of its governors. The Jerusalem Centre for Public Affairs, in a pamphlet supporting reform, reminds Israelis that:

The European experience in the 1930s proved, in a most tragic manner, the consequences of a democratic régime based on proportional representation ... The paralysis that gripped the democracies of the Weimar Republic, Republican Spain and

pre-fascist Italy, invited the dictatorships that arose on the ruins
of the failed parliamentary institutions.[10]

So we have another happy scenario. If Israel's system leads
the nation to the edge of the precipice, its people may choose
dictatorship to put things back together. And who's to say that's
not a better choice than an anarchy so profound, Israel will be easy
pickings for its Arab neighbours?

HELP! SOS! MAYDAY! EMERGENCY! MAN OVERBOARD!
Israel has suffered from a deeply tainted political and economic
system since its founding and now the vice is spreading from the
decaying body. But let the reader be reminded again, the system
is to blame, not the vast majority of Israelis. As a symbol of the
country's present predicament, a few years before this writing, the
Yad Vashem Holocaust memorial board threatened to close down if
it didn't receive government funding. Inside Yad Vashem is a library
containing the names of most of the victims of the Holocaust and an
eternal flame in memory of the Jews murdered in Europe. Lack of
funding from a bureaucracy threatened to extinguish the flame of
sorrow that links Israel with the tragedy that justifies its existence
forever.

And sheer incompetence is promulgating a worldwide lie that
Israel's existence is unjustified. From 1948 to the mid-1950s, there
was a demographic exchange in the Middle East: 500,000 Arabs left
Israel while 800,000 Jews were pressed to leave their homes in Arab
countries. Neither group were compensated for their losses but while
Israel accepted the Jewish refugees and gave them homes, the Arabs
rejected the Palestinians and caused them to remain stateless. That
is a summary of the whole issue that dominates world diplomacy.

And bungling, paralysed Israel has made sure only one side of
the argument is an issue. Israel may soon sink under the weight
of the defamation.

The shift in worldwide public perception has trained Israel's
position in the regional peace talks of 1991/92. After four meetings
in Madrid and Washington, the Syrian delegation did not agree
to sit with the Israelis and discuss simple issues like water and
environmental protection. Yet as the talks inched towards collapse,
Israel received the brunt of the blame for its 'intransigence'
on the issue of Palestinian autonomy. While Syria, a vicious
totalitarian régime, has no need to explain its support of terrorism
or torture, Israel cannot get across the obvious message that an

Arab-controlled West Bank would be used as a military base against the heart of the Jewish state, if not within a year after such relinquishing of control, then almost certainly within a decade.

Israel's wrongs are not external, no matter how many people may think so. Her greatest crimes are not against anyone but her own sorrowful people. And that includes not only the poor Israelis but world Jewry, which desperately needs some sort of inspiration to go on existing.

After the Holocaust, Jews suffered a severe loss of faith. The rise of Israel offered Jews renewed belief. In an increasingly secular world, Israel replaced the Jewish religion as the primary focus for continued Jewish existence. It turns out this was a huge case of misplaced hope.

According to a report in *Newsweek* in August 1991 and confirmed by many similar studies, 52% of American Jews marry out of their religion and only 20% of their offspring are raised Jewish. The figures in Europe and South America are no more hopeful. There are clearly many other factors, but since the founding of Israel, the Jewish people, as never before in their history, have voluntarily decided to opt out of their heritage.

If Israel is not entirely to blame for the quickening disappearance of the Jewish people, she has hardly provided a reason to carry on. As the memory of the Holocaust fades, a new generation of Jews seeks pride in their nation of Israel and finds instead mostly crime, corruption and greed.

The author is a stubborn and proud Jew and Israeli. It is for Israel that he has risked his life in combat before and is willing to do so again. But he has no desire to witness the Fall of Israel. Inculcated in the Jewish tradition are all the values required to run a stable, fair and prosperous nation. The rulers of Israel have strayed from the greatness of their heritage and are dragging the nation headlong into a collision with calamity.

And unless those in power wake up to the tragedy they have foisted upon their nation and take the appropriate measures, the country will fall as sure as God watches over Israel. And this time no power in heaven will ever create a sovereign Jewish nation again.

Notes

CHAPTER ONE

1. David Horovitz, 'Shas's Deri accused of blackmailing local government', *Jerusalem Post (JP)*, 26/11/89; Dan Izenberg, 'Deri's defenders caught up in special government funding', *JP*, 22/6/90.
2. Asher Wallfish, 'Shas in fight for its life', *JP*, 1990.
3. Norm Guthartz, 'Panel gives retroactive OK for NIS 400,000 to Shas schools', *JP*.
4. Dan Izenberg, 'Controversial tape enmeshed in complex legal tangle', *JP*, 5/9/90.

CHAPTER TWO

1. Yosef Goell, 'The steep price of Haredi support', *JP*, 2/12/90.
2. Yosef Goell, 'A plague on both your houses', *JP*, 7/90.
3. Ismar Schorsch, 'Who's a Jew – again', *Jewish Echo*, 12/4/90.
4. Shmuel Flatto, Sharon's criminal involvement in France.
   Ma'ariv, 22/12/88, p 2.
   Government posts for the religious parties in the National Unity Government of 1988 were as follows:
   Shas:
   Rabbi Yitzhak Peretz – Absorption Ministry.
   Rabbi Arye Deri – Interior Ministry.
   National Religious Party:
   Zevulon Hammer – Religious Affairs Ministry.
   Avner Shaki – Minister without Portfolio.
   Agudat Yisrael:
   Rabbi Moshe Ze'ev Feldman – Deputy Minister responsible for the Labour and Welfare Ministry.

CHAPTER THREE

1. Sarah Honig and Michal Yudelman, 'Labour promised Aguda more', *JP*.
2. *Ma'ariv*, 13/11/88, p 1,2.
   Controversy regarding the Who's a Jew legislation: '27 major Jewish organizations oppose Who's a Jew'.
   Ma'ariv, 18/11/88, p 1.
   'As a result of the storm amongst American Jewry, Shamir says that a broad government is necessary.'
   Remark: The proposed 'Who's a Jew' legislation is an amendment to the

Israeli Law of Return, granting all people, born of a Jewish mother or converted to Judaism, the right to obtain Israeli citizenship. The religious parties wish to amend the law to disqualify conversions which do not conform to Rabbinic Law. This would exclude Reform and most Conservative conversions that are performed, mainly in the United States. As a result the Reform and Conservative Movements are strongly opposed to the amendment.'

3. *Ma'ariv*, 27/4/90, p B2.
Arye Deri's involvement in the collapse of the National Unity Government in March 1990 from the viewpoint of the Labour Party once it became clear that they could not form an alternative government.

4. *Ma'ariv*, 6/4/90, p 4.
Promises made to Avraham Sharir in return for crossing the lines and almost presenting Shimon Peres with the opportunity of forming a government. Sharir agreed to leave the Likud after he felt that he was humiliated by Shamir, by not receiving a post in the 1988 National Unity Government. He agreed to join the Labour government in return for cabinet posts in the Transport and Tourism Ministries. When Peres failed to form his government, Sharir returned to the Likud and ostensibly did not receive anything in return.

5. Allocations to the religious parties in the coalition agreements which formed the present Shamir government in June 1990.
Ma'ariv, 29/3/90, p 1.
229 million shekels were allocated to educational and cultural institutions connected with the religious parties by the Finance Committee of the Knesset, after a struggle between the Likud and Labour to see who could grant more funds. This was seen as an attempt by both parties to win the religious parties (18 seats out 120 in the Knesset) over to their side.
Ma'ariv, 8/6/90, p 8.
The cabinet posts received by the religious parties in the Shamir cabinet were as follows:
Shas:
Rabbi Arye Deri – Interior Ministry.
Rabbi Rafael Pinchasi – Communications Ministry.
Rabbi Yosef Azran – Deputy Minister in the Finance Ministry.
National Religious Party:
Zevulon Hammer – Education Ministry.
Avner Shaki – Religious Affairs Ministry.
Yigal Bibi – Deputy Minister responsible for the Environmental Affairs Ministry.
Degel HaTorah:
Rabbi Avraham Ravitz – Deputy Minister in the Housing Ministry.
Rabbi Moshe Gafni – Deputy Minister in the Religious Affairs Ministry.
Agudat Yisrael:
Rabbi Menachem Porush – Deputy Minister responsible for Labour and Welfare Ministry.
Rabbi Shmuel Halpert – Deputy Minister in the Labour Ministry dealing with the National Insurance Institute.
Rabbi Avraham Verdiger – Deputy Minister responsible for the newly created Jerusalem Affairs Ministry.

Remark: Agudat Yisrael refuse to take up ministerial posts on ideological grounds.
Faction of Eliezer Mizrachi:
Eliezer Mizrachi – Deputy Minister in the Health Ministry.
Remark: Mizrachi's quitting of the Agudat Yisrael Party, after they had signed an agreement with the Labour Party, foiled Shimon Peres' efforts to form a government. He was thus highly rewarded by the Likud for his action.
Faction of Rabbi Y. Peretz:
Rabbi Yitzhak Peretz – Minister of Absorption.
Remark: Peretz quit the Shas party (of which he was the chairman) on the day after the National Unity Government fell. This was done as a protest of the fact that Shas had brought down the government and on orders from Rabbi Shach. His resignation was the first and probably fatal blow which prevented Labour from forming a government. He was thus highly rewarded by the Likud.
Ma'ariv, 27/4/90, p 3.
Publication of coalition agreements as a result of a Supreme Court decision.
Further promises made to the religious parties.
Shas:
– Radio channel to broadcast programmes for the haredi public.
– Continuation of peace process.
– Inner Cabinet post and diplomatic posts.
– Status quo on religious matters.
– Blocking of Human Rights legislation.
– Enforcing of existing legislation on religious matters.
– Blocking changes in the electoral system without the consent of Shas.
Degel HaTorah:
– Appointments to senior posts in government ministries.
– 96.7 million shekels for institutions affiliated with Degel HaTorah.
– Blocking changes in the electoral system without the consent of Degel HaTorah.

CHAPTER FOUR
1. *Yediot Achronot*, 12/6/86, p 19.
Begin's lack of knowledge of Sharon's actions in the Operation Peace of Galilee (1982–85). Based on Arye Naor's (Cabinet Secretary at the time who later resigned from the Likud) book, *Government at War* (published by Lahav in Hebrew).
2. *Ha'aretz*, 9/2/83, pp 13–19.
Kahan Report on the Sabra and Shatilla Massacre regarding Ariel Sharon's responsibility for the massacre. The commission found that while the Maronite Christian Phalange Militia was directly responsible for the massacre, Sharon was indirectly responsible because he did not take into account that the massacre could take place under the circumstances that existed at the time (the assassination of Bashir Jemayel, President-elect of Lebanon and the animosity of the Maronites for the Palestinians). Sharon was also found responsible for not taking actions to prevent

the massacre. The commission recommended that he should resign as Minister of Defence.

3. Alisa Odenheimer, 'Sharon is Slammed for conduct at Ministry of Industry and Trade', *JP*.

4. *Ma'ariv*, 23/4/90, pp 1–2.
St John's Hospice in Jerusalem. Jewish residents moved into a building in the Christian Quarter in Jerusalem. They claimed that they had permission to occupy the premises from a company, registered in Panama, that had sublet the premises from the protected tenant who had rented the premises from the Christian Church. Under very complicated rental laws (inherited from the Turkish and British Mandatory Administrations), this would allow them to remain there. The church rejects the Jewish residents' claims.
The Ministry of Housing published an official statement admitting that they had provided $1.8 million for the rental of the premises, under a paragraph in the State Budget which facilitates purchases of land not owned by the Israel Lands Authority (which owns over 93% of Israel's land). The purchase had been approved by the Treasury.
Ma'ariv, 20/5/90, p 1.
The American Congress added $1.8 million to the commission that Israel had to pay for the loan guarantees, approved earlier by the congress, in reprisal for the purchase.

5. *Ma'ariv*, 19/11/90, p 8.
Shamir's statement connecting *aliya* (immigration) with territory.
He said that Israel needs 'the Land of Israel from the Jordan to the Mediterranean for the large *aliya*.'

6. Sarah Honig and Michal Yudelman, 'Sharon's private war', *JP*, 4/91.

7. *Ma'ariv*, 3/4/90, p 1.
Modai's demand for $10 million bank guarantee for the promises made by Shamir to his four-man break-away faction. The promises included the Finance Ministry for Modai and placement on the Likud list for the next election.

8. Alisa Odenheimer, 'Sharon blasts Modai in wild panel session', *JP*.

9. Joel Bainerman, 'Petty corruption Israeli-style', *JP*, 20/8/90.

10. Asher Wallfish, *JP*, 1/7/91.

11. *Ma'ariv*, 8/6/90, p B1.
Levy forcing his way to the Foreign Ministry. From the article it is clear that Levy's support for Shamir was conditional on his appointment as Foreign Minister.

12. Jonathan Schachter, *JP*.

13. *Ma'ariv*, 1/11/90, p 4.
Levy reporting President Mitterrand's statements in closed discussions with Levy. Mitterrand said that Israel would never have to give up Jerusalem. This was a far-reaching policy statement which does not reflect French foreign policy.

14. Michal Yudelman, 'Peres blasts Levy on debt waives issue', *JP*, 1990.

15. Roy Tower, *Glasgow Herald*, 3/91.

16. Yosef Goell, 'Wrong man, wrong job, wrong time', *JP*, 3/91.

17. Michal Yudelman, 'Controversial character in cabinet', *JP*.

18. Personal interview.

19. 'Our elected representatives must be clean', *JP*, 15/2/91.

CHAPTER FIVE

1. Yosef Goell, 'Status quo that never was', *JP*.
2. Michael Rotem and Haim Shapiro, 'Son of Shas leader spurs new police probe into party's affairs', *JP*.
3. Haim Shapiro, 'Shas: family feud', *JP*.
4. Six weeks after his disappearance, Levy returned to Israel. The rotund MK claimed he had lost weight while hospitalised.
5. Haim Shapiro, *JP*, 21/6/91.
6. Herb Keinon, 'Peretz: Limit non-Jewish immigration', *JP*, 28/11/90.
7. Susan Hattis Rolef, 'The psychology of the Peretz probe', *JP*.
8. Michael Rotem and Michal Yudelman, 'Election bribe probe', *JP*.
9. Gil Sedan, 'Minister's alleged misuse of funds', *JP*; Dan Izenberg, 'Harish cancels funding after Shaki link revealed', *JP*.

CHAPTER SIX

1. Weizman's comments from *Yitzhak Rabin*, a biography by Robert Slater in Hebrew, Idan Publishers, p 85. The paragraphs in the book are based on a document released by Weizman to *Ha'aretz* (published on 22/4/74), on Weizman's book *Lecha Shamayim, Lecha Aretz*, Ma'ariv Publishers and on an interview with Weizman in May 1976.
2. From the *Los Angeles Times*, 1985.
3. Uriel Lynn, 'No point in renewing the unity government', *JP*.
4. *Ha'aretz*, 4/10/81.
5. Sarah Honig and Michal Yudelman, 'Bei'lin flies to Egypt despite Labour anger', *JP*.
6. Joel Bainerman, 'Labour Party's days are finished', *JP*.

CHAPTER SEVEN

1. From *Yitzhak Rabin*, p 75 (see Note 1, Chapter 6).
2. Dan Margalit of *Ha'aretz*.
3. *Ma'ariv*, 22/5/85.
4. *Ma'ariv*, 11/8/88.
5. *Ma'ariv*, 24/5/89.
6. *Ma'ariv*, 22/5/88.
7. *Ha'aretz*, 29/9/89, Supplement, p 15.
   Kibbutz debt. The kibbutzim owed as of 29/9/89, $4,000 million. They subsequently signed a deal which forgave 1/4 of the debt and spread another 1/2 of the debt over a period of 30 years at preferred interest. The remaining quarter was to fall on the kibbutzim.
8. *Ma'ariv*, 25/11/87.
9. *Ma'ariv*, 10/12/87.
10. Yehuda Aharoni, 'An end to the *intifada* revelry', *JP*, 4/12/90.
11. Matthew Griphs, 'Givati 4 are convicted; judges rap senior officers', *JP*.
12. Uriel Lynn, 'Surprise! Surprise! is no excuse', *JP*, 29/11/90.
13. 'Avoidable accidents', *JP*, 19/7/90.
14. Yosef Goell, 'Lessons of the Tze'elim tragedy', *JP*.

15. *Bemachane*, 29/8/90.
16. Asher Wallfish, 'Public Heroine No. 1 – Comptroller Ben Porat', *JP*.
17. Bradley Burston, 'IDF barn-door of opportunity', *JP*.

CHAPTER EIGHT
 1. *Ma'ariv*, 6/3/87. Because of Pollard's Iraqi intelligence, Israel was
    prepared for a gas attack on its population during the Gulf War.
 2. *Ma'ariv*, 13/3/87.
 3. Dan Izenberg, 'Klein guilty of illegal military sales', *JP* 11/89.
 4. Two articles by Joel Bainerman, 'From arms to avocadoes' (ic) and 'The
    secret world of Amiram Nir', *JP*.
 5. Joel Bainerman, *JP* 30/11/90.
 6. Nancy Gibbs, 'Unsolved Mystery', *Time Magazine*, 1/7/91.
 7. Jonathan Schachter, 'Israeli "sting" victim freed by U.S. court', *JP*.
 8. Louis Toscard, *Triple Cross*, Birch Lane Press, pp 97, 98.
 9. Ibid p 108.
10. *Ma'ariv*, 30/10/90.
11. 'Inside the Dotan Debacle', *JP* 21/12/90. Apparently the full extent of
    Dotan's crimes is not yet revealed. By the spring of 1991, an associate of
    Dotan's, working for General Electric, was implicated in a $33-million
    theft from the Pentagon.
12. *Ma'ariv*, 20/12/90.
13. Abraham Rabinovich, *Hatsofeh*, 'Judgment on the Temple Mount'.

CHAPTER NINE
 1. Ezra Sohar, *Israel's Dilemma*, Shapolsky Publishers, New York, 1980.
 2. *Hatsofeh*, 7 September 1990.
 3. *Ha'aretz*, 11 April 1986.
 4. Judy Seigel, 'Health fund may see NII to force census recount', *JP*
    1990.
 5. *Ha'aretz*, 18 April 1986.
 6. Ezra Sohar, 1980.
 7. *Jerusalem Post Magazine*, 10 May 1991.
 8. *Ma'ariv*, 24 May 1983.
 9. 'Israeli doctor in US awaits ruling on extradition hearing', *JP*, 1991.
10. Lea Levavi and Alisa Odenheimer, 'Modai trims Olmert's bid for more
    medical staff', *JP*.
11. *Contact*, 31 May 1991.

CHAPTER TEN
 1. Martha Meisels, *Choice*, 7 June 1991.
 2. From special TV programme on the environment, *Halilah* (*Tonight*),
    June 1991.
 3. David Rudge, 'Kinneret's salinity increasing', *JP*, 1991.
 4. David Rudge, 'Red tape threatens to close vital Kinneret research lab',
    JP, 10 June 1991.
 5. D'vora Ben Shaul, 'Pesticides threatening wells', *JP*, 5 July 1990.
 6. Judy Seigel, 'The Health Ministry that wasn't', *JP*.

7. *Ha'aretz*, 24 August 1989.
8. *Ma'ariv*, 15 December 1989.
9. *Davar*, 11 October 1988.
10. *Contact*, 7 June 1991.
11. State Comptroller's Report, 1991.
12. Lea Levavi, 'Most dangerous waste not disposed of safely', *JP*, 3 June 1991.
13. Lea Levavi, 'Bank-shares crisis pales compared to water crisis', *JP*.
14. *Ha'aretz*, 17 May 1991.

CHAPTER ELEVEN
1. 'UJA raises over $1 billion in 1990', *JP*.
2. Charles Hoffman, *The Smoke Screen*, Eshel Press, New York, 1989.
3. Ibid, p 103.
4. Ibid, p 41.
5. Tom Sawicki, *The Jerusalem Report*, 27 June 1991.
6. Hoffman, p 172.
7. Yossi Klein Halevi, 'Dinitz: centre stage at last', *The Jerusalem Report*, 27 June 1991.
8. Tom Sawicki, *The Jerusalem Report*, 27 June 1991.
9. Hoffman, p 47.
10. Ibid, p 178.
11. Tom Sawicki, *The Jerusalem Report*, 27 June 1991.
12. Hoffman, pp 84–86.
13. Ibid p 73.
14. Ibid p 79.
15. Ibid p 226.
16. Ibid p 226.
17. Ibid p 225.
18. Ibid p 38.

CHAPTER TWELVE
1. Louis Toscano, *Triple Cross*, Birch Lane Press.
2. Hoffman, p 140.
3. Ran Kislev, *The Israel Yearbook 1990*, IBRT, p 102.
4. Leah Abromovitz, *JP*, June 1991.
5. Ran Kislev, p 113.
6. Ibid, p 117.
7. David Rudge, 'Traumatized olim remain puzzled', *JP*.
8. Herb Keinon, 'Ethiopian anguish', *JP*, 28 June 1991.
9. Kislev, p 124.
10. Bill Hutman, 'Newcomers from Ethiopia to go to religious schools – Hammer', *JP*, 3 June 1991.
11. Moshe Tutnauer, 'The Ethiopians will find their own way', *JP* 21 June 1991.

CHAPTER THIRTEEN
1. Sarah Honig, 'Schach-mate', *JP*, 1991.

2. Herb Keinon, 'Peretz accuses Treasury of sabotaging absorption', *JP*, 29 October 1990.
3. 'PhD streetcleaners', *JP*.
4. Evelyn Gordon, 'Immigrants' health coverage lapsing', *JP*.
5. Alisa Odenheimer, 'Immigrants moving to unsuitable areas, says Treasury', *JP*.
6. Bill Hutman, 'Red tape strangles US builders', *JP*, 30 September 1990.
7. Adek and Scott Apfelbaum, 'Housing in the dumps', *JP*, 1990.
8. Herb Keinon and Alisa Odenheimer, 'Cabinet fiddles while olim sizzle', *JP*, 26 October 1990.
9. Herb Keinon, 'Plans unveiled to accommodate immigrants in private homes', *JP*, 1990.
10. *Chadashot*, December 1990.
11. *Ha'aretz*, 14 March 1975.
12. Bill Hutman, 'Amidar to inspect after immigrants complain', *JP*, 1990.
13. Bill Hutman, 'Sharon has new plan to get olim into empty caravans', *JP*, 1990.
14. Bill Hutman, 'Is Amidar using scare-tactics?' *JP*, 22 February 1991.
15. Naftali Greenwood, 'The nightmare of Israeli small business', IASPS, January 1990.
16. Dan Izenberg, 'Easy prey for swindlers', *JP*.
17. Joel Bainerman, 'Little brother should watch big brother', *JP*, 12 October 1990.
18. Melvin Cohen, 'Housing for today and tomorrow', *JP*, 1990.
19. Jonathan Schachter, 'US Jews must carry most of absorption load, says Modai', *JP*.
20. *Forum*, June 1990.
21. Yosef Goell, 'Hard-headed thinking on absorption', *JP*, 1990.
22. *JP*, March 1991.
23. Bill Hutman, 'Demo by Soviet immigrant doctors', *JP*.
24. Asher Wallfish, 'Peretz, Namir deplore growing prostitution among immigrants', *JP*.
25. *Weekend Magazine*, May 1991.
26. Joel Bainerman, *Moment*, April 1991.
27. 'Just too many olim', *JP*, 17 May 1991.
28. Yossi Klein Halevi, 'The cellist in the mall', *The Jerusalem Report*, 4 July 1991.
29. Asher Wallfish, 'Knesset told of olim's worries', *JP*, 1991.
30. *Forum*, February 1990.
31. Ziv Hellman, 'Cash grants instead of tax relief approved for some olim', *JP*, 1991.
32. *JP*, 1991.
33. Ziv Hellman, 'Modai seeks lower standard of living', *JP*, 1991.
34. Wendy Blumfield, 'We can't afford low mortgages', *JP*, 23 May 1991.
35. Manfred Gerstenfeld, 'Looking beyond Utopia to pragmatism', *JP*, 1991.

CHAPTER FOURTEEN
1. Dan Izenberg, 'Their day in court', *JP*, July 1991.

2. Ibid.
3. 'The defendants: look at them now', *JP*, 12 July 1991.
4. *Ha'aretz*, 3 October 1985.
5. Alvin Rabushka, 'Scorecard on the Israeli economy. A review of 1990', IASPS.
6. *Yediot Achronot*, 16 April 1989.
7. *Ma'ariv*, 5 February 1989.
8. *Ma'ariv*, 4 December 1987.
9. Galit Lipkis, 'Bank manager suspected in $10 million embezzlement', *JP*, 3 September 1990.
10. *Ha'aretz*, 27 April 1989.
11. *Ha'aretz*, 13 June 1989.
12. *Yediot Achronot*, 18 July 1986.
13. *Ha'aretz*, 27 June 1986.
14. *Yediot Achronot*, 18 July 1986.
15. *Yediot Achronot*, 5 January 1990.
16. Galit Lipkis and Alisa Odenheimer, 'Official: Begin sale of banks on course', *JP*, 1991.
17. Alisa Odenheimer, 'Panel raises eyebrows', *JP*.

CHAPTER FIFTEEN
1. Daniel Brod, 'The kibbutzim and their debt: policy considerations', IASPS, May 1990.
2. Ibid.
3. *Ha'aretz*, 28 December 1989.
4. Ibid.
5. *Ha'aretz*, 4 December 1989.
6. Brod, May 1990.
7. Abraham Rabinovich, 'Which way do we go?' *JP*, June 1991.
8. Ezra Sohar, *Israel's Dilemma*, 1989.
9. Ibid.
10. David Krivine, 'A way out for doomed moshavim', *JP*.
11. *JP*, 1990.
12. 'Untying the farmers', *JP*.

CHAPTER SIXTEEN
1. 'A visit and a scandal', *JP*, June 1991.
2. 'What public servants are for', *JP*, May 1991.
3. Judy Seigel, 'Education Ministry – totally out of touch', *JP*, 1991.
4. Judy Seigel 'Failing marks for educators', *JP*, 1991.
5. Bill Hutman, 'Out for the count', *JP*, 28 June 1991.
6. Alisa Odenheimer and Michal Yudelman, 'Studies at yeshiva cost more than college', *JP*, 1991.
7. Dan Izenberg, 'Arrest, remand, then investigate', *JP*, 1991.
8. Ibid.
9. Andy Court, 'The untouchables: charges of police brutality aren't probed', *JP*, 1988.
10. Ibid.
11. Jack Menes, IASPS, October 1990.

12. *Ma'ariv*, 27 July 1990.
13. 'Confidentiality and confidence', *JP*, 1991.
14. Ezra Sohar, *Israel's Dilemma*, p158.
15. *JP*, 3 November 1989.
16. Larry Derfner, 'Greater Tel Aviv is crawling with congested roads', *JP*, 1989.
17. Margot Dudkevitch and Ron Kampeas, 'Road Safety stalled in bureaucracy', *JP*, 24 August 1990.
18. Asher Wallfish, 'Driver's sentence outrages law chairman', *JP*, July 1991.
19. Michael Rotem, 'Police widen Tel Aviv parking tickets probe', *JP*, 1991.
20. Michal Yudelman, 'Scandal no surprise to hassled Tel Avivians', *JP*, 1991.
21. Ibid.
22. State Comproller's Report, 1988.
23. Moshe Glazman, 'Public transport in Israel today: Proposals for reform', IASPS, December 1989.
24. Greer Fay Cashman, 'Aid funds check in to some doubtful hotels', *JP*.
25. *Ma'ariv*, 27 January 1984.
26. *Ha'aretz*, 2 December 1990.
27. *Yediot Achronot*, 7 April 1989.
28. *Ha'aretz*, 20 November 1988.
29. *Ha'aretz*, 9 January 1989.
30. *Contact*, 8 July 1991.

CHAPTER SEVENTEEN

1. Ziv Hellman, 'What we need is just a *little* more unemployment', *JP*, 12 July 1991.
2. Ziv Hellman, 'Small entrepreneurs lose ground in Israel', *JP*.
3. Alisa Odenheimer, 'Cabinet fracas over '91 budget' *JP*, 26 November 1990.
4. Carl Schrag '... And 25,000 shekels for a cup of coffee', *JP*, 27 June 1990.
5. S. Zalman Abramov, 'Histadrut – state within a state', *JP*.
6. Ibid.
7. Alvin Rabushka, 'Scorecard on the Israeli economy; a review of 1990', IASPS, 1990, p 45.
8. David Rudge and Lea Levavi, 'Soltam head fired in "dogs" affair', *JP*, 28 September 1990.
9. Rabushka, 1990, p 34.
10. Ronald Glover, 'Stanley Gold is still giving chase', *Business Week*, 4 March 1991.
11. 'The Histadrut jihad', *JP*, 1991.
12. S. Zalman Abramov, 'The last Mohicans of World Socialism', *JP*, 1991.
13. 'Business Roundup', *JP*, 1991.
14. Evelyn Gordon, 'Lower customs, improve our lives', *JP*, 1991.
15. Ezra Sohar, *Israel's Dilemma*, 1989 p 189.
16. Paul Rivlin, 'Industrial subsidies in Israel', IASPS, May 1991.
17. Joel Bainerman, *JP*, 2 March 1990.

18. Galit Lipkis, 'Can the Clal empire last without Dovrat?', *JP*, 21 December 1990.
19. Joel Bainerman, 'Independent at any price', *JP*, 12 October 1990.
20. Ezra Sohar, 1989, pp 203–204.
21. *Ma'ariv*, 20 April 1984.
22. Evelyn Gordon, 'Cabinet opens door to ICL purchase of Rami Refractors', *JP*, 12 August 1991.
23. Ziv Hellman, 'The hurdles still facing privatisation' *JP*, 19 July 1991.
24. *Ha'aretz*, August 1991.
25. *JP*, 28 December 1990.
26. *JP*, 21 December 1990.
27. *JP*, 7 June 1991.
28. Evelyn Gordon, *JP*, August 1991.
29. Ibid.
30. Daniel Doron, 'Blame the system, not the hapless worker,' *JP*.
31. Yigal Kotzer, 'Trash business run by national cartel – Police', *JP*.
32. *JP*, 12 August 1991.
33. *JP*, 28 September 1990.
34. 'The new governor's task', *JP*.
35. Alvin Rabushka, 1990 (Foreword).
36. Daniel Doron, 'Free enterprise hasn't been given a fair chance', *JP*, 1991.
37. Loewenberg, 'Scorecard on the Israeli economy – a review of 1990', (Foreword) IASPS.
38. Joel Bainerman, 'The downside of foreign aid', *JP*.
39. Joel Bainerman, 'Cut off aid to Israel and watch it thrive', *Wall Street Journal*, 27 July 1991.
40. Burton M. Halpern, 'The "victim" image has its price', *JP*, 28 September, 1990.

CHAPTER EIGHTEEN

1. Dan Izenberg, '17 MKs fail to file income statements', *JP*.
2. Carl Schrag, 'Unclog the system', *JP*, 26 July 1991.
3. *JP*, 26 July 1991.
4. Sarah Honig, 'Poll Shows Labour at all-time low', *JP*, 1989.
5. *Ma'ariv*, August 1991.
6. *Haolam Hazeh*, 24 June 1991.
7. Yosef Goell, 'New rules for the political game', *JP*, 1991.
8. Ibid.
9. *JP*, June 1991.
10. 'Changing the system of government in Israel', The Jerusalem Centre for Public Affairs.

Index